College Libraries
and the
Teaching/Learning Process

College Libraries
and the
Teaching/Learning Process:

Selections from the
Writings of Evan Ira Farber

**Selected and Edited by
David Gansz**

Earlham College Press

Jacket design by Karen E. Roehr.

ISBN 978-1-879-117-18-1

Earlham College Press
801 National Road West
Richmond, Indiana   47374-4095

**In Loving Memory of
Hope Wells Farber
(1931-2006)**

Contents

PREFACE

by David Gansz

No intelligent discussion of college librarianship can fail to mention Evan Farber, since he clearly stands as one of its most influential theoreticians and practitioners from the last third of the 20th century. Were it not for his tireless efforts to define and promote it, "bibliographic instruction"—or "B.I.," as it came to be known, for short—might not have entered the lexicon of higher education, nor would it have dominated academic library circles for decades (as it continues to do today, under the slightly revised monikers of "information literacy" and "information fluency").

A dedicated family-man and not one to seek to make a name for himself, Evan entered the profession as so many of us did, with tremendous admiration for education, learning, wisdom, the research process—and the information that can, potentially, lead to all of the aforementioned—without feeling called to specialize in any particular academic discipline to the doctoral level, although he clearly had the capacity to do so. A generalist in the best sense of the word, he became College Librarian at Earlham College, a Quaker school in Indiana, in 1962, at the age of forty—his first direct involvement in a small, private liberal arts college environment.

In short order he grasped those quintessentially important aspects unique to a college library's mission and, in 1974, published the outstanding and seminal "College Librarians and the University-Library Syndrome" as a chapter in a book of essays honoring his mentor, Guy Lyle. Now more than three decades old, this work rings as true today as the day it was written—as witnessed by its republication at 14-year intervals. Many of us who direct or have directed college libraries have come to think of it as required reading for our new hires. It stands as the first chapter in this chronological volume of Evan's 'selected works,' spanning the years 1974 through 2004.

The centerpiece of the volume (chapter 14, beginning on page 82) consists of excerpts from "The Library in Undergraduate Education," written in 1985 by Evan for the Boyer Commission funded by the Carnegie Foundation for the Advancement of Teaching. As Tom Kirk, the current College Librarian at Earlham, states in a recent letter, "It so clearly represents the best thinking about college libraries in undergraduate education up to that time. In many ways it foreshadows developments of the 1990's and early 21st century. Therefore the document has historical importance." Heretofore it has remained an unpublished manuscript.

Evan's career in the Earlham library (which did not end with his retirement in 1994, but continues today with his status as Emeritus Librarian), is marked by his insistence that each and every interaction with a student is a potentially "teachable moment." In so doing, he is the instructional-librarian *par excellence*, who has done much to raise the status of the role of librarians as educators.

We are firmly entrenched in the so-called 'information age.' Yet, "Where is the knowledge we have lost in information?" asks T.S. Eliot. When so many college professors view information as a destination, rather than a journey, it seems, as Carl Jung states, "We have become rich in knowledge but poor in wisdom." Evan Farber is not afraid to address the relationship between information, knowledge, and wisdom (see page 187). He invites librarians to help restore the quest for wisdom back into the student journey.

Librarians help researchers re-phrase their questions. The reference interview that elicits the student's deeper question-within-a-question invites the telling of a story. The aim is for students, in the process of retelling their tale, to arrive at a new understanding of their life's quest—via the assignment at hand. The result is a new question that reorients the individual, putting him or her back on a deeper path of self-inquiry. This becomes the true "re-quest" for understanding, a much more fruitful mode of learning than the standard informational question.

Farber's premise is that any attentive librarian should facilitate the dialogue that invites such a transformation to take place in the library researcher. Students must be given an opportunity to reflect and reformulate themselves and their questions such that the need for learning beneath the surface of the assignment is honored. The quest is in every question. And, as James Hillman asks, "Is not the cure, after all, merely a linguistic conversion?"

Most new students—as well as non-traditional students unaccustomed to new technologies—continue to approach the library in fear and trembling. They bring to it their deepest thirst for knowledge, and all the anxieties accompanying that undertaking. Librarians are responsible in the etymological sense, implying that they are able to respond, from the Latin word meaning, "to promise." Responsibility may be defined as "to perform one's part in a solemn engagement." Learning should be engaging, and instructional librarians need to reach out to engage information seekers. In so doing, they promise our students a future bright with possibilities, where the liberal arts accomplish what they were intended to do, to liberate us from the shackles of our own ignorance.

Evan's daily activities over the decades have always left room for personal interaction whenever and wherever possible, endearing him to generations. It is not by mistake that, due solely to his infectious enthusiasm, Earlham has arguably graduated more students who have gone on to become professional librarians than any other school of its size.

In addition to his steadfast focus on undergraduate students, Evan worked as diligently during his career to educate those in his profession. Under his direction, Earlham hosted Bibliographic Instruction conferences between 1977 and 1986 and, in the 1990s, he was also active in founding and assisting the Association of College and Research Libraries' "Mentor" program under which experienced college library directors provide guidance and assistance to librarians newly-appointed to such posts.

Evan was always willing to share his knowledge and experiences working with faculty and ensuring that librarians are integral, rather than peripheral, to the teaching/learning process. As a result, Evan graciously accepted most of the more than two hundred invitations to speak, lead workshops, and present at conferences over the years. Thus, in addition to his considerable published output of journal articles and book chapters, his hitherto unpublished speeches also contain important observations. The best of them are included herein.

Beyond this book's title, his works have touched on aspects of libraries that are pertinent to colleges, universities, and special libraries alike. His career bridged the world of paper-based resources and access tools (embodied in the card catalog) and that of emerging electronic information. He embraced the new with a healthy skepticism, and never confused technology as an instrument of education with thinking and learning itself.

As is so often the case in academia, graduate schools are slow to recognize, celebrate, and pass on the extraordinary knowledge and advances in their particular fields during the lifetimes of the individuals who are their *avant-garde*. So it is that, as recently as a decade ago, library schools did not require their students to familiarize themselves with Evan Farber's ideas. One can only hope that this situation might be remedied.

What follows, then, is an arrangement of Evan's thinking, each facet of which is briefly (and recently) prefaced by Evan himself regarding the circumstances under which his words first took form. Of course some repetition of themes and, in some instances, even phrases is present throughout the volume. This we have let stand as a testament to the constantly evolving "work in progress" that is one's life, and the dedication it takes to revisit themes of great importance from various vantage points along the way.

For those of us who have had the great pleasure to work with him and/or learn from him, Evan's presence in our midst alone would suffice to validate our decisions to embrace the academic library as a vibrant and ever-changing institution deserving of our deepest reverence and respect. For those in the future who read what he has to say, it will become readily apparent that his ideas are heartfelt, insightful, and inspirational.

My thanks to Evan for access to his extensive archives of personal papers, Scottie Cochrane, Director of Libraries at Denison University, for suggesting the need for this collection and supplying the personal interview with Evan (and her transcription thereof) that comprises Appendix A, Richard Werking for his close and careful reading of the manuscript, and to Doug Bennett, President of Earlham College, Len Clark, Earlham College Provost and Academic Dean, and Tom Kirk, Library Director and Coordinator of Information Services at Earlham College, for facilitating this publication.

David Gansz,
Dean for Learning Support and Information Literacy,
Edison State Community College,
Piqua, Ohio

INTRODUCTION

The Library as an Instrument of Education:
Appreciating Evan Farber

by Richard Hume Werking

Evan Ira Farber has been the pre-eminent college librarian of the past thirty-five years, with a career that spans half a century. Born in the Bronx in 1922, he grew up in New York City and in its suburb of Great Neck. After receiving his B.A. in 1944 from the University of North Carolina at Chapel Hill and then attending Princeton for two years, he taught at Massachusetts State College, what is now the University of Massachusetts, Amherst. He subsequently returned to Chapel Hill, earning first a Master's degree in Political Science in 1951 and then in 1953 a Bachelor's in Library Science (today the equivalent of the MLS).

Evan's first professional position was at Livingston State Teachers College in Alabama (1953-55), followed by a seven-year tour as serials librarian at Emory University, where he worked for his mentor, Guy Lyle, author of the multi-edition classic, *The College Library*. While at Emory, Evan came to national attention in the profession by editing the fourth edition of *Periodicals for College Libraries*, published in 1957.

But it was as chief librarian at Earlham College, from 1962 to 1994, that Evan would hit his stride, becoming his profession's most articulate spokesman for college librarianship and bibliographic instruction. This book is a collection of his writings on these two subjects.

The move from a major, prestigious university to a small college in Indiana (enrollment then about 1,000) did nothing to diminish Evan's career. In 1967 he was elected chair of the College Libraries Section of the Association of College & Research Libraries, and he would use his CLS program at the 1969 ALA annual conference to speak, before a huge and enthusiastic crowd, about the Earlham library's new bibliographic instruction efforts. In 1977 he was elected President of ACRL and in 1980 received that association's Academic/Research Librarian of the Year award, only the fifth recipient of the award and the first college librarian so honored.

Meeting Evan Farber

I first met Evan in January 1975, less than four months after enrolling in library school at the University of Chicago. I had just read about Earlham's bibliographic instruction program in Billy Wilkinson's book, *Reference Services for Undergraduate Students.* Wilkinson concluded that Earlham's program of library instruction was outstanding, indeed "unparalleled at any college or university in the country."[1] Here was a topic that interested me greatly, and I wanted to talk with this successful college library director, to pick his brain about instruction and college librarianship.

In those days the Midwinter meeting of the American Library Association usually convened in Chicago, handily enough. I went uptown to the conference headquarters, found Evan's name and conference hotel on the list of registrants that ALA's conference managers had posted, gave him a call, and offered to buy him a cup of coffee the next day. He graciously agreed to meet a graduate student who was a complete stranger, and our conversation in a diner across the street from the Palmer House Hotel was an important step in my journey into librarianship. Evan talked about college libraries in general and about Earlham in particular, about how he had become interested in library instruction, and about two book chapters he had recently published—coincidentally the first and second chapters in this book.

In the months and years that followed, Evan became my most important mentor. During 1976-77 we both had grants from the Council on Library Resources' Library Service Enhancement Program, and my first of many visits to Earlham occurred in conjunction with that project. He got me onto a program at the 1977 LOEX conference, and we both spoke at Cerise Oberman's first bibliographic instruction conference at the College of Charleston in 1978. When I was library director at Trinity University (Texas), Evan was one of three speakers at our library's dedication ceremony in 1983; his succinct, ideational, and well-honed remarks are included in this volume as chapter 10.

Why This Collection?

Why this collection?—for a number of reasons. These essays and talks provide a combination of information and stimulating reflections on instruction and on academic libraries, librarians, and librarianship—especially librarianship—over a thirty-year period, by one of our profession's leading thinkers, practitioners, and critics. Collectively, the contents of this volume provide a window into college librarianship during the last few decades, from the pen of its most articulate spokesman. Although many of these pieces have been published before, some more than once, others appear here in print for

---

[1] Billy R. Wilkinson, *Reference Services for Undergraduate Students: Four Case Studies* (Metuchen, NJ: Scarecrow Press, 1972) 304.

the first time. (One especially important piece, hitherto unpublished, is Evan's 1985 report to Ernest Boyer's Carnegie Commission, chapter 14). Moreover, Evan's introductions are all new, and they provide useful context. In addition, Earlham's program has long served as a model for other colleges and also for universities; hence librarians, and instruction librarians in particular, will have in one place the products of much of Evan's writing and thinking about instruction and academic libraries, many of which they may not have seen or heard before. Also, faculty and academic administrators will doubtless find these pieces stimulating and pertinent for their work. And, finally, library school faculty and their students will encounter here a number of issues as they contemplate the present and future of academic librarianship.

Some Themes

Some of Evan's themes and expressions will be quite familiar to many academic librarians. Foremost among these, perhaps, is his insistence that while the college library is very important, it is *not* the "heart of the college"; that place is reserved for "the teaching-learning process." Other familiar themes include: 1) the "university-library syndrome" that has afflicted college librarianship and the (related) unfortunate tendency for some college libraries to build unnecessarily large collections;[2] 2) the advantage that college libraries have over university libraries because they can be centrally concerned with students' (and the faculty's) education—"the library as an instrument of education," as Evan put it in a talk to librarians at his alma mater in 1988 (chapter 17); and 3) the historical development of bibliographic instruction, with specific attention to the contributions of Harvie Branscomb, Louis Shores, Patricia Knapp, and others.

Nevertheless, there are additional themes and examples here that deserve more attention from academic librarians than they probably have received. For example, in these articles and talks Evan gives much

---

[2] To some extent Evan and I disagree about the pluses and minuses of relatively large collections in college libraries. The strongest enunciation I know of his view was stated in 1975, in a book edited by Dan Gore, when Evan wrote: "We should be just as wary of the oversized college library as we are critical of the undersized one....When a college library becomes much larger than necessary, its most important role, education, may have to be sacrificed in order to maintain the seldom-used, or even unused, major portion of the collection." (chapter 3)

On this subject we have simply agreed to disagree. Evan's willingness to speak at our Trinity Library dedication in 1983 was both ironic and another example of his generous nature, considering that at the time we were in the process of doubling the size of the collection, to 600,000 volumes, during a seven-year period.

weight to the importance of interpersonal relationships, especially with faculty and with students, and readers will be reminded of the importance of personality—particularly of the positive impact it can have—in both local and extended environments. Another theme is Evan's view that college libraries and their librarians need to be innovative and dynamic, and how library instruction can help stimulate such innovation. A related point concerns the importance of recruiting to the profession librarians who are creative, energetic, not "stodgy," and who see the library not as an end in itself, but as an educational tool. There is also the repeated reference to one-on-one reference service that is personable, helpful, and even sympathetic. And finally, beginning in the 1980s, Evan paid increasing attention to the proliferation of electronic information and its resulting impacts in several areas: student use of the library, the teaching/learning process, and even the librarian's role on campus.

Although in his report to Ernest Boyer's Carnegie Commission Evan called for more attention to evaluation of bibliographic instruction, it was not an issue with staying power for him.[3] Rather, he would point to the popularity of his methods with Earlham faculty and students, taking that as preferable to formal assessment. I remember him telling me once, with an appropriate amount of pride, about his talk to faculty at Carleton College about bibliographic instruction, when a professor asked him how he could assure them that what he was talking about actually worked. Before Evan could respond, another faculty member spoke up in support of the guest speaker and effectively closed that paragraph of the conversation, saying "my son goes to Earlham, and he knows more about how to use a library than I do."

The Farber Persona

An important factor in Evan's success at Earlham and beyond has been his engaging personality. He is friendly and generous, as well as thoughtful. But he combines those traits with a refreshing directness that many of us Midwesterners associate with street-smart New Yorkers (an association that in this instance is most appropriate). So far as I know, Evan has never failed to tell me—always politely, but never beating around the bush—when he disagreed with me, whether it had to do with my decision to accept a particular library position or a point I had made in an article.

Evan has been an educator for most of his life, coming to librarianship after several stops along the way: graduate studies at

---

[3] See Richard Hume Werking, *The Library and the College: Some Programs of Library Instruction*, (Educational Resources Information Center [ERIC] Document #ED127917, 1977), 24.

Princeton for two years, teaching college for a year, a Master's in Political Science, and then library school. He has encouraged college librarians to see themselves as educators too, teaching students to use library research to learn that scholars disagree with one another, and hence that they themselves, although "only" students, can become part of the academic conversation. As an educator, he has surrounded himself— through conversations, acquaintances, and other associations—with like-minded people. (I have heard him remark a number of times that instruction librarians are interesting people and enjoyable conversationalists.) He was a hands-on library director, working at the reference desk and observing the difficulties students were having, while also being struck by how quickly students would learn to use subject tracings on catalog cards, to the benefit of their research (chapter 1).

Evan is "a generalist in the best sense of the word," David Gansz says in his preface to this book; the chapters that follow demonstrate the truth of that description. In a fashion decidedly uncommon in the literature of librarianship, he weaves into his remarks observations by intellectuals and other writers such as Alfred North Whitehead, Kenneth Boulding, Irving Howe, Martin Buber, philosopher Susanne Langer, and educational psychologist Nevitt Sanford, among others. Many years ago I experienced first-hand the breadth of Evan's reading when he sent me a review of my book that he had chanced upon while perusing the latest issue of the *Wisconsin Magazine of History,* a periodical to which this small college in Indiana subscribed for almost eighty years.[4]

Among Evan's most important characteristics are his creativity and penchant for innovation, traits that he very much wants to see in librarians. In 1965 he hired as the college's science librarian a young man who was just graduating from Earlham with a degree in Biology. Tom Kirk worked at Earlham as science librarian for four years while earning his Master's in library science from Indiana University, and continued to hold that position for ten more years; in 1979-80 he served as acting director of the Learning Resource Center at the University of Wisconsin, Parkside, while on leave from Earlham. He left Earlham in 1980 to become library director at Berea College and returned to Earlham as Evan's successor in 1994. Ten years later, Tom received ACRL's award for Academic/Research Librarian of the Year, the same

---

[4] For additional examples of Evan's breadth of reading, as well as a wealth of other pertinent information, see Pyke Johnson, Jr., "A Day with a College Librarian," *Publisher's Weekly* (January 9, 1978), 43-46. (Appendix B, p. 239, of the present volume).

award Evan had won in 1980. It is the uncommon library director who will put talent ahead of degrees.[5]

Indeed, as with the case of Tom Kirk, it was the quality of Evan's interaction with students, often combined with their involvement as student employees of the library, that led many of them to become librarians. The profession is now peppered with Earlham graduates who have been heard to say they are in librarianship because of Evan. Examples include Susan Barnes Whyte, Rebecca Watson-Boone, Barbara Baumgartner MacAlpine, and Kristina Macpherson, along with Tom.[6]

Surely some of Evan's personal characteristics first engaged and then sustained his involvement in ACRL's Mentors Program for new college library directors between 1992 and 2001. During that time he worked closely with Larry Hardesty to help develop this group of professionals. And high on their list of priorities, no doubt, was communicating the college library's role as educational tool.

The Earlham Approach to Bibliographic Instruction
The instruction program at Earlham has reflected its leader — thoughtful, practical, and oriented toward educating students broadly. Evan's experience working with government documents at Chapel Hill and with serials at Emory spurred his determination to see that these important resources — neglected in many college libraries — would be used. During our very first conversation, he shared with me the story about his shock at encountering in the Emory library a Biology graduate student who had never heard of *Biological Abstracts*.

As readers will see, Evan did not share the wildly unrealistic views of Louis Shores and his "library-college" movement, which advocated a merger of faculty and librarian roles. And although he appreciated Patricia Knapp's theoretical contributions, he did not share her enthusiasm for making bibliographic instruction a separate discipline. Instead, he wished to use instruction to enable students to do better academic work and become more independent learners, even to help teachers, freeing them from restrictive assignments and "spoon-feeding," encouraging them to have higher expectations of their students. Apparently beginning in the 1980s, he began to place considerable emphasis on an additional, longer-term benefit — helping students

---

[5] Patricia Battin, another exceptional librarian, has noted: "If the choice lies between credentials and talent, I think we must opt for the talent." Battin, "Developing University and Research Library Professionals: A Director's Perspective," *American Libraries*, 14 (January 1983), 22.
[6] Tom Kirk contributed this paragraph's substance and much of its wording.

succeed in a society where success was increasingly based on their ability to find, evaluate, organize, and use information. This latter goal would be both substantively and rhetorically at the core of the so-called "information literacy" movement that emerged in the late 1980s and is still going strong.

The Earlham program did not emerge from educational theory; instead, it began as a practical response. When librarians at the reference desk found themselves getting very similar questions from students in the same class about finding information for assignments, they quickly concluded that a more efficient way of educating the students was needed. Moreover, their early efforts in the classroom were not very successful, because they spent their time describing and explaining various reference works. They soon discovered an important truth, one much underpublicized in the literature of bibliographic instruction—that many of the reference sources in and of themselves are simply not that interesting, especially to undergraduates. Hence the Earlham librarians soon moved to a "case study" approach, taking a sample topic and showing students how to compile a bibliography for it. As Evan puts it in chapter 2, "only by *using* the reference works can students really know and appreciate them."

Although Evan properly emphasized the quality of the classroom presentations that librarians gave to students and faculty ("There's no faster way of killing a bibliographic instruction program than giving deadly presentations"—chapter 6), he and his librarians understood that the most important learning activity happened outside the classroom, as students went about their academic work. It is a lesson that many college faculty are slow to discover. Not only is there a "university library syndrome" that affects college libraries; it is part of a more general "university syndrome" that has featured, even in small colleges, the lecture as the typical classroom activity, rather than a combination of lecture, demonstration, and structured conversation with students, among other things.

As news of Evan's instruction program spread in the profession, boosted by his CLS program in 1969, by reference librarian Jim Kennedy's article in *Library Journal* the following April,[7] and by Evan's two chapters published in 1974 (chapters 1 and 2, below), increasing numbers of librarians traveled to Earlham to talk with Evan and his colleagues about what they were doing. It soon became a problem similar to what the Earlham librarians had encountered at the reference desk—a large number of repetitious questions. Hence they again

---

[7] James R. Kennedy, Jr., "Integrated Library Instruction," *Library Journal*, 95 (April 15, 1970), 1450-53.

combined practicality and pedagogy, and began offering workshops to visiting librarians, faculty, and administrators, to discuss what they were doing and how. In time, Earlham librarians and faculty would travel to other campuses for such workshops, often at Eckerd College in St. Petersburg, Florida, a more congenial meeting location than Indiana in February.

Recently, William Miller and Steven Bell, respected academic library leaders, have suggested that faculty should assume responsibility for offering bibliographic instruction.[8] Evan repeatedly has declared that this would be a bad idea, believing that neither faculty nor librarians can do each other's job. Indeed, he has written that it would even be a mistake for subject specialists, like bibliographers, to offer instruction, because like faculty they tend to be "beholden to their disciplines." He courageously tells us how, when he was teaching a course at Earlham, he was so caught up in the details of teaching the course that he forgot to provide bibliographic instruction for his own students (chapter 22).

Farber at Earlham

Contributing to Evan's successful career were certain features of a small campus community. For one thing, for forty years until her death in 2006, Evan was married to Hope Farber. Not only was Hope a respected figure on the Earlham campus in her own right, she was Evan's secretary during his entire tenure as library director; as Evan would tell audiences, "I married my secretary." During one of my visits to the Earlham library I was impressed to see Hope on the phone arranging some meeting that was to be held in the library, while speedily checking in the library's daily shipment of periodicals. Perhaps generalizing a bit too much from this demonstration of efficiency, I suddenly understood how it was that Evan had all this time to think, read, write, give talks, and play tennis almost every day. In addition to Hope's many contributions, Evan could rely as well on other members of his very capable staff. Especially noteworthy in this context was Phil Shore, head of technical services, who ran the library on a day-to-day basis and also handled budget matters.

Nevertheless, Evan was more involved and engaged in the daily life of the library than many directors; he regularly worked the reference desk one evening a week and every fifth weekend, and was an active

---

[8] William Miller and Steven Bell, "A New Strategy for Enhancing Library Use: Faculty-Led Information Literacy Instruction," *Library Issues: Briefings for Faculty and Administrators* (May 2005), and William Miller, "Enhancing Students' Academic Honesty and Respect for Research," *Library Issues: Briefings for Faculty and Administrators* (May 2006).

participant in the instruction program that was his principal focus. Obviously he is a person who is organized as well as imaginative. Tom Kirk has written perceptively that observers from outside Earlham, focusing on the content of the library's instruction program, have often overlooked Evan's success as a manager who was simultaneously "teacher, implementer of the possible, leader, and visionary."[9]

Evan and his staff practiced what they preached about the importance of reference materials and reliance on inter-library cooperation to get materials that the library did not own. In the 1970s this small college library began acquiring the new and expensive *Social Sciences Citation Index* well before the University of Chicago library did, and Earlham was the first institution in Indiana to subscribe to the *Science Citation Index.*[10] The library also used a van that ran three days a week, to receive materials from Miami University in Ohio, about thirty miles away.

Evan's combination of intellect and personality made him a significant force on the Earlham campus, a community that was marked by its close-knit and informal character. (At least at one time, the second-most important criterion for faculty promotion and tenure—the first was "effectiveness as a teacher"—was not the usual language of publications or scholarship. Instead, it was "quality of mind," which could be demonstrated in a variety of formats and venues.) He was highly regarded by faculty, administrators, and students, and even had a voice in faculty hiring. For at least ten years he was a member of the campus personnel committee. On one of my first visits to Earlham, I encountered first-hand the weekly luncheon meeting of "Farber's Friends," over which Evan presided. There were only two rules: no private conversations, and no shop-talk—nothing about campus matters.

Evan's highly respected place at Earlham, with close personal and professional relationships with the faculty, almost certainly influenced his views about college librarianship—particularly the importance of the faculty's confidence and the relationship between that confidence and their perception of librarians as teachers rather than "housekeepers." His standing in the community doubtless helped spread the instruction program, to the point that in the 1970s Earlham's statement of educational aims included "competence in the skills of information retrieval and the use of the library for research purposes."

---

[9] Thomas G. Kirk, "Introduction," in Larry Hardesty, *et al.*, eds., *Bibliographic Instruction in Practice: A Tribute to the Legacy of Evan Ira Farber* (Ann Arbor, Michigan, 1993), viii.

[10] The information about the *SCI* was provided by Tom Kirk.

The committee that drafted the statement did not contain a single librarian.[11]

Conclusion

Critical to Evan Farber's professional success has been the confluence of several factors: his personality and intellectual breadth; the surge of interest in bibliographic instruction that began in the 1960s, which provided a receptive climate; and his affiliation for so many years with Earlham College. That institution has been not only a hothouse environment in which B.I. has flourished, but it is also a school that has seemed to some librarians, those at a distance and especially those who traveled there to see for themselves, the ideal of what a college should be.

For many readers, the chapters that follow will be an introduction to the ideas and the persona of a great librarian. For many others, even the large number of Evan's friends who are generally familiar with his publications, this is a volume that will remind, refresh, re-inspire, and re-energize us. In addition to teaching students and faculty, Evan has been a most effective educator of his fellow librarians. His legacy may be found in them, in their libraries and on their campuses, and in the society at large. A good life's work.

Richard Hume Werking,
Library Director and Professor of History,
U. S. Naval Academy,
Annapolis, Maryland

With thanks to Victoria Hanawalt and Tom Kirk for their considerable assistance.

---

[11] Werking, *The Library and the College,* 22.

College Librarians and the University-Library Syndrome
(1974)

*I had gone from being an administrator in Emory University's library
to director of Earlham College's library in 1962, about ten years before this
essay was written. During those years I'd been struck many times by the
differences between the two experiences and yet, I felt, too many college
librarians did not recognize those differences (as I had not at first) and so did
not really take advantage of them. Why not? Well, having to write an essay for
a collection of essays honoring Guy Lyle gave me the opportunity to explore the
answers to that question. The idea for this collection of essays began with a
discussion between Ruth Walling and myself. While I was at Emory Ruth was
Head of Reference and, when Guy Lyle was away, Acting Director.*

*Later, in the Foreword to the collection I wrote: "When, a few years
ago, Ruth Walling and I met at an ALA conference and began to reminisce
about our years working together at Emory University we suddenly realized that
Guy Lyle's retirement was near. Both of us felt enormously grateful to Guy for
the rich experience afforded by working under his direction, and we wanted to
pay him tribute. After some deliberation we decided that most appropriate
would be a group of essays by persons who had been associated with Guy in a
variety of contexts." The group of essays was published in 1974 as* The
Academic Library: Essays in Honor of Guy R. Lyle. *Mine was the lead essay.*

*I think that the essay was especially appropriate for this collection,
discussing the two areas in which Guy Lyle had worked and was nationally
known and respected. Though when the essay first appeared it didn't attract
much attention, it's gratifying to note that since then it's been reprinted several
times and that references to it or to the concept of the "university-library
syndrome" still appear in the literature.*

— Evan Ira Farber, 2006

Of the various types of academic libraries, college libraries
should find it easiest to achieve their purposes. Their manageable size
should permit a focus on the kind and level of materials they acquire and

Farber, Evan Ira, and Ruth Walling, editors. *The Academic Library: Essays in
    Honor of Guy R. Lyle.* Metuchen, New Jersey, Scarecrow Press, 1974.
    Pages 12-23.
Reprinted in:
Hardesty, Larry, John P. Schmitt and John Mark Tucker, editors. *User
    Instruction in Academic Libraries.* Metuchen, New Jersey, Scarecrow
    Press, 1986. Pages 243-253.
Farber, Evan Ira. "College Librarians and the University Library Syndrome."
    College & Undergraduate Libraries. Volume 7, Number 1 (2000).
    Pages 61-69.

distribute, and the relative clarity of institutional goals should point out more or less precisely the services they perform. Their personnel are almost always deeply dedicated, not merely to the profession and to the needs of their immediate clientele groups, but to the academic and social objectives of the parent institutions. Their students and faculty comprise a clientele who are, for the most part, captive, and with whom the library can establish almost any relationship—in kind and in depth—it wants. And yet...is there any knowledgeable observer who can say that college libraries are really doing the job they should?

That the undergraduate library in the large university has shortchanged the university undergraduate is fairly common knowledge. For those unaware of the situation, it has been documented in Billy Wilkinson's *Reference Services for Undergraduate Students.* He studied two of the more prestigious undergraduate libraries, those of Cornell University and the University of Michigan, and compared them with libraries in two liberal arts colleges.

> The basic conclusion...is that full advantage has not been taken of the opportunities afforded by the creation of undergraduate libraries. The librarians in the Cornell and Michigan undergraduate libraries have not closed the 'gap between class instruction and library service'. Reference services are of low calibre. Too often the assistance given students is superficial and too brief. Although the references services in both undergraduate libraries have been in a state of decline for several years, there have been almost no attempts to discover why or to make changes from traditional practices.[1]

One might infer from the comparisons made in this study that college libraries are doing a much superior job. And, indeed, if one were to assume that the services afforded by the two college libraries (Earlham and Swarthmore) which Dr. Wilkinson studied as a contrast to the

---

[1] Billy R. Wilkinson, *Reference Services for Undergraduate Students; Four Case Studies* (Metuchen, N. J.: Scarecrow Press, 1972) 347.

universities' examples were typical of college libraries, the inference would be more than justified. But the services given in those two college libraries are not typical—far from it—and undergraduates in even the smallest colleges are also being shortchanged.

For what reasons? Is it a lack of funds? To be sure, most college libraries have not been well supported, but one could respond that the lack of support results—in part, anyway—from libraries not doing an effective job. Even more to the point, however, is the fact that many college libraries that have been relatively affluent have not done as well or as much with their material resources as have other, poorer, libraries. Is it conservatism, inertia, smugness? Lack of faculty cooperation or administrative support? There's not much question that all of these factors have contributed, in one way or another, in one institution or another, and at one time or another, to inadequate college library service, and in many books and articles they have been duly recognized and inveighed against. And while I do not discount their effects, I think another factor has been at work here which has been just as detrimental. Just as detrimental, but even more deplorable because its impact—if it were recognized—could have been prevented or at least reduced. This factor is what I call the "university-library syndrome." It is a pattern of attitudes which causes college faculty, administrators and librarians to think of their libraries in terms of university libraries—and thus to imitate their practices, attitudes and objectives.

The Teaching Faculty

It is neither unfair nor inaccurate, I think, to point out that so many college faculty members suffer from this syndrome, and it is especially true of newer, younger faculty. Time after time prospective faculty members—many of whom turn out to be excellent teachers—ask me about our library, but these questions almost invariably are about reserve book procedures, how one orders materials, the size of the collection, facilities for interlibrary loan, or borrowing privileges for faculty wives and children. Rarely are the questions in terms of how students use the library, and certainly never in terms of what the library staff is doing to contribute to the teaching program—other, of course, than supplying materials. The assumption such faculty members make is

3

that all the teaching takes place in the classroom, and the library is there if the students are sent to it.

What else can one expect? These faculty are in many cases "junior members" of their disciplines, often only recently out of graduate school, and they view the college library's relationship to their teaching much as they viewed their university library's relationship to their graduate studies. That the graduate schools have been most responsible for the poor quality of undergraduate teaching is no secret. Their emphasis on research, in particular, has caused university faculty members to slight the teaching of undergraduates, not only by turning over such teaching to graduate assistants so that the senior faculty can focus on their research and their graduate courses, but also by training graduate students for research rather than teaching.

> The assumed unimportance of preparation for instructional responsibilities reflects the academic value hierarchy of the graduate school. American graduate study was modeled after the nineteenth century German university, an institution established to produce the scholar-researcher rather than the scholar-teacher...This system forces the embryonic professor to read prodigiously in order to gain a command of his special brand of knowledge, and disciplines him to analyze, synthesize, and hypothesize as his professors do. Inevitably, he learns to judge his own accomplishments by the values his graduate professors honor. It is when this modeling has occurred that the trainee is judged ready to strike out on his own. Meanwhile, the novice professor has been graduated without teaching preparation, and imbued with the values of a system which deemphasize its importance.[2]

---

[2] Raymond P. Whitfield and Lawrence M. Brammer, "The Ills of College Teaching: Diagnosis and Prescription," *Journal of Higher Education*, 44 (1973), 5.

The attitude of members of the teaching faculty toward the staff of the college library is also affected adversely by their experience in the university library. University graduate students and faculty have had their closest library relationships with those members of the university library staffs who work in the same subject areas, who have the same academic interests; these have increasingly been the subject specialists on whom the research scholar could depend for information and for maintaining the usefulness of the subject collection. As subject specialists have become increasingly prevalent in university libraries they have been replacing the general reference librarians as the handmaidens of the researcher.[3] For the purpose of research, and for building collections in depth, such subject specialists are important, but their particular competencies have meant that the scholar has perforce become less dependent on the general reference librarian and has put a lower value on his services and worth. Such an attitude carries over to the college library, though the need for the subject specialist isn't there. As a matter of fact, his approach isn't even desirable in working with undergraduates, but the college professor, because he assumes that the college library's purposes are similar to the university's, while also noting that the college library staff doesn't know as much about his field as did the university library's subject specialist whom he'd always depended upon, takes upon himself the library responsibilities for his students and for the collection even though the college librarian is much

---

[3] Reference service to undergraduates, which, as has been pointed out earlier, has not been good in university libraries, is being handicapped even more by this development since such reference service receives, when its needs are weighed against those of the subject specialists, a lower priority. Eldred Smith, in his essay [contained in the same volume] on the "Impact of the Subject Specialist Librarian on the Organization and Structure of the Academic Library," asks: "Should general reference stations be staffed by a few reference specialists, supplemented by subject specialists, by new library school graduates who stay only a year or two, or by non-professionals?" A few years ago the suggestion of using non-professionals for any reference work would have been considered unthinkable. With the increasing demands of the subject specialties and the decreasing financial ability to meet them, the undergraduate libraries, which have no one speaking strongly for them in the rarefied atmosphere of the upper echelon university administrator, are being caught in the squeeze, and services for them will be kept at their present minimal level.

more suited for this than the specialist would be. Thus, many college faculty reject the reference librarian's offer of bibliographic instruction to their students and also insist that the purchasing of materials in their areas be left up to the departments.

The faculty member's academic background and training work against an understanding of the proper role of the college library. He has been trained as a scholar-researcher and is not really interested in *how* his students use the library; he, after all, learned to use it in his discipline and he assumes students can also. Moreover, if students need help, they can either come to him and he'll recommend titles they should use, or they can of course ask the reference librarian. Rarely does it occur to him that learning *how* to use the library intelligently and independently is not only a desirable part of the educational process but will also permit students to do better work for him, and certainly the idea that anyone else can lead his students through the intricacies of his discipline's material is foreign to him. Similarly, his selection of library materials is based primarily on the scholarly reviews, and so he requests specialized monographs, sets of primary sources, and foreign language commentaries which the scholarly journals emphasize.[4] No one who is serious about higher education would deny the importance of many of these for college libraries, but too often they are purchased at the expense of materials that are less highly regarded by specialists but are more appropriate for undergraduates.

The teaching faculty's lack of confidence in their librarians as colleagues in the educational process has another unfortunate consequence: the librarian's role is viewed as a passive one, one devoted to housekeeping, to getting materials quickly and making them accessible with dispatch and efficiency, and to being available when needed for answering questions, compiling bibliographies, or putting materials on reserve. Deans and presidents, most of whom have come from faculty ranks and are prone to the same attitudes, want their librarians to "run a tight ship" — to keep their accounts balanced, to make sure all student assistants and clerical help are working hard, and to

---

[4] Fortunately, the growing practice of distributing *Choice* cards to faculty members is reducing their dependence on reviews by specialists for other specialists.

answer the needs of the academic departments. Whether the college's students are really deriving much benefit from the library is rarely questioned. Lip service is paid to the library's being "the heart of the college" but as long as faculty members don't complain, as long as the size of the collection and other standards meet a level acceptable to accrediting agencies, the administration is happy to let the library alone.

And, unfortunately, too many librarians like it this way.

The Librarians

Why are so many college librarians caught in the university-library syndrome? Why have not more of them been able to focus on the special mission of the undergraduate library, just as many college teachers (though still not enough, certainly) have been able to focus on their mission—teaching—rather than on research? Is it simply a response to what librarians think faculty and administrators think of them? Partly, but there are also reasons which derive from within the profession itself.

The outlook of university librarians is constantly impressed upon college librarians through the fact that university librarians are the spokesmen for academic libraries. They are the ones who edit the journals, write most of the books and articles, and hold the positions of eminence not only in library organizations but in councils of higher education which bring together administrators, teaching faculty and librarians. It is quite understandable: most university library administrators are more articulate, travel more widely, have a greater breadth of experience, possess more academic credentials, and have more time because of their larger staffs, and so they do tend to dominate the academic library scene and set its tone. Hopefully, this is changing: better salaries in colleges, disenchantment with the bureaucracy that is necessarily a part of large library systems, and the appeal of smaller, more personal situations for many younger librarians should mean more able college librarians who can establish their own patterns of objectives. But in the meantime, the university librarian is dominant.

Another influence is the fact that so many college librarians either began or spent an earlier portion of their careers in university libraries. They were, to begin with, trained in library schools which were associated with, if not located in, university libraries, and many of them

7

worked in these same libraries while they were going to library school; also, a sizeable number of each year's library school graduates go into university library work. Now, it would be ridiculous to assert that experience in a university library should be regarded negatively when, say, one is interviewing candidates for a college library position, and I hope I have not implied that: surely the desirability of having staff members who have had contact with the expertise, the approach to scholarship, the breadth and depth of materials that only experience in a good research library can provide, is too apparent to need more than simple mention. The point, however, is that desirable as this experience is, the mind-set that too often accompanies it, a mind-set resulting in not really understanding the difference between the purposes of a research library and those of an undergraduate library, should be recognized and must be deplored.

Perhaps the most egregious and widespread indication of college librarians ignoring this difference is the handling of government documents, especially in those libraries that are selective depositories. I've seen too many college library documents collections that are in basements or out-of-the-way corners of the library and are seldom used. The location of documents collections in many university libraries is, to be sure, not very much better, but in those libraries one assumes that the location is not that crucial since their clientele—faculty and graduate students—*must* use them, wherever they are located. But undergraduates are rarely *required* to use documents and if the collections are relatively hidden, these superb resource materials are virtually unused. While some of the blame can be attributed to teaching faculty who don't direct students to documents, college librarians must accept much of it for taking the attitude that all that need be done is acquire and organize the material, and for doing nothing to insure or even encourage its use.

Just as graduate study in the disciplines has done little to prepare Ph.D.'s for teaching undergraduates, so have the library schools done little to train reference librarians to work in college libraries. Reference courses have taught that the function of the reference librarian is to provide answers or information—quantitative data, biographical identification, bibliographical citations, comprehensive or selective

8

bibliographies, or whatever; to become experts in information retrieval; accuracy and expedition are of the essence. To be sure, one should not off-handedly denigrate these objectives—that function is an extremely important one—but when it displaces the educational function of the reference librarian, then its appropriateness for the undergraduate library must be examined. The role of the information expert is a tempting one, indeed. What reference librarian doesn't glow under the admiration and gratitude of a college student for whom he has found that elusive information in a matter of minutes or even seconds after the student had spent precious hours and had finally, in desperation, asked for help? But what has the student learned—other than to ask for help the next time? He has his information, of course, and can proceed with his work. True also, that if he needs similar information again, he will know where to look for it. But how much more the reference librarian could have done! At that moment the student was interested in finding out about something and was open to instruction, so that not only could he have been given the information he needed, but he could have been taught something about how one goes about finding information on one's own and he might perhaps have begun to understand something about search strategy. This is the process of education, and this is what college librarians should be engaged in.[5]

Not too long ago Guy Lyle, in preparing for a new edition of his *Administration of the College Library*, asked me for the names of some college libraries that were doing exciting, innovative things for their students. It was hard to think of any, and it occurred to me then how far ahead of college libraries the public libraries are in imaginative programs which reach out to their publics, even though the college library's clientele is so handy and so much more identifiable. Why don't college libraries serve their communities—their administrators, the staff and their families as well as students and faculty? Compare, just for

---

[5] I've been struck by how quickly students, when they're shown how, learn to use subject tracings to go from one subject to another in the card catalog. Yet I know that for students in most libraries they mean nothing; in one college library I was appalled to see that subject tracings were omitted from all but the main entry cards, even though, since the cards were computer-produced, tracings on the subject cards would have entailed no additional expense.

example, the browsing areas of a sampling of college libraries with a sampling of public libraries. Why isn't the encouragement and enjoyment of reading part of the college library's responsibility to its community just as a public library's is? Limited funds, shortage of personnel? Perhaps. But more important, I think, is the attitude that the library exists only to support the academic program—and that in a most traditional way, reflecting the university-library syndrome.

The result of this syndrome is so dismaying because it so effectively vitiates the potential role of the library in undergraduate education. Most universities are by their very nature—their size, their bureaucratic patterns of operation and governance, their political accountability—unwieldy and educationally hidebound: educational reform and innovation is slow and sporadic and so often as not retreats after a brief flurry of change. Colleges, on the other hand, by virtue of their variety, independence and size, are much more capable of innovation in the teaching and learning process. Sad to say, however, they have not taken advantage of these attributes nearly enough, and most colleges don't live up to their potential or even to the statements in their catalogs. Nor have their libraries.

Undoubtedly some of the reasons for each falling short are different; there is no question, on the other hand, that the same factor— the emphasis of the university on research and on graduate study rather than on teaching undergraduates—has had sufficient impact on the university's products so that even when they shift to a different educational context that single influence has worked to the disservice of both the classroom and the library.

Insofar as college teaching is concerned, this detrimental effect has been recognized and a variety of corrective approaches have been suggested and are being tried to ameliorate the situation. But the university's impact on college libraries has not been recognized. College libraries are quite different from university libraries, not only in quantitative terms but in their educational roles. They have their own goals and purposes and unique opportunities to achieve them. Only if the differences are kept in mind can college librarians begin to work successfully toward these goals.

2

Library Instruction Throughout the Curriculum:
Earlham College Program
(1974)

At the American Library Association Conference in 1969 I gave a presentation to the College Libraries Section on Earlham's instruction program. We had anticipated an audience of a few hundred at most but to our surprise (and some embarrassment—we'd prepared enough handouts to supply just the expected audience) a crowd we estimated later at about 800 turned the meeting into an SRO event. Obviously, we'd misjudged interest in the topic: the size of the audience, the questions following the presentation along with later inquiries about it indicated there was a much greater interest in instruction than anyone had realized. With that realization Jim Kennedy, Earlham's Reference Librarian, wrote an article further describing our instruction program ("Integrated Library Instruction," Library Journal, April 15, 1970). The talk and the article, and the interest aroused by them caused John Lubans to request a piece for his forthcoming book. What I tried to do in that piece was to provide the program's rationale, to describe "the underlying points that define the present program..." In retrospect I must say that those underlying points have mostly stood the test of time and continue to serve the program. In particular, working closely with members of the teaching faculty has been the program's centerpiece.

— Evan Ira Farber, 2006

Before I came to Earlham, I had no professional experience with library instruction. Indeed, I had done little thinking about it. Perhaps, though, one incident, which happened in the late 1950s while I was at Emory University, engendered later thinking. Surely it was not uncommon, and it seemed insignificant at the time. I had asked a student who was wandering around in the stacks what he was looking for, since he was obviously puzzled. I don't remember his exact question, but it had something to do with articles in biological journals. "Did you look in *Biological Abstracts*?" I asked. This drew a blank look, and I asked him what year student he was. When he told me he was working on his M.A. in biology, I was incredulous—a graduate student in biology who didn't even know *Biological Abstracts*. I urged him to speak to the science librarian, but when talking the matter over later with other staff members, I found out that this sort of thing was not at all unusual.

Lubans, John Jr., editor. *Educating the Library User*. New York, R.R. Bowker Company, 1974. Pages 145-162.

After coming to Earlham and working my turn at the reference desk, I realized that despite the very good teaching, there were many students who didn't know how to find information; at the same time, as an administrator, I also realized that requiring the reference librarian to answer approximately the same question 20 different times for the students in one class was a terribly inefficient use of professional time. With this latter observation as an appeal, I asked a member of the English department if I could talk to his class. He agreed, and the results were sufficiently encouraging for me to approach other faculty.

There was another incentive to my growing interest in instruction. As librarian, I had to justify (in a practical way) to the college administration and to myself my budget requests for additional materials—especially new subscriptions and back files of periodicals— that my training and experience had convinced me were essential for a good academic library. But if they were not being used much, why were they essential, and how could the request for funds be justified? The answer, of course, was that they were not used—or at least not used enough—because students didn't know about the indexes, bibliographies, and abstracts that would lead them to these periodicals, and if students were only shown the existence and usefulness of these tools, then the periodicals would be used.

...Here, then, are the underlying points that define the present program.

Flexibility and Variety. Perhaps the outstanding features of the program, flexibility and variety, are made possible by the size of the institution and the close relationships the library staff has with students and faculty. These relationships enable us to know when library instruction is needed and to find out what the situation demands in time, format, and purpose. The willingness, even eagerness, of the librarians to try new approaches and presentations also contributes to this flexibility. And so we have formal lectures and informal discussions; lectures to large classes at one extreme and individual conferences at the other; instruction spread over almost an entire term, building from basic techniques to sophisticated concepts, and spot lectures, some only ten minutes long, focusing on particular reference works. Some instruction is given through written exercises, but most by demonstration and oral directions. The locale may be the library's projection room, the reference area, the regular classroom; or even the librarian's office. The materials used include transparencies, brief bibliographies, lengthy handbooks with annotated entries, and sample pages from complex reference works. The determining criteria are simply what is feasible and what will be most effective, and since the two are sometimes in conflict, the result is often a compromise.

During the 1972-1973 academic year we gave some 70 lectures

for 48 different courses, divided among the social sciences, natural and physical sciences, and humanities. These do not, of course, include conferences with individual students or discussions with small groups.

Use of structured examples and illustrations. Whereas at the start of the program most lectures merely described and explained the various reference tools appropriate for particular subjects, we've come to realize that going over one reference work after another—no matter how fascinating they are to librarians—is for students fairly tedious and mostly ineffective; only by *using* the reference works can students really know and appreciate them. And so we have more and more used the process of compiling a sample bibliography, step by step sometimes, and let the annotated listings of reference works that are handed out to classes serve to point out specific works.

What we are trying to do, then, is to get across concepts by way of example. The *Pathfinders,* developed by Project Intrex at M.I.T. and now being published by Addison-Wesley, use a similar approach, but most of their topics are too broad for our use. Our hope is that what students learn from the *Pathfinders* by inference, and more directly from our lectures, is a workable search strategy that begins with introductory works—encyclopedias, handbooks, and other guides—and then proceeds to selective bibliographies and other reference works that give more specific information, and finally takes them to the card catalog for items in the library. The idea of search strategy is reinforced in the individual sessions with students, which leads to the next feature of our instructional program.

Personalized reference service. One of the major benefits of giving lectures to classes is the rapport established with students, who come to realize that librarians are approachable, knowledgeable, and interested in students' library problems. Because of this rapport, it is easier than in most library situations to make responses to reference questions an element of library instruction and, whenever possible, to show how looking for the particular information requested fits into a pattern of search strategy. At the same time, when individual reference works are consulted, their nature and uses are explained. The reference interview, then, is viewed as a potential educational experience and an important part of library instruction.

Librarians as instructors. In view of these features and the concepts mentioned below, it seems almost superfluous to say that we feel the teaching faculty cannot give adequate library instruction. On the other hand, we encourage—almost insist upon—faculty members attending the library instruction sessions for their courses, not only because their absence would say something to the class about the lack of importance they attach to the sessions but because they can, and often do contribute to the discussions by their knowledge of particular items that come up in the lectures, and by relating points in the lecture to aspects of the course and its assignments.

But teaching faculty are discouraged from giving library instruction, and even from preparing explanatory material for assignments that entail bibliographic tools, without consulting with librarians. For too many times we've found such explanations incomplete or incorrect, and while talking about this with some faculty members takes a good bit of discretion, the message can usually be gotten across by pointing out that there are additional sources they may have overlooked, or that some reference works they were familiar with have changed their nature or been superseded by newer, more useful ones, and—most important—that it takes someone who knows how students use and misuse these sources to guide them in using the reference sources. We disagree strongly here with some devotees of the library-college concept. We feel that while the teaching faculty have the central responsibility in the educational enterprise, librarians can help them carry out that responsibility much more effectively and at the same time enhance it. While the two groups—teaching faculty and librarians—can and should work together, neither one can do the other's job.

There is really no way of determining how much staff time is used—though we know it's considerable—since the lecturing time is only the tip of the iceberg. The other five-sixths (nine-tenths?) of the iceberg is taken up in discussing the approach and specific materials with the teaching faculty and with the staff, and then preparing the bibliographies and transparencies, in which several staff members are involved. To make the computation even more difficult, the load is spread irregularly throughout the academic year, with most of the lectures coming in the third through the sixth week of each (11-week) term, while the preparation for these weeks of lectures is carried on sporadically during the preceding weeks. If I were asked to give a rough estimate, I would guess that about ten to 15 hours a week are given to class presentations during those weeks of lectures, but as indicated, this is a small portion of the total staff time.

Extending the library's resources. If students are going to be shown how to use indexes, abstracting services and other bibliographical tools, the library must be willing to provide, as far as it is possible, the materials discovered through these tools. Otherwise, the frustration of finding just the right item in a bibliography, and then not being able to examine it—a frustration encountered again and again—will soon cause students to return to dependence on the card catalog, so they can be sure of having the materials available. Obviously, a college library must lack many important items, but it can give priority to materials that are indexed, and even more helpfully can provide ways for students to use

14

the resources of other libraries by a number of means: improving interlibrary loan service and making its availability known; providing union catalogs; joining periodicals banks and state or regional systems; cooperative arrangement with local or nearby libraries. We have done all these.

Objectives

By using these features and applying these precepts, what are we trying to convey to students? How do we want them to act, and what do we want them to understand and put into practice? Do we want them, really, to become junior reference librarians?

The last question can be answered very quickly: No—though we do want them to know how reference librarians approach a search for answers or information. To imply that we should even try to do much more than this would be to severely denigrate the professional training and role of reference librarians, to indicate a very restricted notion of what reference librarians are and a very simplistic notion of what they do. We would be attempting a dangerous thing, the substitution of second-class knowledge for first-class skills.

What, then, do we want?

At first, we want students to be struck by the difference between a high school library and a college library. Perhaps this was not such a difficult assignment years ago when there was little or no library instruction in the school systems, but now most of our students know— or think they know—how to use a library when they get to college, and after all, what is the difference on first sight? A college library is larger, of course, and the call numbers are different, but there's the card catalog and near it the *Readers' Guide*—what else do you need? What we librarians must do, in some way, is convince students that an entirely new approach is called for, a new approach that makes use of a bibliographical apparatus they never dreamed existed and techniques that may have been unknown to them, but are necessary to make the most of that apparatus.

Leading directly from this, we want them to realize that there are relevant reference sources for almost any topic. Since their biggest problem is rarely going to be a lack of material, but rather identifying the most important and pertinent items, the ability to find and use these reference sources is essential.

A third point is that certain principles comprise a search strategy that can be applied to almost any library research topic. The details of course will vary from topic to topic, but if one has grasped these basic principles, materials can be found much more effectively and efficiently.

And fourth, students should realize that no student, no matter

how well trained, can be aware of all the useful reference sources.
Students should work with a reference librarian when exploring new
territory.

     *Finally, because the information one wants may appear in so
many places, and because our library is necessarily limited in its
resources, the library should be used for doing the bibliographical
searching, but one should be prepared to go outside it, either by
borrowing materials or using other libraries...*

3

Limiting College Library Growth: Bane or Boon?
(1975)

In 1975 the Associated Colleges of the Midwest, a consortium of twelve liberal arts colleges, held a conference in Chicago on Space, Growth & Performance Problems of Academic Libraries. Faced with the adverse economic conditions of higher education, the conference dealt with these questions: did academic libraries really need to continually enlarge their collections and buildings? What were the alternatives to unlimited growth? What ways could growth be contained and what were the implications of containment?

Daniel Gore, Librarian of Macalester College, one of the brightest, most creative, most interesting academic librarians I've ever known (he was also one of the most controversial, but that's another story) was the organizer. Dan did a masterful job, obtaining as speakers an impressive list of librarians and persons who, in one way or another, had connections to the library world. Among the fourteen speakers were Eugene Garfield, Michael Buckland, R.W. Trueswell, myself, and others whose names were well known then, but probably are not now. The proceedings were published the following year in Farewell to Alexandria: Solutions to Space, Growth, and Performance Problems of Libraries, *edited by Daniel Gore (Greenwood Press, Westport, CT, 1976). The volume is still worth perusing.*

— Evan Ira Farber, 2006

My point here is that a college library is very different from a university library, not just in size but also in purpose. Moreover, the needs of college undergraduates have to be determined by different criteria than those used for university students. A college library must have, first of all, a collection of cultural and recreational materials that can expand students' horizons; second, a good basic collection that will meet most of their curricular needs; and, third, a good reference collection that will serve as a key to the immediate library, and to

Talk given at the ACM Conference on Space, Growth, and Performance Problems of Academic Libraries, Chicago, April 17, 1975.
Published as:
Farber, Evan Ira. "Limiting College Library Growth: Bane or Boon?." *The Journal of Academic Librarianship*, Volume 1, Issue 5 (November 1975). Pages 12-15.
Reprinted in:
Gore, Daniel, editor. *Farewell to Alexandria: Solutions to Space, Growth, and Performance Problems of Libraries.* Westport, Connecticut, Greenwood Press, 1976. Pages 34-43.

resources elsewhere. Only after these three needs are met should we think about a collection to fill the occasional research need. We should aim for a well-chosen basic collection that meets the first two needs, plus enough advanced materials to meet most of the students' research needs, and then depend on outside sources for the remainder. One implication for space in this connection is that the reference collection cannot be limited by the same criteria as the rest of the collection. But *use* of the reference collection, which is the key to the library's resources (and those outside the library), must be developed. College librarians should be thinking of "reference-centered" libraries, not "book-centered" (that is, warehouse-type) libraries. Every student should know how to use the reference collection, or at least know its potential so he can ask the right questions.

At Earlham, which has a fairly typical curriculum, I have gone out on that limb I spoke about before and have told the administration that, to meet those three needs, a library building for 350,000 volumes should be sufficient for us indefinitely. I am not talking about a steady-state library of 350,000 titles; rather, I am saying that a library accommodating 350,000 volumes in today's terms has sufficient space for continuing growth, albeit at a much, much slower rate. What I am counting on, of course, is that space-saving devices and technology will permit our future students to have more than 350,000 volumes in the same space as well as fairly quick access to almost anything else they might need.

But what I really want to make sure of is this: assuming that our basic collection is well chosen, our students will make good use of it. A 750,000-volume library sounds good in the college catalog, will assuage any accrediting team, and will please faculty members who are pursuing their own research, but will it really do the freshman or sophomore much good? We should be just as wary of the oversized college library as we are critical of the undersized one. An enormous collection overwhelms, probably inhibits, the beginning student. Moreover, when a college library becomes much larger than necessary, its most important role, education, may have to be sacrificed in order to maintain the seldom-used, or even unused, major portion of the collection.

This is where the "boon" comes in. By being forced to limit collection size, college librarians can devote their resources and energies to doing what a college library should be doing. Too many college librarians have been caught in the university-library syndrome and have thought of their libraries as small university libraries, conscious of only the superficial differences—fewer resources, less scholarly expertise, fewer relationships with other libraries and information centers, and less availability of electronic technology. These differences are limiting, of course, but the one difference between the two types of libraries that we

18

should focus on is that the college library, in contrast to the university library, can establish a unique program, one tailored to the needs and character of its constituency. It has, so to speak, a captive clientele, usually small enough to know as individuals. With that clientele the library can establish as intimate, as helpful, and as educational a relationship as its imagination, energy, and desire allow.

There are many things the college library should be doing better to enhance this relationship, but for me the most important is to teach students how to use the library effectively. Limiting the growth of a library makes it all the more important for students to know bibliographical resources. In most undergraduate research relatively few items *must* be in the library for the work to get done, but the student is not likely to think so. We should help him be imaginative and ingenious as well as efficient in his search, rather than merely diligent in plowing through everything. Students can and should learn to appreciate the importance, even the fascination, of searching for useful materials—that is, to realize that part of their learning is the skill of information retrieval and that such learning entails qualitative as well as quantitative searching. It is here that teaching search strategy becomes important. Moreover, if students are going to have to go outside the library's own collection for some of their needs, the intelligent selection of materials becomes crucial, and only by using the bibliographical apparatus can those selections be made intelligently. This is certainly obvious with terminals to an information bank. If students do not know the structure of indexing vocabulary—another objective of bibliographic instruction— a search through the computer can be very expensive *[...meant literally when written, but just as accurate figuratively now (ed.)].*

Faculty should be willing to accept the concept of a trim collection as long as students use that collection really well and as long as there is relatively quick access to other sources. Without doubt, students can thereby improve their performance, and most faculty should be willing to make the tradeoff of a more limited collection for better work in their courses. But there needs to be some additional re-education of faculty, so that rather than accept term papers that can be done overnight, they should insist on preliminary bibliographies and rough drafts and evaluate the quality of their students' sources as well as their spelling and footnote form.

The library can also help the college in practical ways. To a minor extent, by raising funds from donors or by grants. To a somewhat larger extent, by saving money through efficient operation. The library can usefully help, though, by enhancing the college's appeal to prospective students. The answer given by the Carnegie Commission on Higher Education to the financial problems of the liberal arts colleges, is not simply to cut costs or cater to the changing needs of students.

Rather, the answer lies in each college defining its unique educational character and role, and then develop its program to make that character and role a reality.[1] It is here that, by realizing its educational potential, the library can make a real contribution to its college's quality and character.

Not only can this contribution be a significant one, but it is in the library's self-interest. The Carnegie Commission, in noting the economies that educational institutions will have to make, felt that perhaps one-third of them could be made by fairly obvious efficiencies, but that the other two-thirds would require hard policy choices.[2] If libraries are not to suffer from these "hard choices," they will have to make themselves much more important factors in the college programs, and this is really what I am pleading for. Nothing I have said is very new, but it needs retelling for the urgency is greater now.

---

[1] Carnegie Commission on Higher Education, *Reform on Campus: Changing Academic Programs* (New York: McGraw-Hill, 1972) 36, 37.

[2] Carnegie Commission on Higher Education, *The More Effective Use of Resources: An Imperative for Higher Education* (N. Y.: McGraw-Hill, 1972) 152.

4

Book Reviews: Two Selections
(1976 and 1982)

I was a regular reader of book reviews even before keeping up with them became one of my professional obligations. What mostly appealed to me—aside from the sense, or maybe the illusion, that I was becoming widely read (or was able to impress others that I was)—were the differences of opinions, the intellectual disputes between authors and reviewers, or between two reviewers of the same book. Over the years I wondered why, in the undergraduate curriculum, more attention wasn't given reviews in order to document the important fact that scholars can disagree honestly and openly. In my BI presentations to classes whenever it was appropriate I mentioned the usefulness of book reviews and sometimes when working with teaching faculty on changing their assignments I suggested ways of getting students to use book reviews.

This interest in current reviews had been reinforced by a project I'd worked on at Emory, the Guide to General Books, *mentioned below. My interest in older reviews really began with helping design assignments, especially assignments for courses that had some historical parameters. I soon realized that it was very difficult finding reviews of books published more than several decades ago, especially reviews in scholarly journals or in "little" but important literary periodicals. That difficulty led to a discussion with a friend, Bill Buchanan, who had created the Carrollton Press, a discussion that eventually led to the publication of the* Combined Retrospective Index to Book Reviews in Humanities Journals, 1802-1974, *and the other retrospective indexes. The Introduction reproduced below was used almost verbatim in each of the other sets.*

The first piece below is from a talk given at an ALA conference in 1976. I was one of a panel of four (as I remember it) talking about the use of book reviews in book selection. I, presumably, represented the librarian's viewpoint. The others represented publishers, book reviewers, and book distributors. The audience (again, as I remember it) did not contain many librarians; it was made up mostly of those interested primarily in the making and selling of books.

— Evan Ira Farber, 2006

"Book Reviews in the Education of Undergraduates"

The more interesting part of my remarks—at least to me—is on the use of book reviews, not in selecting books for purchase, but in the education of undergraduates. It's more interesting—and more

---

Talk given at the annual conference of the American Library Association, Chicago, 1976.

21

important—because my major purpose as librarian (and I think this true for all college librarians, and probably many university librarians) is to enhance the teaching-learning process, to contribute in whatever ways I can to the education of students. Only by doing that, I feel, do we college librarians really justify our existence.

How do book reviews fit into this?

First, let me state the claim that one of the aims of education, especially higher education, should be to develop a healthy skepticism. As one commentator on American higher education put it (in one of the Carnegie Commission essays), skepticism—or, as he phrased it, "organized skepticism"—provides "the only basis from which man is able to contemplate the possible directions in which human society could be moving."

Now, whether or not you agree that skepticism is that basic, you must be aware that—and this is my next point—undergraduates are much too credulous, too uncritical about the printed word. They are not skeptical at all: they are willing to accept almost any statement, any point of view, any argumentation, if it's in print—and especially if it's in a scholarly work and on the library's shelves. Students know that novels can be criticized, and films, and recordings—but a scholarly work? It comes somewhat as a shock to them to look in the *Book Review Digest* and see criticisms of books they've been using, to see scholars arguing with one another, criticizing a single work for different reasons, and from different points of view. This is my third point, then: by using book reviews, students can learn to question the authority of a book, to read critically, and can begin to understand that a keystone of scholarship is challenging ideas, data, and arguments.

But how to get students to use book reviews? At the reference desk, to be sure, but this reaches a relatively small number. And so I pull out once again on my favorite soapbox, the one marked the need for giving instruction in use of the library. One of the purposes of library instruction is to wean students away from dependence on the card catalog and the *Readers' Guide*, to get them to know and make use of the whole gamut of bibliographical tools, and one very important category of those tools is of course book reviewing sources.

In talking about bibliographical materials to classes we stress the use of book reviews for two purposes: first, to help select books before reading them. Are they worth reading and spending time on? Or are there better ones on the same topic? The card catalog, students are reminded, doesn't tell whether a book is good, bad or indifferent, nor anything about its thrust or thesis. Why spend time reading it, and then discover it wasn't worth the time? (Remember, one of the payoffs of library instruction for students is making more effective use of time in the library.) Secondly, after reading a book, and deciding to use it as an authority, look up some of the more extensive reviews (I wish all book review indexes would indicate the length of reviews, as the *Book Review Digest* does). Long reviews not only evaluate books, and comment on their viewpoint, or data, or method, but may themselves be important contributions to the subject matter—that is, the review is used as much to express the reviewer's own viewpoint as it is for evaluating the book, and there's no reason why a student can't cite such a review in his bibliography just as an article on the same subject.

But also, get teaching faculty to encourage students to use reviews. Get them away from the tired assignment of the traditional term paper, an assignment that is so often given only because of lack of imagination. Compiling an annotated critical bibliography, for example, by using a variety of reviews, can be a much more worthwhile assignment. It forces students to particular works, to become aware of divergent points of view, and to try to fit them into a single scheme.

There are other ways to make students aware of reviews. Along with displays of book jackets, or in the new books area, why not display reviews of some of those books? Most of us are aware of the debate over Edward Wilson's book, *Sociobiology*, but how many students are? Displaying the initial positive reviews along with the range of later comments, calls attention to a dramatic case of scholarly disagreement, showing how a major work of scholarship has been interpreted so diversely. Or, if students who are interested in Irving Howe's *World of Our Fathers* were led, say, to the superb review of it in the most recent *New York Review of Books*, not only would they get some insight into the book, as well as suggestions for other materials related to the subject, but by being introduced to the *New York Review* as well as to other book reviewing media, they might just become regular readers of reviews.

The result of introducing students to reviews, then, is to make a contribution to their education by making them aware of intellectual diversity and perhaps helping them think more critically; and if we can go even further, that is, make students regular readers of reviews, so much the better. Reading, we believe, is contagious—"hooked on books" as the slogan says. Reading book reviews can also be contagious, and once we've got students hooked on reviews, they should become more dedicated readers and even book buyers—and that's what we all want.

For the second part of my remarks, I take my cue from a statement of Guy Lyle's, my mentor and friend, who wrote some years ago that good college library collections

> ...are not developed by an excessive dependence
> upon recommended book lists. There is no
> substitute for a thorough acquaintance with

23

books through the reading of critical reviews and
the books themselves.

But which reviews? I admit to being a compulsive reader of
reviews, not only for selecting books, but also just for the pleasure of
reading them as a genre of literature. I read too many, though, and
perhaps too few books...Well, what to say about them from the college
librarian's viewpoint? First, let's keep in mind some of the differences
between college libraries and university libraries. The latter are
(generally speaking) supposed to be comprehensive in collecting and
current in the latest research materials. College libraries not only cannot
collect widely nor, in most cases very deeply, but moreover they should
not want to—a college library with a well-selected, relatively limited
collection is much more useful for, and usable by undergraduates. (Too
many faculty, of course, would not agree—they'd like their college
library to be a miniature Widener—at least in their particular areas). But
with today's budget crunch, the care with which books are selected is
even more important.
　　　　Also, the college library should serve as a community library,
not just a scholarly one. It can do this well in most cases because its
community is more limited and defined. Book selection can be more
personal, more tailored to the community, and in smaller colleges like
ours, for example, the selection will reflect the librarian's tastes and
manifest his or her perception of the community. And, as with the public
library, and unlike the university library, the general reviewing media are
important. If one function of the college library is to encourage students
to read, and to be aware of what's going on in the book world, and
another function is to act as a community library—for faculty and staff as
well as students—it must keep up with current trade books. Using the
standard reviewing titles, of course—the *New York Times* (I use the daily
reviews as well as Sunday's), the *Saturday Review* (not used nearly as
much as formerly) the *New Yorker*, *Bookletter*, etc. I think *Business
Week's* reviews are superb, and as a regular Today Show viewer, I often
note titles to buy when authors are interviewed. I regularly scan *Science*,
not for its reviews of technical works, but for more general titles,
especially those in natural history and the history of science. Also the
Chronicle of Higher Education—it has a few long, thoughtful reviews,
but its listing of new books on higher education should be checked by
every academic library...I used to read *Times Literary Supplement*
conscientiously and carefully; in addition to its reviews of scholarly
works it is one of the few places to find reviews of Asian and African
English-language fiction and poetry...I regularly look through a few
periodicals which pick up books neglected by the standard journals—for
example, *Booklegger* for its materials on women, or *Parnassus* for its

24

reviews of books of poetry. Perhaps the reviews I read most regularly, even religiously, are those in *Publishers Weekly*...Though I've learned to be a little chary of some of *PW's* enthusiasms—especially in non-fiction—I find the reviews for the most part quite reliable...

What about scholarly books? Certain major items would probably be caught through those periodicals mentioned above, but by far the largest number—perhaps a half of the scholarly works we purchase—are ordered from *Choice* cards, which are distributed to the departments, then routed to individual faculty members, initialed and returned to be used for the order file, and then mounted on the inside front cover of the book after it's been processed. Several college librarians I know report a similar dependence on *Choice*, and I think it's probably a continuing trend. The long bibliographical essays in *Choice* are also very useful, particularly for checking one's holdings in a special area.

The scholarly journals, then, which used to be the mainstay for book selection, even in college libraries, are relatively seldom used now—the reviews are written by scholars for other scholars, and while the titles may be significant, their usefulness for undergraduates is usually not indicated, or even considered. And as budgets have gotten tighter, the appropriateness of titles for undergraduate use has become more important. College libraries do—must—focus more on titles that will be used; they can no longer purchase as widely, and certainly not as casually.

"Introduction to the *Combined Retrospective Index to Book Reviews in Humanities Journals, 1802-1974*"

Why an index to book reviews in humanities journals? At first glance, it might seem to most knowledgeable library users that there are ample points of access to book reviews. *The Book Review Digest* springs immediately to mind, followed by such titles as *Current Book Review Citations, Index to Book Reviews in the Humanities,* and others. But, on second thought, when one considers that *BRD* has severe limitations for scholarly use, and that most other general book review indexes that include humanities journals have been in existence a relatively short time, the need for a broadly-based retrospective index to book reviews in humanities journals becomes more obvious.

This need was brought home to me while working with teaching faculty at Earlham to develop course assignments that entailed scholarly book reviews. We prepared some fairly complicated sets of instructions for the students in those courses, and while I was at the Reference desk explaining the various search steps that would be required, I realized how much better it would have been for them to have access to a cumulative single source, especially one that would be easy to use. The result of this realization was the *Combined Retrospective Index to Book Reviews in Scholarly Journals 1886-1974.* But even before publication of this set, as soon as the data acquisition phase had been completed, I pointed out a parallel need for the retrospective indexing of book reviews in literature and other segments of the humanities.

The Value of Book Reviews in Scholarly Journals

Scholarly book reviews have been a special interest of mine for a long time. Most librarians have some interest in them, but mine was heightened while I was on the library staff at Emory University. There we had issued a little-known but (in our and its hundred-plus subscribers' opinion) valuable *Guide to General Books* that necessitated our combing reviews in all sorts of journals for books of general interest. I was intrigued by two things: first, the difficulty of locating some of the best reviews; and second, the importance of those reviews for not only evaluation purposes, but for fresh insights into and new perspectives on the subjects treated by the books.

Most students are aware of reviews in the mass media, especially reviews of films or recordings, and occasionally they may have read

Farber, Evan Ira (Exec. Ed.). *Combined Retrospective Index to Book Reviews in Humanities Journals, 1802-1974.* Woodbridge, Connecticut, Research Publications, 1982. Pp. Vii-viii.

reviews of current fiction or popular non-fiction in *Time* or *Newsweek*. But they are usually unaware of the existence—let alone the importance—of the reviews in scholarly journals even though they may have used articles from the same journals in other aspects of their research.

In order to gain the proper perspective of the value of these reviews, students should first recognize that they provide a crucible in which the output of scholarly research is examined, tested, and responded to. Through these reviews, they can trace the acceptance or foundering of individual reputations, and follow intellectual debates, not only between author and reviewer, but also among reviewers themselves. For the first time, perhaps, students can see that scholars disagree— openly and often emphatically—and that simply because something is published and in the library is no guarantee that it is completely credible. One important objective of higher education is to teach students to question assumptions, to teach "organized skepticism" as one writer has put it, and book reviews can help in this purpose.

Secondly, students should begin to understand that many book reviews do much more than simply evaluate the book at hand. A reviewer will often use the occasion for reviewing a book as an opportunity to reflect on the subject itself, and the review—or "review-essay" which is what it may then have turned into—could be an important contribution to the critical literature of the discipline. Indeed, there are even cases in which a review of a book became more important—in the long run—than the book itself.

Book reviews, then, are important not only for helping evaluate particular books, but also for understanding the critical context of a period, and for discovering new insights about the subjects under review.

5

Position Statement on Course-Related Instruction
(1977)

When I first looked at the piece below sent to me by the editor of this book, I had no doubt that it was by me, but hadn't the vaguest notion of where or when I had delivered or written it. It read like boiler plate for Earlham's BI program—that is, its very basic information could have been used by me at any number of occasions or for almost any audience not familiar with that program. So the content was no help in identifying its source. The only clue was the citation at the end: Literary Research Newsletter, *a publication I'd never written for, ever read or even heard of (and I considered myself somewhat of an expert in the field of periodicals). But then, getting a copy on interlibrary loan clarified everything.*

I'd forgotten that I'd given a paper at a Modern Language Association Conference to a special section's mini-conference on "Recent Developments in Teaching Research Methods and Papers: From Theory to Practice." The four papers given at that session, including mine, were then published as part of a Special Issue of the LRN *(volume 6, nos. 1 & 2, Winter and Spring, 1981). As I recall the MLA event, the audience was fairly large and consisted primarily of English teachers, for most of whom of course BI was an unknown. The piece below, then, the "boiler plate," was necessary for that audience and actually was only the first part of my talk, the remainder suggesting ways of implementing that basic information.*

The audience's response? They were attentive but, as I remember, their questions and comments related almost solely to the problem of plagiarism, an issue which none of the papers had addressed. Disappointing? Sure, but anyway I hoped that at least they then knew what BI was, and perhaps I'd partly paved the way for librarians at their home institutions.

— Evan Ira Farber, 2006

In the public relations literature of higher education, one often reads the statement that "the library is the heart of this university (or college, or whatever the institution)." It may be heretical coming from a librarian, but the statement is simply not true. What is—or should be—the heart of the college or university is the teaching/learning process. The library can and should be used to enhance this process, and *that* is its

---

Written for a meeting of the Modern Language Association at Illinois State University, February, 1977.
Incorporated into:
Farber, Evan Ira, "Library Instruction at Earlham College," *Literary Research Newsletter*, Volume 6, Numbers 1 & 2 (1981), pages 35-48.

most important contribution to its institution. But too often it is not used in this way. In fact, for most institutions, the library's resources are not used effectively at all.

Why not? A particular library may be well administered, with an attractive and comfortable building, a competent staff, adequate facilities and resources, yet still not be an effective partner in the educational program. Here are some of the reasons:

1. Student attitudes toward libraries and librarians are generally negative.
2. Most students and many faculty are minimally aware of the library's services and resources.
3. Course assignments don't make the best use of library materials.
4. Library faculty and teaching faculty don't interact very much in the teaching/learning process.
5. Students (including graduate students) don't know how to find materials effectively or efficiently.

Some, perhaps all of the above, are interrelated. What I want to propose is that a program of library instruction can respond to every one of those, and can help make the library an effective instrument in the teaching/learning process. Stated in very basic terms, such a program will teach library users how to make more efficient and effective use of library materials: efficient because it will help them get to materials more quickly; effective because it will help them get to better, more appropriate materials. Do not confuse library instruction with library orientation; library instruction *may* include the traditional introduction to the layout and procedures of the library, that would only be a small part of it, and is not even necessary to it. Nor is it a *separate* course in how to use the library—such courses may be useful, but they reach only a small number of students and do not relate to what students—and professors— are most interested in: the subject matter of their regular courses.

My appeal, then, is for course-related instruction, that is, instruction that works through the courses students already take, but makes the library applications of those courses more effective.

What are the objectives of such instruction?

First, and most immediate, to improve the work done for particular assignments (research papers, in most cases).

Second, to teach students how to search for information, not just the individual indexes, abstracting services, bibliographies and other reference materials they will use for particular assignments, but the strategy of search. The truly educated person is one who's learned how to learn, who can go beyond the textbook, even beyond the professor in searching for information. Much of what students are learning now will not be very useful to them fifteen years hence, but if they know how to search for information and how to evaluate it—and this is the third, and long-run objective—they will possess an important ability.

How does course-related instruction work?

Basically, by classroom presentations that introduce students to progressively more sophisticated library materials and methods whenever those are appropriate to particular assignments. Teaching faculty and librarians working together should decide when and how those presentations take place, and there are enough examples from many colleges and universities to help select the most effective method.

The major hurdle is faculty cooperation. By this time, librarians have read and heard enough about library instruction to recognize its importance and potential. But most faculty members do not realize that their students do not know how to use libraries or, if they do realize it, don't know how to help them. Nor have most faculty thought about librarians helping them *except* in the traditional ways—that is, by acquiring, organizing and servicing materials for their courses or research, and by answering questions at the reference desk. But that librarians might act as helpmates in the teaching/learning process, and the library play an active, not just responsive role, has not generally occurred to them.

The advantages of course-related instruction is that it relates to what students are most interested in (their immediate assignments), that it's flexible (it can be used with large and small classes, for many types of assignments and with all kinds of materials), and that it can—no, should—be built into the structure of the course itself so that it becomes a natural and expected part of many courses. When that happens, course objectives and library assignments become mutually reinforcing, students perform better, both in the library and on their assignments, and the library has begun to realize its most useful role in the teaching/learning process.

6

Bibliographic Instruction and Library Organization:
Problems and Prospects
(1977)

This paper was given at a conference at Indiana State University in 1977. The purpose of the conference was to examine issues and trends that were effecting changes in the administration of academic libraries. Eight papers, mine included, were given, and all were later published in a volume, Emerging Trends in Library Organization: What Influences Change *(Pierian Press, 1978). Now, in reading my paper over, I was struck by the comment in the opening paragraph that in all the time I'd given to speaking or writing about BI none was given to "relating to the structure and process of library administration" and that the same lack of attention was true throughout the profession, even by those actively involved with BI.*

"I was struck," as I said, because I realized that even after that conference, maybe even presently—that is, even since BI had become a significant service of so many academic libraries—there was still little attention given to its place in library administration. And then I thought of a couple of reasons. Since most BI programs were started and then administered by Reference departments, top administrators were content to leave it that way. Also, the role of information technology had become increasingly important and expensive—not just for the library, but for the entire campus—so that administrators necessarily focused on it.

— Evan Ira Farber, 2006

    I suppose I should have welcomed the invitation to present this paper. Like almost everyone else who's been actively engaged in bibliographic instruction, my time has been spent mostly in doing it and at other times talking about it, or proselytizing for it. The times I've had to think about it have been spent mostly on content and method, with a good bit less attention to rationale and to evaluation. As for any time spent on relating it to the structure and process of library administration, that has been relatively minuscule, yet when one thinks about it, one can almost immediately see that that relationship should be a basic consideration. Yet I don't think my lack of attention to the subject is unusual. For example, John Lubans' book, *Educating the Library User* (the most useful single work on bibliographic instruction) contains

Talk delivered at a conference at Indiana State University, October 20, 1977.
Published in:
Lee, Sul H. (ed.). *Emerging Trends in Library Organization: What Influences Change.* Ann Arbor, Pierian Press, 1978. Pp. 49-59.

almost forty essays, case studies and research reports, none of which are on the relationship of bibliographic instruction to administration. There are of course occasional comments about administrative support, or staff participation, but no sustained attention, not even for a few paragraphs. Nor does the extensive bibliography in the book include anything on administration. The only published work I know of that focuses on the subject is Allan Dyson's brief study comparing English and American patterns,[1] but even his conclusions are limited to organizational patterns, and as useful as that subject is, it does not treat the many other ramifications administrators should think about. So, as I said, I should have welcomed the opportunity to devote some time to thinking about the relationship and its ramifications.

However, it didn't take me long to realize that it was going to be a much more difficult job than I'd thought initially, not because of the lack of documentation (that may have made my task easier, really) but difficult because of the variety of current practices, because of the fact that almost every program—although drawing upon the experiences of others—has been created and then modified to meet the needs, the demands, the obstacles, the problems of the local situation. There *is* no accepted pattern, or patterns; there *are* no criteria or standards, and there has certainly been no evaluation of organization as it affects practice. On the other side of my agenda, the theory of library administration has been discussed, described and analyzed from every possible vantage point.

What I realized I had, then, were two kinds of information—one consisting of a body of principles, more or less agreed upon, based on long experience and many case studies and observations; the other, a mélange of practices and ideas, some seemingly successful or at least useful, but with very few deducible principles or generalizations—and what I was thinking of doing, juxtaposing them and making connections, was at best awkward and probably logically impossible. I concluded, therefore, that I could not posit a scheme or solution; rather, all I could do was raise questions and suggest directions for thinking about the administrative and organizational aspects of bibliographic instruction. My format, then, will be to examine those aspects that seem to me most significant. Some of them are interrelated, either because they affect or overlap with others, but I'm not concerned with logical categories, and the order in which I'm presenting them has no particular significance.

First, though, because most of you are administrators and perhaps not personally involved with bibliographic instruction, let me begin with a little background. The idea of teaching students how to use

---

[1] Allan J. Dyson, "Organizing Undergraduate Library Instruction: The English and American Experience," *Journal of Academic Librarianship* 1:9-13 (March, 1975).

library materials effectively is hardly a new one, and attention was given to it even in the nineteenth century. There were early isolated programs, but it wasn't until the movement away from the classical curriculum, the decreasing dependence on textbooks and increased use of term papers and independent studies, that the need for instruction became readily apparent. Harvie Branscomb's *Teaching With Books*, published in 1940, called attention to the underused libraries of colleges and universities, but he did not point to a program that would help other than suggesting that teachers make more use of library materials in their courses. Pat Knapp's work at Knox College and at Monteith in the 1950s was very advanced—too advanced for others to emulate at the time—but it provided a useful theoretical framework. (Indeed, it is still useful.) The "Library-College" movement, begun by Louis Shores, then taken up by Robert Jordan and others in the 1960s, got many librarians interested in teaching the use of library resources, but its refusal or inability to grapple with reality caused many of those who believed in the basic idea to strike out on their own. In June, 1969, at Atlantic City, bibliographic instruction was the topic of the combined general meeting of the Junior College and College Libraries Sections of ACRL. The overflow audience then and the subsequent questions and mail responses later brought to the surface the widespread interest in the subject. As yet, however, it was an inchoate interest that was not only unorganized but individually unaware of what others were doing, and in 1971, as a response to this situation the Ad Hoc Committee on Bibliographic Instruction was established and the first Conference on Library Orientation held. These two agents are still at work: the former has evolved into ACRL's Bibliographic Instruction Section, and the latter has not only held six succeeding conferences at Eastern Michigan University, but also gave rise the establishment of LOEX, the Library Orientation Exchange, which provides a central point for materials and information on bibliographic instruction. Much of the subsequent activity has emanated from these two groups, some of it with the assistance of the Council on Library Resources and, more recently, the National Endowment for the Humanities. I've sketched this history hastily and superficially, because what I simply wanted to call attention to was that most of the development has taken place only recently and within a period of less than ten years. Furthermore, even in this recent decade, the most prestigious libraries—the ARL group—had for the most part ignored the movement, or had only a few isolated staff members working on bibliographic instruction. This is no longer the case, and more than just a few of them have started programs.

What all of this means—this recent history and rapid growth—is that there's a lot of scampering going on, and this further justifies my reasoning that it would be impossible to came up with any really useful generalizations relating to bibliographic instruction and library organization.

Now, while there is a wide variety of practices, of formats and devices used, there is one type of instruction that is used more than any other—and that is "course-related" instruction, instruction that teaches use of library resources by means of assignments in individual on-going courses. I won't go into the rationale for the popularity of this method, but will just assume throughout this paper that it is the method used. Another assumption I'm making is more or less traditional library administrative and personnel structure. I'm not, for example, using Sangamon State as a model, because whether or not one believes it is the model to emulate, it is unique, and its solutions are not especially relevant for other libraries just now.

Given this background and these assumptions, let me move to specific aspects of library organization.

Typically, bibliographic instruction begins with one or a few reference librarians starting instruction on their own. As long as this is limited to a few staff members, usually giving the instruction on their own time, and not detracting from other library functions, there's no problem. But what happens when more and more staff time is devoted to it? When it becomes obvious that it is impinging on other activities, that there is no coordination with resultant conflicting demands for time, for clerical help, for supplies, and most unfortunate of all from the viewpoint of those who are interested in bibliographic instruction, that it is an inefficient program with many gaps and some overlap? It then becomes obvious that some planning and organization is necessary as noted in this analysis from librarians at the University of Texas:

> The absence of a comprehensive program
> of user education has contributed to a tendency
> for each library unit to operate in a vacuum,
> regardless of what is being done in other units.
> Due to the lack of well-defined user education
> goals, objectives, and areas of responsibility,
> there is little pattern in the activities which have
> taken place. Instead of directing their energies
> toward the development of on-going cumulative
> programs, librarians have generally responded to
> the usually ad hoc, spur of the moment, requests
> that are made of them.[2]

---

[2] *A Comprehensive Program of User Education for the General Libraries, The University of Texas at Austin* (The University of Texas at Austin, The General Libraries. Contributions to Librarianship, No.1, 1977) 24.

But then the question is: who does the planning? Assuming an office, where in the organization is it located? What are the relationships to departments, to subject specialists?

Before talking about the more basic questions let me discuss for a moment the relationship to subject specialists, because there is an interesting and perhaps instructive parallel between the role of the subject specialist and that of the instructional librarian. Now, I know there are some who think that the two roles can be joined, that bibliographic instruction can be left to subject specialists, and I want to dispute this immediately. Subject specialists are created in response to faculty demands, primarily to help with collection development, bibliographic assistance, and perhaps bibliographic instruction for graduate or upper level courses. Their training, their interests are in disciplinary areas, in research materials and procedures, and *not* in the educational process. I know they can be useful in helping with bibliographic instruction, particularly with upper level courses, but subject specialists (at most libraries) are not responsible for, nor interested in the general student, yet that is where most of the effort must be made. (The Northwestern University Library has a grant now to use librarians with subject Ph.D.s not only as subject specialists, but to give bibliographic instruction to undergraduates, and it will be interesting to see how this works.)

So when I said there is a parallel in looking at the role of subject specialists and the role of bibliographic instruction librarians, I'm not at all implying that the two can or should work together; as a matter of fact, I believe that their roles are probably incompatible, and there is a real tension between them. The parallel is from their correspondingly anomalous roles in the administrative structure. The administrative structure of most libraries follows the flow of materials, so that "responsibilities are limited, explicitly defined, and latitude is restricted so that it does not interfere with efficient workflow." The subject specialist, on the other hand, represents an opposite trend. "Although he may be located in one or another library department, his combination of activities...carries him across departmental lines."[3] So it is with the bibliographic instruction librarian, who, while mostly concerned with the reference function, must also be concerned with cataloging, with acquisitions and with circulation policies — and perhaps with others.

That is the parallel, but there it ends. Subject specialists are beholden, as I said, to their disciplines, and they may well be doing their work independent of, even oblivious to, the work of other subject

---

[3] Eldred Smith, "The Subject Specialist Librarian," in *The Academic Library: Essays in Honor of Guy R. Lyle* (Scarecrow Press, 1974) 71-81.

specialists. Bibliographic instruction librarians, on the other hand, whose purposes should relate to students' total education, must work together, so that there can be a logical, coherent program, so that individuals' experiences and material resources can be shared, so that desirable changes in policy resulting from instruction can be implemented more effectively. The response to this must be a coordinator, and the more decentralized the library system, the more important such an office is. It is also particularly important for an undergraduate program, because of the need for building upon previous experiences and to avoid overlap. It is perhaps not as important at the graduate level, where instruction may be given by subject specialists.

Assuming that a coordinator is desirable, where should the office be?

It is probably best to set up such an office as a staff position at first, preferably responsible to the director rather than one of the second-line administrators. The reason for this is that at first—at least at first—decisions will have to be made on the reallocation of resources, and continual verbal support for the program will be needed. After the developmental stage, when the program becomes established and taken for granted as a budgetary item, one might consider moving the position of coordinator to a line position, but that should be done only after there is general commitment—because unless there is, there will be too many tensions to permit the staff to work together. Assuming that happy state is reached, where in the line organization? Public services? Resources? A line position on a level with other major areas? That, it seems to me, depends on the extent of the program—its breadth and depth. To what extent, in other words, has it become a major part of the library's program, and how much further development is anticipated?

I've referred several times to the problems and tensions that bibliographic instruction can create or exacerbate, and since the pattern and practices of administration will partly be shaped as responses to these, I should spell out their sources. I take them up in no particular order.

Staff Relationships. In her article, "Some Effects of Faculty Status on Supervision in Academic Libraries," Martha Bailey points to the "unsettling effect" on administration that faculty status may bring.[4] The patterns of academic rank, the ways in which faculty interact do not correlate well with traditional library organization, which is bureaucratic and hierarchical. Bibliographic instruction may intensify this incompatibility: not only will instructional librarians have rank, but their

---

[4] Martha J. Bailey, "Some Effects of Faculty Status on Supervision in Academic Libraries," in *College & Research Libraries* 37:48-52 (Jan., 1976).

major responsibilities—the planning, implementation, and evaluation of course-related instruction—will bring their roles and their self-perceptions closer to the teaching faculty.

Indeed, this will bring them in much closer physical and intellectual contact with faculty—and with students—with the educational process, if you will—so that librarians who remain behind the scenes—those in technical services, for example—may become resentful. Avoiding this morale problem is not easy, but an attempt can be made at it by at least offering the opportunity to give instruction to anyone who wishes it. But that solution can lead to other problems. Beside the obvious one of alienating the head of, let's say, technical services, who resents the time taken away from departmental business, there is the problem of dealing diplomatically with the staff member who's eager to give instruction but whose talents are just not appropriate. (There's no faster way of killing a bibliographic instruction program than giving deadly presentations.) One possibility is making use of the person, or office, on the faculty who is concerned with teaching improvement. If they can't help the misguided librarian improve, they can at least suggest his or her talents are better used elsewhere—and the source for the hurt feelings is at least not on the library staff.

Professional Development. There's not much point in administrators expressing their commitment to a program of bibliographic instruction without recognizing the need for professional development on the part of its participating librarians. And this entails release time, even at the risk of other staff members being envious. The need for release time is not only to permit keeping up with the subject matter of the courses with which they're working, or even attending those courses, and with the literature of bibliographic instruction and with the materials and programs of other institutions (for these have provided by far the most productive sources of ideas and practices). There is also the need for time to develop teaching skills, to meet with faculty individually and in departments in order to plan courses. All of these are important and useful. They are, however, useful for getting a program underway and for keeping it current, and what is also needed is time to develop some expertise in areas such as evaluation (generally acknowledged the weakest aspect of the entire bibliographic instruction movement) and computer-assisted instruction, which only a few programs have dabbled with, yet which has enormous potential, but also which very few instructional librarians have the expertise to explore.

Relationships With Faculty. The ultimate level of course-related instruction is, in my opinion, when it is totally integrated with the courses—that is, when teaching a subject and teaching the effective use of that subject's library materials are mutually reinforcing and not separable without damaging both. This should be an objective of every program and, if achieved, will surely change relationships with the faculty. Librarians will be regarded not as custodians of or even as experts in the processing and servicing of scholarly materials, but as partners (junior partners, to be sure) in the educational process. What this means is that librarians will participate in the planning of courses, even the planning of total programs, meeting with departments as well as individual faculty, and serving on those committees (curriculum, educational policy, teaching and learning) concerned with the content and structure of the educational program. It is obvious that this has implications for the status of librarians, for tenure considerations, for other personnel practices. What may not be so obvious is the impact on recruiting. Criteria used in recruiting librarians will change, and whereas administrative or technical expertise used to be paramount, now such qualities as initiative, presence, articulateness, even teaching experience, will become important. Teaching faculty may want a greater voice in screening applicants if, after all, they are going to work with them.

Reallocation of Resources. I've left this to last, because it's the most fundamental and most difficult — difficult for some to accept, and probably for all to effectuate. There are a number of reasons reallocation is so fundamental — the demand for additional personnel is obvious — and one of the reasons attaches to its symbolic value. Allan Dyson's study, which I mentioned earlier, concludes that the most important factor in determining the success of bibliographic instruction programs "is the extent of commitment to it by the library administration."[5] This is hardly surprising — the same is probably true of any other program; I think, though, it is particularly relevant to bibliographic instruction programs because they are so unfamiliar to many librarians, and because the staff tensions they can create can jeopardize their continuance and development unless administrative support is obvious, and the willingness to reallocate resources is surely the most obvious form of support.

Connie Dunlap has pointed out that "service programs designed to teach students the effective and efficient use of a large library" must be extended, that "we cannot continue to justify the expenditure of millions of dollars each year to build collections which are only minimally used," and, given present economic conditions, "the cost of such programs may have to be funded, to some extent at least, at the expense of the book budget."[6] The reallocation of personnel entailed to meet this shift raises serious problems, and I can do little more than list

---

[5] Dyson, p. 13.

[6] Connie R. Dunlap, "Library Services to the Graduate Community: The University of Michigan," *College & Research Libraries* 37:247-51 (May, 1976).

them, since each should be discussed at length. First, it seems to me, is the basic process of selection. If technical services librarians are to be shifted, which ones? No one should be dragged or pushed, kicking and screaming, into giving instruction, but if the experience of some libraries (including Columbia University) is any criterion, there are a number of technical services librarians who are not only willing, but capable and eager to give instruction. This can be a real advantage for the program, giving it a broader base of staff support. It means, though, that the coordinator will have to select carefully, will have to encourage the development of instructional skills, and will have a more difficult job of coordination.

If a large number of the staff can be involved in instruction, the benefits for their morale are considerable; for the first time, perhaps, they'll feel that they're really part of the institution's major purpose—the education of students.

I might note at this point that I've not talked about the implication of bibliographic instruction for planning physical facilities. I could have devoted some time to it—almost nothing has been written on it—but it seemed to me not quite central to the administrative matters I've discussed. But administrators should be aware of some of the considerations—space for teaching, the restructuring of reference areas and the card catalog area, the increased public use of terminals, easier access to bibliographic materials, just to name a few.

I've spoken all along of the problems, the challenges, that a bibliographic instruction program raises for administration. What opportunities does it offer? Surely the most important is making the library a more active participant in the educational process, an admirable and desirable aim, but there may be an additional important effect. Pat Breivik has noted how "a major change on campus, either in personnel or direction, best facilitates a significant change in the educational role of academic libraries."[7] By "major change" she means a change in top library administration, or a change in the institution's educational thrust, or (most opportunely) both. These can provide the opportunity for changing the library's program, policies and procedures, and from her viewpoint, provide the occasion for instituting a bibliographic instruction program. Such an opportunity doesn't come along readily, but if we reverse the circumstances, how can instituting an instructional program change the library? Because an effective instructional program is so

---

[7] Patricia Senn Breivik, "Leadership Styles and Management Support for Teaching Libraries." Paper given at Leadership Conference for Integrating Libraries into the Educational Mainstream, June 13-15,1977 [Sangamon State University, Springfield, Ill., 1977] 4.

different from traditional library services, a fresh look should be taken at many of the traditional roles and relationships—roles and relationships which were once created for an effective library, but perhaps have since become outmoded and ineffectual.

If I've sounded as though I mean to elevate bibliographic instruction above all other library functions, I don't really intend that—and I have always stressed the importance of maintaining the high quality of other services. Perhaps this is unnecessary to say to those librarians who feel that instruction, if not a frill, is a service that should be offered only after the traditional library functions and services have received the resources and attention they need. But even if we heed Connie Dunlap's advice, and bibliographic instruction is given priority, the importance of maintaining other services must be constantly kept in mind. The success of course-related instruction is, and as far as I can tell, will continue to be dependent on faculty cooperation. Until teaching faculty change radically (and radical change is not a characteristic most faculty are noted for) the most important library services for them will be the adequacy of the collection, how fast books are processed, or are put on reserve, the availability of an SDI service, etc., and faculty will not readily accept librarians as partners in the educational process if the quality of these services, which they regard as librarians' main responsibility, deteriorates. But the day will come when the quality of bibliographic instruction is valued at least as highly as other services.

I've tried to show that because bibliographic instruction diverges in a number of ways from other library functions, and is only in its adolescence, with the attendant inconsistencies, problems, and pains of that stage, individual instruction programs can be shaped and be used to make their libraries more effective. There are many aphorisms about change—its desirability or its undesirability, but most refer to its inevitability. I like Alfred North Whitehead's observation that "the act of progress is to preserve order amid change and to preserve change amid order." By anticipating the problems of bibliographic instruction, by recognizing the challenge it presents and, most important, by welcoming the opportunities for change it provides, librarians can be assured of a more creative and effective role in the educational process.

7

Librarian-Faculty Communication Techniques
(1978)

In September, 1977, I received a letter from The College of Charleston inviting me to speak at the Southeastern Conference on Bibliographic Instruction that was to be held the following March. According to the Conference Coordinator, Cerise Oberman, "The conference will be composed of five sessions chaired by different speakers...your session [is] 'Librarian-Faculty Communication Techniques'." The audience, she noted, would be "rather diversified" and suggested that my session should cover "the value of involving faculty members in library instruction; the role of the librarian and the techniques employed to involve faculty with bibliographic instruction; various techniques and their success or failure rates; and successful and unsuccessful integrated programs..." but "Please feel totally free to discard, redefine, and/or supplement these suggestions."

How could I refuse? Charleston in March? And to speak on a subject about which I'd talked or written many times, and furthermore, to be given such leeway? Of course I could not refuse, and so spent a few days there, giving my talk and then enjoying the city, its history, and its culinary attractions.

That may be the first talk I gave in which I addressed the problem of getting faculty to use innovative methods in their teaching, a problem I often spoke or wrote about later. I thought that one likely solution to the problem was to convince a faculty member that using BI in his or her course would improve students' work. The best way to do that, I felt, was to get testimonials from other faculty who could testify to their successful experiences using BI. I had used Earlham faculty members in various workshops to do that, but our connection could make their testimony a bit suspect. Fortunately, I had made a videotape of a talk by Goodwin Bergquist, a distinguished professor of rhetoric at The Ohio State University, who'd used BI in his History of Rhetoric class that had several hundred students. As one might expect from a professor of rhetoric, he was a superb speaker, and had a delightful sense of humor. His testimony was most effective, not only because of his style, but also because he represented the experience of a large university faculty member (as opposed to one teaching at Earlham with 1100 students) as well as providing some compelling results with his students. I used that tape frequently in later workshops.

— Evan Ira Farber, 2006

Talk given at the Southeastern Conference on Approaches to Bibliographic Instruction, The College of Charleston, Charleston, South Carolina, March 17, 1978.
Published in:
Oberman-Soroka, Cerise (ed.). *Proceedings from Southeastern Conference on Approaches to Bibliographic Instruction* (Charleston, SC, 1978), 70-87.

The communication techniques which we in the library use with the teaching faculty are important for any aspect of academic librarianship, but especially important for bibliographic instruction. The form of bibliographic instruction I'm talking about is course-related bibliographic instruction, not a separate course. I won't go into the arguments for or against separate courses now, and will simply assume, with ample justification I think, that most of us are or will be working with course-related instruction. Because such involves courses taught by and traditionally planned by the teaching faculty, it is necessary for us to establish effective communication with them.

In course-related instruction, the librarian's input is relatively minor. This is not to say that it is unimportant, nor that it is inferior, but it *is* subsidiary—subsidiary, that is, to the major thrust of the course, which is planned primarily by the teaching faculty. In my ideal course using bibliographic instruction the disciplinary objectives of the course and the library objectives are mutually reinforcing. That is to say, the instructor's objectives in teaching the subject and the librarian's objectives in teaching search strategy and sources of information work together and call for cooperative planning. This obviously necessitates communication.

There is a cliché that appears in many college catalogs—and you will hear many administrators, even some librarians, perpetuate it—that the library is the heart of the college. Now that is simply not true. The heart of a college or university is the teaching/learning process. Although I may say that for political reasons (that is, to dissuade any teaching faculty or administrators from believing that my sole interest is the library), I believe it, too. But while I do consider that the heart of the college or university is the teaching/learning process, I also believe that the library should be used much more effectively than it has been for enhancing that process, and the greatest enhancement, I think, occurs when that ideal situation is achieved: when the disciplinary objectives of a course and the library objectives are mutually reinforcing.

What the library must do is pursue those goals implicit in the cliché. It should be used to make the whole teaching/learning process more effective, and at the same time help students learn how to find information. This certainly seems sensible, and most faculty and administrators agree that it is—in principle. If it is sensible, why then is it difficult to get many faculty to work with librarians in planning courses, or even let librarians talk to their classes. It would seem that we are all interested in the same end—that is, the teaching/learning process and better education for students. Why then are librarians regarded as enemies or suspect? Why is there not more cooperation?

One can approach the question of the lack of faculty cooperation from two points of view. First is the sociological or institutional context;

second, the psychological, individual traits and qualities. These categories are not mutually exclusive, and both factors are encountered at most institutions, but in varying proportions. Let me define what I mean by sociological. Bibliographic instruction is an innovation, particularly to teaching faculty. In the article, "Faculty Receptivity to Organizational Change: A Test of Two Explanations of Resistance to Innovation in Higher Education," the author states: "Faculty respond to innovation in terms of whether the innovation would bolster or present uncertainties to the prerequisites accruing to them in their present statuses. The greater the risks and uncertainties they perceive, the lower their receptivity."[1] In other words, if the institution rewards innovation, the faculty will respond. Unfortunately, most institutions do not. Nor do the disciplines—that is Political Science or History or English—reward innovation. So most faculty play it safe, and teach as they were taught.

But this really cannot be the total explanation. Earlham College, for example, an innovative institution in terms of teaching, encourages innovation in all kinds of ways. But even in this supportive environment some faculty have remained unresponsive to the overtures of the library. So I suggest a second explanation, which is the psychological or personal. I know psychologizing is risky, and that categorizing individuals so easily is not only an oversimplification, but also unfair. Nevertheless, I will go ahead.

Most teaching faculty tend to be discipline-centered, as contrasted with student-centered. Discipline-centered faculty see their task as training students in the respective disciplines, primarily by imparting to them the technical aspects of methodology and procedure. In this kind of teaching, the library has no role except to store information and to make it available on demand. The teacher, according to this point of view, is the real source of knowledge, and the library is simply a storehouse where items of information are kept that will validate that source of knowledge.

Also, a classroom teacher's training is toward individualism, toward expertise. Librarians, then, who long to show students other points of view, other ways of getting information, may be regarded as threats to the entire training and background of teaching faculty. Many teachers have fragile egos, and because someone wants to work with their students—someone who can point out materials and methods with which they may be unfamiliar—it is easy for them to infer that others think them inadequate.

---

[1] Carole Kazlow, "Faculty Receptivity to Organizational Change: A Test of Two Explanations of Resistance to Innovation in Higher Education," *Journal of Research and Development in Education*, 10:2 (W 1977) 87-98.

Moreover, cooperating with librarians takes time. It means changing assignments and perhaps modifying objectives, and that complicates a teacher's existence. It is, in other words, trouble as well as a possible threat. And these days, when the pressure to publish is great, a non-tenured faculty member will want to spend as much time as possible on his or her own research and not be bothered with experimental courses. Further, most teaching faculty have never met librarians serving in a teaching capacity, and cannot think of librarians as peers with whom one can share the responsibility of teaching.

I have intentionally oversimplified, drawing a caricature perhaps, a caricature of teaching faculty who are interested only in conveying information, who are defensive, who are condescending to librarians, and who are reluctant to share their space, their students and their time. But fortunately those are not the only members of the teaching faculty. There are those who are student-centered, who have adopted a developmental model of education. These are teachers who are as much concerned with the process of learning, with the development of students' capacities and abilities as with the transfer of knowledge and skills. They can see that learning to retrieve information can be taught, that it can perhaps make their courses more interesting, can improve their students' work in the future as well as in the present, and that it is an important part of the educational process. I am quoting one of Earlham's faculty members:

> A working familiarity with the use of the library can serve to achieve one of the most basic purposes of a liberal arts college. It can truly liberate the student to be a self-starter. Bibliographic instruction, when it is accomplished in the context of a substantive academic program and is done with practical rather than with a more formal end in mind, really frees the student by awakening her or him to the possibilities of the scholarly task. The feeling of achievement when one comes across a gem of information obtained only because one knew where to look is in a very real sense its own reward.

While not every student-centered faculty member understands this as perceptively and quickly, there are many like him. They are generally innovative teachers. They are not necessarily library-minded, but they can become librarian-minded, and there is a big difference. We have a number of faculty that are library-minded, faculty who know bibliography in and out, who know the library collection very well, but who don't think of librarians as people to work with. There is a big difference between library minded and librarian-minded.

The best way to encourage this librarian-mindedness is to cultivate it in many different ways. Let me just suggest a few ways of doing this. One is to make the librarians known personally, and here I am going to cite some of the things that we do. As soon as a new faculty member is hired, I, as Director of the Library, send him or her a letter saying, "Delighted to see that you are coming to our college. Is there anything that we can do for you? Do you have any bibliographies you want checked, and books you'll be needing, etc? We look forward to seeing you in the fall and working with you." I am always amazed at the response that I get. A new faculty member is frequently someone just out of graduate school who has been teaching perhaps only a couple of years. They are just delighted at the recognition, and even though many of them have nothing for us to do for them, they will just write back a note saying "Thanks very much" or will come in to see us and comment on receiving that letter. It is a little thing, but it immediately gets new persons aware that the librarian knows they are coming and that the librarian wants to work with them. Another thing we do is to talk to new faculty during orientation; I make a point to spend half an hour or so talking about the library. Not about the collection, because they find that out quickly enough, but about what we can do for the faculty in terms of getting materials, in terms of helping. Where that kind of occasion is not available, some kind of reception for new faculty should be held.

After the individual is on campus, we try to make the library known for its services. We get to know the individual instructor's courses, his research projects, even his personal interests. At the talk that I give to new faculty, one of the things I do is ask them to let us know the kinds of things they are working on. Not their courses, because those we may already know or we can find out about easily; rather, what specific subjects outside their courses they want information on. Then we will try to send them notices of books, articles, etc., items they would not be likely to see. In other words, I will not send a psychologist items from the American Psychological Association journals because I assume that the psychologist looks at those journals regularly; I might send an item from the *Journal of Marriage and the Family*, things that I don't think the person will ordinarily be looking at.

Do work with faculty on collection development. I think the use of *Choice* cards distributed to departments and then departments routing them to individual faculty members is a very good way of keeping faculty involved in collection development. Ask the advice or opinion of a faculty member; make faculty recognize that you are interested in what they are doing. That is the major objective: to get faculty to see that the librarians are interested in what the faculty members are doing in their research and in their teaching.

Librarians are in a good position not to be threatening, but rather to be helpful, and that is my point, to emphasize that role of helpful friend, to establish confidence in the library and the library staff as librarians. Because if we are not as good at what we are traditionally supposed to do, why should anyone think that we can work in areas where we are not trained? If the faculty does not have confidence in the way the library is run, why should faculty members listen to our overtures to help them in their teaching? Before any librarian thinks about offering bibliographic instruction, he or she should make sure the library is being run well. Establish your reputation for doing what you're traditionally expected to do, then build on that.

Planning Instruction

Be aware at the Reference Desk where the need for instruction is demonstrated. Indeed, this is the way I started instruction at Earlham. I can remember the class well—it was John Hunt's course in American Literature. I had worked Reference one evening and got a number of similar questions from John's students. So I said to John the next day, "Look, John, ten of your students came to the Reference Desk yesterday and were asking how to find information on Faulkner. It really doesn't make any sense, you know, for the Reference Librarian to spend twenty minutes with each of those students. It is not very efficient. How about letting me come to class and show the class at one time how to find information on Faulkner?" And he said, "Sure, fine." So I did. The Reference Librarian has to be aware of times and ways to give better reference help than individually, such as by giving a basic instruction to an entire class.

This may require "instant lecture" or may mean looking to the future. Students will come to the Reference Desk and say, "We have an assignment to do such and such. How do I find information?" This alerts us—too late, of course—but we call the instructor the next morning and say, "Look, some of your students are looking for information quickly. Can I come into your class and give a quick lecture?" But that is not efficient. There is no time for planning the instruction or the assignment. This may, however, lead to instruction later on—begin wherever you can. If it is necessary to work up a lecture very quickly, you do that because it may lead to a better planned bibliographic instruction next term.

Planning is most desirable, and that is planning as early as possible—with individuals, with departments, with entire programs such as black studies programs, programs in family relations, programs in peace studies, as we have. Try to plan an entire bibliographic structure

46

throughout a program because most programs have a core of courses that students have to take. And if you can relate instruction to those courses, it really works out very nicely.

Are there departments or programs that are restructuring right now? Are there departments that are looking over their entire curriculum? Are they reorganizing or re-planning courses? Try to get in on the planning stages. A library component is best inserted when the course itself is being planned. Target those courses that are most crucial, those that are introductory to an area, which are basic for all majors, that provide the foundation for later work. What is the content of those courses? What kinds of assignments do they have? How can bibliographic instruction be related to that content and to those assignments? For example, one of the things we are doing now in Economics is giving beginning Economics majors a test in government documents. Many of them have had instruction in government documents before. But now the head of our Economics Department, who incidentally used to be quite resistant to library instruction, is convinced that it is important for Economics majors to know how to use government documents, and he has agreed to have them given the test. And if they do not pass the test, we will give them special instruction.

Focus on those faculty who might be receptive. As I talked about before, what are their courses, their interests, their plans? And as I said, for the discipline-oriented faculty members, point out how bibliographic instruction can be useful in those disciplines, because it is only by appealing to their interest in having their students become better majors that you can persuade them. Do all this in person, not by memo, not by form letter. Talk to people individually. Go to their offices if necessary. Call them up on the phone. But talk to them individually. Talk about what *they* are trying to do. Keep in mind the particular course. What is the instructor trying to accomplish? What are the objectives and the content of the course?

Bibliographic instruction can be flexible. We can adapt bibliographic instruction to almost any kind of course, but most faculty are not flexible in terms of what they want to teach, in terms of the course structure. So keep the course in mind and adapt to *it*.

Timing Instruction; Flexibility

The timing of instruction is very important. We do not usually give instruction early in the term; rather, it should be given to students when they need it most, when the students are up for it. When an instructor says to me, "Can you come in the first day of the term or very early in the term and talk about the library?" I say that that is no good. At that point students are not even interested in the library. Students become interested in the library only when they have an assignment in mind and they feel a little bit frustrated: "Is there enough material? How am I going to find it?" And actually some of our assignments are planned to insure that students are frustrated. I often ask instructors to have students do a preliminary search before any kind of instruction so that they have begun to worry about finding materials. *This* is the point at which we want to come in and say, "Here is how you find the material."

In one Spanish class, for example, we gave the class a bibliography after the first few days of class, with a very brief, general lecture. This was to help students choose a topic and then begin to look for materials. Then about the fourth week, we gave another lecture, this one more explicit, and then worked with groups of three, since each group had its own topic. The students did not actually have to write a paper, but prepared an annotated bibliography on each of the groups' subjects. To make these individual searches of value to the entire class, each group gave an oral presentation to the rest of the group on their accomplishments.

(The teacher involved in this course is unusual. She told me that one of her colleagues in the Languages Department had accused her of being anti-intellectual, of watering down her courses, of catering to students, that she was not demanding enough. That encapsulated for me the dichotomy, the contrast, that I was talking about earlier: The discipline-centered and the student-centered faculty member. He is the former; she, the latter. She is a delight to work with; he, almost impossible).

Here was a case of relating bibliographic instruction to the assignments. Though we began with the general, we then followed the course pattern, going from the general to the specific, finally working with individual groups of three about the fifth or sixth week of the term. At that time we talked about the progress each group had made so far, and showed other bibliographies or indexes that they had missed. Since the students had already had some library instruction, we did not have to teach them about using the card catalog or the subject heading book. What we needed to do in this course was to teach them those sources that were specifically for that particular course. This, then, was an example of flexibility that makes course-related instruction such an effective method.

Obviously, not everyone can do this kind of thing. But we had laid the foundation for it in our structured program. With an instructor who is receptive and flexible, and students who have been given a foundation in library search techniques, it works very nicely.

Instruction

Everything that I have talked about up until now has led up to the instruction itself. The instruction has to be effective, but let us recognize the unique difficulties of library instructors as compared to the difficulties of a classroom teacher. First of all, in bibliographic instruction you do not have a developing relationship. It is generally a one-shot situation. If an instructor bungles the first day of class or even the first week of class, he has the rest of the term to make it up. We do not have that luxury. We have to be effective immediately. Secondly, the material is just not that interesting. Abstracts and indexes, for example, are fascinating to me and to you, but to students they are not— at least not initially. In addition, they are difficult to talk about, hard to show.

Most students come to college thinking that it is fairly easy to use the library. They went through high school using the library without any trouble, so what do they need besides the familiar *Reader's Guide* and the card catalog? We must dissuade them of this, and show them that those tools are not all there is to bibliographic searching. We have to persuade them on the one hand that finding information is more difficult than they think, but on the other hand that it is not so difficult that it can't be learned. And striking that balance is not easy to do.

Also, searching for information stands between the students and their assignments. It complicates their lives. The goals of bibliographic instruction, of the search for information, search strategy, all of those kinds of things that we want students to learn, are seen as peripheral by most students. Of course they are not, but students need to be convinced of this.

And finally, librarians' instruction efforts can be subverted. Students can get through four years without really knowing how to use the library or without even using the library very much. The student who is facile, articulate and can write well, can write a term paper on the last day of class and, unless the instructor is careful, the student can get away with it.

There are responses to all these difficulties, and they add up to being interesting, relevant and organized. The bibliographies that we prepare for students at Earlham are structured in a way that we hope students will use materials, beginning with encyclopedias or handbooks for general and background information, then proceeding from the general through the specific, with each reference work described as to its contents and usefulness. One of the things that we have begun using frequently is a sample search, and most of the bibliographies that we prepare now contain this sort of sample. What we do is reproduce portions of the particular reference works that are in those annotated bibliographies and show how one goes from one work to another. We take a sample topic and explain the way we would go through a search on that topic. The student has this sample on which to pattern his own.

8

The Library as a Minimal Resource Base
(1980)

This talk was given in December, 1980, to the Association of American Colleges Conference on Issues and Trends in Intercultural Education. I presumed I was invited because of Earlham's successful experience with and national reputation for its incorporation of Japanese studies into many areas of the educational program. The attendees were primarily administrators and faculty who were involved with some aspect of non-Western studies, and so I felt I needed first to say a bit about the basic purpose of bibliographic instruction.

Earlham's interest in Japan had been a longstanding one, but the impact of Japanese studies on the curriculum really began in the late 1950s under the leadership of Jackson Bailey. Jackson graduated from Earlham in 1950, then went on to Harvard, where he studied under Edwin O. Reischauer. After receiving his doctorate in Japanese history he was persuaded by President Landrum Bolling to return to Earlham to teach. With his dedication and what seemed to be limitless energy—plus funding from the Ford Foundation—he began a program of Japanese studies that in a few years became a model for area studies in colleges around the country. That program, incidentally, made excellent use of bibliographic instruction, and provided me with many examples for my proselytizing. I didn't talk about Earlham's program at this ACM conference because another speaker did.

— Evan Ira Farber, 2006

Let me start with a point that—for a librarian—is close to heresy: the library is not the heart of the college. Despite what your catalog or other publicity may, probably does, say, the library, I repeat, is *not* the heart of the college. What is? The teaching/learning process—those activities, those interactions that go on in the classrooms, in lecture halls and in laboratories between teachers and students. Plus, of course, what students derive from those interactions—not just how well they've learned the material so they can do well on exams, but how their own ideas have developed, their values enriched, their prejudices challenged, their abilities to look at issues with an informed skepticism sharpened. These are some of the cognitive objectives of higher education, of course, and in particular perhaps, of intercultural education.

Well, where does the library fit in? What should its role be in this teaching/learning process? The library's primary role is not just to

---

Talk given at a conference on "Issues and Trends in Intercultural Education in the Independent Colleges," Wingspread Conference Center, Racine, Wisconsin, December 9, 1980.

support, but to enhance that process, to enhance it in two ways: first, by permitting teaching to be more effective and second, by contributing to those student outcomes I just mentioned. Sure, the library does other things, but its basic purpose—its basic purpose in an undergraduate institution—is to enhance the teaching/learning process. That's one side of my first point.

The other side of this point is that in most colleges (and even more surely in universities) the library is not fulfilling that role, i.e., the resources that go into the library—the books and periodicals, the personnel, the maintenance—are to a large extent a wasted expenditure. Too many students, if they use the library at all, use it reluctantly, and when they do use it, use it only superficially and with great inefficiency. They have not, after all, been taught how to use it well, and they bring to college the same library habits and patterns they learned in high school, patterns that may have been appropriate then but are quite inadequate later for making use of the more sophisticated and greater variety of materials in a college library. Nor are students forced, or even encouraged, to change those patterns by the assignments given them, and most students can get through their four years with minimal skills in information retrieval. And that condition, that lack of skill, is serious in today's world.

> High-speed communications in oncoming years, some critics fear, can either produce the most informed and aware generation in history—or reduce the globe to a second "tower of Babel," collecting and transmitting much information but offering little comprehension of what it all means. (*U.S. News*)

To put it another way, we're moving into an information-based society, a society in which, when, as one commentator put it, the measure of one's success or failure will be directly related to one's ability to find, organize and use information. So far we have not been turning out students who are now or will be later discriminating users of information, and thus we're failing in one of our more important objectives.

My first point, then, is that the library should be used to enhance the teaching/learning process, but that it is not. It is, in other words, a resource that—by most students—is unused or misused, or both, and a lot of money is being wasted by supporting it and then not insuring its effective use.

My second point is that in these days, in these times of financial stress, talking about adding library resources in any substantial way is not only unrealistic but—to go one step further—even if we could add much, I'm not sure the results would be worth the expenditure, unless research efforts on the part of the faculty developed significantly, and the additional expenditures were fairly massive and continuing—and neither of those criteria is likely.

I'm basing that observation on several things. First, on experience from the early '60s, when an earlier wave of interest in international studies was widespread. As a result of that interest in the early '60s, a number of colleges, with government and foundation support, began building area studies collections. The impetus was great, and so was the initial interest, but with only a few exceptions that interest and support has flagged, and one can visit a number of college libraries today and only be depressed by seeing the evidence of a moribund interest—an area studies collection that's outdated and little used. There are several reasons for this, but one of them, it seems to me, was that college libraries made the mistake of attempting to emulate the university libraries—they fell prey to what I call the "university-library syndrome"—a syndrome that creates many problems for college libraries, and in this case focusing on *collecting* materials appropriate for research, rather than focusing on what undergraduates need or can use. Moreover, not only did they collect unnecessary materials, but then they didn't even bother to teach the students how to access those materials.

What they should have done—and in hindsight it seems so obvious—was buy carefully, selectively, to get the necessary reference materials—the bibliographies and indexes—teach students how to make use of them, and then to depend on the larger libraries, on cooperation, on interlibrary loan for access to less frequently used materials.

Another reason large expenditures on intercultural materials may not be necessary is that libraries already have more than they realize. "Intercultural," after all, does not necessarily mean exotic; intercultural materials simply means materials from which students can learn about other cultures. "For anthropologists," a commentator wrote just last week,

> ...the arrangements of the Western world
> will always remain but one set of possibilities
> among others; a new and unexpected
> configuration is always waiting across the next
> tributary of the Amazon or the next Papuan
> mountain—or in the next neighborhood of their
> own home town.

Your libraries undoubtedly already contain a good bit of material to help students understand that their way of life is but one among many possibilities, and to appreciate other traditions, other ways of living and thinking. It is, again, a matter of getting these materials used: first, giving assignments that will necessitate their use, and then getting students to use the library effectively, to mine the resources at hand and to use the means available to get information from other libraries.

Please don't misconstrue what I've said. When I said a large investment in new materials is not essential, that there are in most libraries already materials that can be used in intercultural studies, I don't mean to imply that your collections are all they should be, but I do mean that you probably have a better start than some might think. Probably what's needed is a bit more breadth, and very little depth. I think it's important, for example, to have a small but good collection of browsing materials—especially periodicals—so that students can keep up to date with what's going on in other cultures. A few hundred dollars expended for them can go a long way. And, again, I don't necessarily mean foreign-language publications. Nor are long runs of these journals necessary. Which specific titles would depend very much on your interests, on particular courses, and assignments. But in order to provide for even these relatively small expenditures, the library's budget should be structured to insure support for materials in whatever cultures or areas are given attention.

Perhaps even preliminary to this should be the encouragement of librarians to support this development. While the professional training of most librarians has, for the most part, neglected cross-cultural materials, this same training has attuned them to think across national and disciplinary lines. A library collection, after all, is a superb example of cultural amalgamation, of blurred religious and racial barriers. One role the college president can play is to help define the goals of intercultural education in broader terms than the departmental or divisional. The librarian, then, is a natural ally of the president in that broadening role. And to encourage librarians' participation in this endeavor, their level of expertise in and empathy for cross-cultural studies and materials should be raised, so that they may become as comfortable selecting and servicing cross-cultural materials as they are now with servicing, say, English literature or American history. Librarians ought, for example, to be given the opportunity to audit courses about other cultures, to participate in faculty activities and committees that treat cross-cultural matters, or they might take courses at a university or by extension. And the best way of encouraging this is providing some release time or a modicum of financial support. Then the librarian will not only be able to better help students but will be able to work more effectively with faculty.

The most important aspect of building a collection, however, is providing reference materials: the general and specialized encyclopedias, the directories, the yearbooks, the periodical indexes, the abstracting services and the bibliographies—again, a collection with some breadth and little depth. I want to stress the importance of this, because a good working reference collection can serve as the means of access to an enormous body of materials that may be hidden or overlooked, materials either in the college's library or available in libraries elsewhere. But students must know not only that these means of access exist, but also how to use them, and that entails teaching students how to use a library. Together—a good basic working collection of reference materials combined with students who know how to use them effectively—these can make an enormous contribution to the role of the library in the educational program, not only in intercultural studies, but in the entire teaching/learning process.

Let me summarize my points:

1. The college library's primary role is to enhance the educational process. But most don't because students don't know how to use libraries effectively, and assignments don't correct that ignorance.
2. There is no need to spend a lot of money in building collections. Rather, aim for some breadth, focus on reference materials, and make efficient use of what you have.
3. Involve librarians in your development plans. See how their interests can be stimulated, their expertise sharpened. They can and should play a key role—with a little bit of encouragement and support, they can. When that happens, the library resources will be more carefully chosen—and more important, effectively used.

That is your minimal resource base, and in cooperation with stimulating teaching, imaginative assignments that make good use of the library, and a basic collection, student attitudes toward the library and their patterns of library use will change. They will, in their library use, become self-starters, and an important educational objective will be the result.

9

Academic and Research Librarianship in the 1980's
(1983)

In the spring of 1983, I received an invitation from Dick Werking, Director of the Trinity University Library, to participate in the celebration of the opening of the library's new second level and the naming of the building for its principal benefactor, Mrs. Elizabeth Coates Maddux. My role would be twofold: first, to be part of a panel of three, each of us addressing in a 20 to 25 minute talk "Academic and Research Librarianship in the 1980s" (the other panelists were John Cole, Director of the Library of Congress's Center for the Book, and Paul Mosher, Head of Collection Development at Stanford); second, to say a few words (limited to no more than five minutes) at the actual dedication ceremony. Of course I accepted the invitation, and the following piece was my contribution to the panel (followed by the dedication speech). Readers should realize that the text below is an almost exact transcription of the talk as delivered, so there are many liberties with a traditional scholarly style.

I think the axiom I used—the three stages of the impact of a technological development—is one I continued to find applicable in many cases, and I used it several times in other talks. Probably many readers won't recognize Russell Baker, a delightful and perceptive writer on almost any topic, especially political or social issues. I recommend getting acquainted with a collection of his columns.

— Evan Ira Farber, 2006

If one thinks in metaphorical terms—as I often do—then I suppose the word that most readily comes to mind when considering academic librarianship in the 1980s is "watershed." Technically, a watershed is "a ridge or stretch of high land, dividing areas drained by different rivers or river systems." But, as you know, it's come to be used much more generally to indicate a historical turning point, a crucial period, a vitally important "point in time." Now there's probably not one decade over the past few centuries that has not been designated at one time or another, by one writer or another, as a "watershed" for some historical development, some national trend, or some series of events. But surely when we're talking about academic libraries, the term is quite appropriate for this decade. The 1980s are going to be—indeed, already are—a crucial period, a vitally important "point in time" for every academic library. Decisions regarding the procedures and practices of all libraries are going to have to be made soon that will affect those libraries in crucial ways for generations to come.

Talk given at Trinity University, San Antonio, Texas, September, 1983.

But an image that seems to me even more descriptive of where we are now is a whirlpool, a vortex caused by the confluence of two currents. It's those two currents I want to focus on. They are, first, the current deriving from the 19th century (and even earlier, really)—those practices, procedures, materials, even ways of thinking that shaped libraries up to very recently. And the second current is the one leading into the 21st century, the current of the new technology. Until a few years ago, libraries resembled very much what they were at the turn of the century. Students, or faculty members, stepping out of the late nineteenth-century would have little trouble finding their way around and even using most libraries in 1970. The libraries were still organized, both physically and organizationally, around the centrality of the card catalog: books and periodicals were still the basic commodities and materials were still shelved and circulated in much the same ways. Oh, sure, the 1970 building would have looked quite different from the 1870 one—more spacious, more informal, more comfortable, surely with a much larger collection, and there would have been (or should have been) a distinctly noticeable difference in librarians' attitudes toward use and users—but essentially libraries of twenty years ago were obvious products of the 19th century. But beginning in the 1960s and then increasing rapidly in the 1970s with the application of the computer to library operations and services, the vision of what libraries could be changed from a 19th century product to a 21st century one. The "electronic library," or a "library without walls" are a couple of labels recently attached to these visions; whether or not one agrees with those radical visions in all their details, there's not much question that libraries are changing rapidly now, and what happens in the next few years—the 1980s—will determine what academic libraries look like and do in the 21st century.

Thus—the watershed.

Perhaps you can begin to see why I like the metaphor of two currents. On the one hand, we have the current from the 19th century—a current comprised of traditional materials and services. On the other hand, the current leading to the 21st century, a current consisting of radically different materials and services—some not even yet imagined.

Let's drop the metaphor for the time being. You see what I mean. Librarians are caught in a bind, a time-bind, if you will: we have to provide services for our students and faculty now, today, using on the one hand the traditional materials and procedures, and on the other, we have to plan for, even implement services and procedures for electronically manipulated, even electronically created, information, with all the technology that goes along with it. And we've got to do both these quite different, even seemingly incompatible things in the same building, using the same personnel, even offering both types of materials and services side by side.

Do we have a choice? Well, a library could refuse to prepare now for the future and ignore most of the new technology. I suppose some do that—but not many. Aside from a professional matter of pride to keep current and, aside from the educational reasons—that is, preparing students for the world they're going to have to live and work in—aside from those abstract arguments, there are more practical ones: it would not be long before the faculty wondered why they were not getting services other libraries offered, and the Admissions Office demanded to know why perspective students repeatedly declared the outdated library was a reason for their choosing to go elsewhere. So we really can't ignore technological change.

Might others claim we do have the other choice? Opt for the future, and design today's libraries as if all information were electronic? Clarkson College (in upstate New York) did this—or at least the public and media perception was that it did, a perception hardly mitigated by the college's extravagant claims and the Clarkson librarian's definition of education, a definition gleefully cited in the media: education, several sources reported him saying, is "basically an information transfer process." The response was quick and scornful. The *New York Times* editorially deplored Clarkson's solution, and its marvelous columnist, Russell Baker, wrote: "information transfer process indeed! Education is not like a decal, to be slipped off a piece of stiff paper and posted on the back of the skull. The point of education is to waken innocent minds to a suspicion of information." And Ada Louise Huxtable, the *New York Times* critic, noted disdainfully that in Clarkson's kind of education, "there are no great minds, only great computers." She concluded, "The objective of education resists even the most sophisticated programming: it is the application of intelligence, inquiry and sensibility to the development of informed and caring responses to the achievements and dilemmas of the world."

Actually, the Clarkson library is not quite as radical as the publicity would have us believe, but I know there were some who welcomed the vision. That vision of the totally technological library is, for a few people, the wave of the future.

Compare that perception with the observation by Robert Frost, in one of his last public appearances, almost exactly 21 years ago. It was at the dedication of the Kenyon College library in 1962 that I heard Frost describe a college library as a place "where a student can have it out with himself." That is so brief, so laconic, so appropriately laconic from the New England poet—but it is also, as one might expect, an image full of implications. Perhaps the most obvious of those implications is that the library provides the novels or books of poetry in which students can lose themselves, that the library takes the newspapers and journals of opinion in which students check their perceptions of world affairs, and contains the volumes in which are laid out the words and ideas of the great—and, to be sure, the not-so-great—minds. "Books," the plaque in this library reminds us, "are the treasured wealth of the world; the fit inheritance of generations and nations." As Norman Cousins said recently in an interview: "If the book didn't exist and someone invented it and said that years of human experience could be put in your pocket and you could take it wherever you wanted, that you could select whatever you wanted to pursue, it would be called the greatest invention of the ages."

Yes, we must do both: provide students with the materials we've been working with for hundreds of years, those magnificent landmarks and minor evidences of our cultural and intellectual heritage, and we also need to acquire and implement the new technology. And, because the flow, the continuum of information, of knowledge, of ideas does not recognize the limits of time, or of format, we need to do both in the same building, with the same personnel. We have no choice.

But how to do both of these without becoming schizoid, or at least without feeling dizzy, caught in this whirlpool of the two currents?

It hasn't been easy, these past few years and it won't get any easier—not for a long time, anyway.

A few weeks ago, J. D. Watson, who, along with Francis Crick, won the 1962 Nobel Prize for their discovery of the structure of DNA, was interviewed on the occasion of the 30th anniversary of that discovery. He was asked if developments since their discovery had surprised him. His response was that for the first fifteen or twenty years, they didn't— he'd pretty much anticipated those developments. But then, he continued, the nature and increased pace of developments had amazed him.

I think we're reaching that period in librarianship. Some of the technological developments in libraries and information science of the past few years might have been anticipated 20 years ago, but now, with the increased pace of computer technology, combined with recent developments in fiber optics and optical disc technology, the implications for the storage—and even more important—for the retrieval and long distance transmission of information are mind boggling.

In studying the history of technology, that discipline which looks at the interrelationships between technology and society, there's a convenient axiom that describes the development of those interrelationships, a framework consisting of three stages. During the first stage, a basic invention or technological improvement permits us to do what we've done before, only better or faster, or both. In the second stage, it permits us to do things we've not been able to do before. In the third stage it changes our ways of living, working, even of viewing the world. We are at this third stage of library development now. At first, the computer permitted us to keep better records, to catalog faster. Then it permitted us to do new things: it gave management a variety of means of analysis and controls; it gave reference new kinds of indexes and data banks; it has freed us to consider new ways of creating and using the card catalog. In this second stage the computer has given us, in other words, a whole new toolbox for library services and administration. New we're in the third stage and many of our ideas of organization and management, of document delivery, the design of buildings and information networks, are all up for grabs. Combined with other technological developments, electronic information is the current that is carrying us into the 21st century. The limits of its potential are anyone's guess.

How can we best combine that potential, those unknowns, with what we've been doing for a century or more? How do we get our students to straddle the present, one foot in the traditional library, the other in the electronic age without getting confused, or not doing well at either? How do we get our staffs to work in both ages without becoming schizoid? How do we design our buildings and place our materials so there's no artificial gap between past and present information.

None of the answers to those questions will be easy. But they will be very interesting. My mentor at Emory University, Guy Lyle, remarked some 25 years ago that he was glad he was going to retire before technology took over libraries. I don't think Guy was right; technology is not going to take over but is surely going to change academic libraries. By the end of this decade academic libraries will be very different.

But in all this change, there will be one constant—the user—and for us that means our students. We must always keep in mind that academic libraries (and all other types of libraries, for that matter) are not ends in themselves. They are means for promoting, for enhancing the educational process. They help students make "connections between historical antecedents and the...quest for new knowledge, and the meanings of it all for the integration of life with learning." That definition (which is not original) is, I think, a more explicit way of saying what Frost said: "A library is a place where a student can have it out with himself."

If we can keep that purpose in mind, if we can continue to focus on our students and their needs, we won't have any trouble sorting through the problems, the unknowns. The solutions will become obvious. The 1980s are going to be an exciting and challenging decade for us, but if we keep our users in mind the decade will be a rewarding one. We're lucky to be a part of it.

10

Trinity University Library Dedication Remarks
(1983)

I had asked Evan and the other two dedication speakers (John Cole of the Library of Congress and Paul Mosher of Stanford University) to limit their remarks to no more than five minutes apiece, and they did. Evan's presentation was the shortest, at 3 minutes, 20 seconds.

—Richard Hume Werking, 2006

Thank you, Dr. Calgaard.

Ladies and Gentlemen, Mrs. Maddux...

It seems to me that a library dedication should be two-fold: one part conceptual, the other personal.

The first part, the conceptual, was suggested to me by an essay of Susanne Langer, the philosopher. In it she noted that higher education tends to emphasize the growing edge of knowledge, while ignoring the fact that development is possible only as long as there is a vital or growing center of knowledge. Quality education keeps this synoptic relationship in the foreground, keeps stressing that the frontiers of knowledge relate to a growing center of knowledge. And to paraphrase an observation by Martin Buber, the circle of our knowledge can only *really* be described and understood by seeing the radii, the *spokes* if you will, the connections between the center and the edges, by seeing the radii, *not* by identifying the points about the circumference.

An academic library, it seems to me, epitomizes that concept of interconnectedness. And it is to the promulgation of that synoptic concept, and its implications for the educational process, that I would make the first part of this dedication.

The second part of the dedication is to persons. But it is not the administrators, nor the faculty, nor even the generous benefactor I want to acknowledge, though their roles, of course, have been crucial to the vision, the planning, and the construction and expansion of this magnificent building. Acknowledgment of their contributions has come in many ways, and from many sources, including a very gracious editorial in this morning's newspaper. But it seems to me that their greatest satisfaction must come later, seeing the embodiment of their ideas and their ideals in use. And it is to those *users*, those future

---

Speech given at the Maddux Library Dedication, Trinity University, San Antonio, Texas, October 6, 1983.

generations of students, those inquiring, developing minds, those young people, for whom the library will be a place where they can experience and understand the interconnections and begin to explore the frontiers of knowledge, it is to them I would address the second part of this dedication.

They will be the ones to thank you all, and to acknowledge by their lives, and by their deeds, the contributions of all of you who had a part in this.

Thank you very much.

11

The College Library in the Year 2000
(1984)

*Library Issues was (and still is) a bi-monthly newsletter published in
Ann Arbor by Mountainside Publishing. Aimed especially at academic
administrators and faculty rather than librarians, and so intentionally succinct
and non-technical, each issue is four to six pages, usually covering just one
current topic of interest to all groups. I wrote this piece, which appeared in the
November, 1984 issue, hoping to help academic administrators and faculty think
about some of the issues being raised about the future of academic libraries.
My crystal ball may have been a bit cloudy, but considering that I consulted it
more than twenty years ago, my predictions have stood up pretty well. I was
certainly off the mark regarding the use of videodiscs, but even though I
predicted that in 15 years even the smallest library would have electronic access
to "large collections and data banks," I had no inkling of how soon, how
prevalent, and how versatile online information would become. However, my
bits of advice about being flexible, and about the importance of helping students
cope in this new scenario of unlimited information, are still worth repeating.*
— Evan Ira Farber, 2006

What will the college library look like 15 years from now? From
the outside, it will probably look much the same as it does now. When
today's undergraduates return for their fifteenth reunion, they should
have no trouble recognizing it. There will still be the familiar brick
walls, the lovely vistas of the campus from almost every window. As
they enter, they'll still see the circulation desk, but checking out
materials will be done almost automatically and instantly by the user.
The reference librarian will probably still be seated nearby, but rather
than consulting a variety of reference works or indexes to answer a
question or locate a source, he or she will be using a terminal on the
reference desk to find the information. There will still be displays of
new books and periodicals as well as daily newspapers—all arranged
somewhat differently, perhaps, but familiar enough to make the alumni
nostalgic.

Technology Invades
But when those former students begin to use the library, the

Farber, Evan Ira, "The College Library in the Year 2000," *Library Issues*,
Volume 5, Number 2 (November 1984).

differences will become very apparent. Instead of a card catalog (done away with in 1988, let's say), the library's holdings and records will be consulted on any one of the terminals which are scattered around the library or in other buildings on campus, in offices and even in dormitories. These terminals will be easy to use (i.e., "user friendly") and will tell what this library has, whether a particular item is available or checked out, whether the latest issue of a periodical has been received, and it will also tell what is available at other libraries. Individual items can be searched for traditionally—that is, by author, title and subject—but also by key word, and perhaps by language or date of publication, or by any combination of these elements. Pamphlets, government documents, even periodical articles and other publications now listed in separate catalogs or indexes may be included in this general computerized catalog, and thus accessible through those terminals.

And if a book or article that's needed is not in this library, getting it from elsewhere will be a routine matter. It can be done almost instantly by long distance facsimile transmission equipment, either from another library, or from a regional or national storage facility. If it's a brief article, the copier will reproduce the original; if a longer article or a book, what may be transmitted is a miniaturized copy of the original, which could then be enlarged at the user's library. All periodical indexes and abstracting services will be available online, though some of the most frequently used ones, such as the *Readers' Guide to Periodical Literature,* will also be available in printed form. The full text of articles listed in the indexes will also be available online.

Microfilm and microfiche? Where these once represented the cutting edge of library technology, they now seem almost old-fashioned, and their use will increasingly be confined to archival materials. Videodiscs, which only began to be used in the 1980s, will have taken their place. A roll of microfilm contains only one or two thousand frames, while a videodisc can store over 100,000. Moreover, unlike microfilm or microfiche, any of the frames on a videodisc can be retrieved almost instantly, and if one wants a copy, a print of that frame can be made almost as quickly. Videodiscs will be used for many other kinds of information retrieval since they have the capability of combining sound and motion with text. For example, one might look up John F. Kennedy in an encyclopedia that's on videodisc, and not only read about him, but see and hear him making a speech.

Books and Magazines Remain

Will the library, this repository of electronic information, also contain books and magazines? Without any doubt. For some types of writing—in particular, fiction, poetry, or works that depend on design or need a special format—the book is a very efficient package. It can be read in bed, or at the beach, or on a bus, and one can start or stop anywhere in it, or underline it, or write in the margins (though not in library copies, please). Besides, even in the year 2000 there still will be hundreds of thousands of books that have been published over the last 500 years and not available in electronic form. As for magazines, many — in particular the specialized technical and scientific ones — will be available only in electronic format. Many others, though, will still be published as they are today, simply because that format, like the book, is more appropriate for readers. Browsing among the current issues of periodicals, looking at their cartoons, reading an article or a short story here and there, dipping into an interesting looking issue — these are some of the real pleasures of spending time in a library. Could one enjoy terminals the same way? Not likely. For these reasons and for others related to their commercial aspect, magazines in printed format should remain a library staple for a long time.

Flexibility is the Key

What all this adds up to for those now planning a college library, or even a renovation of, or addition to one, is an interesting problem: how do we combine in one building those facilities that can accommodate both the new, rapidly changing technology and the traditional materials and means of using them? The solution to that problem is not easy, but one must work at it by staying abreast of the latest developments and by designing a facility that is as flexible as possible, so that further changes, not even on the drawing boards now, can be incorporated as needed.

The Discriminating Consumer

But there's an even greater challenge: the enormous amount of information that will be available to every student. Imagine undergraduates today working on term papers and having access to the entire collection of the Library of Congress. Where do they begin? How do they get a handle on that mass of information? Every student, fifteen years from now, will be faced with a similar problem because even the smallest library can have immediate access electronically to large collections and data banks. It will become even more important, then, to teach students about sources of information — not so much how to find materials, but how to evaluate them, how to find the best, the most relevant information, how to become intelligent, discriminating consumers of information. That, after all, is one of the purposes of a liberal arts education.

12

Catalog Dependency
(1984)

This piece is an edited version of a talk at a 1983 conference on
Training Users of Online Public Access Catalogs. *The conference was
sponsored jointly by the Council on Library Resources and Trinity University in
San Antonio. The talk went well, but it wasn't until some time later that
preparing it and then editing it for publication had a far-reaching effect on my
approach to teaching students to make effective use of library resources.*

*Keep in mind that the conference was planned in the early 1980s when
the traditional card catalog served most libraries and OPACs were still
something many librarians only read about and marveled at. For years I (and
many other librarians) had observed students using a card catalog, and
deplored their indiscriminate use of it. Their assumption, perhaps because of
their training in high school, validated by the central location and imposing size
of the college library's catalog, was that it was the key to everything in the
library. So most of my talk dealt with that phenomenon as well as ways of
lessening that dependence.*

*But my conclusion shifted the scenario to the future, when I expected
that the OPAC would have become so much easier to use, contain so much more
information, and be so much more accessible. "There's a real danger that users
will regard the catalog even more than they do now as the single key for
unlocking the doors to the universe of information." Later, I came across the
concept of "technological idolatry" and realized that it was exactly what I was
concerned about, and especially about its effect on student use of OPACs and
thus on the teaching/learning process. A few years after, the confluence of those
thoughts led to planning a* Forum on Teaching and Technology. *The
proceedings of that forum, which was attended by college and university faculty,
administrators and librarians, were published in 1991 by the Pierian Press as*
Teaching and Technology: the Impact of Unlimited Access to Information on
Classroom Teaching.

— Evan Ira Farber, 2006

My subject is teaching the use of the traditional card catalog as if
it were 20 years earlier and an online catalog was something that existed
only in science fiction, if even there. Let me make it clear that this is not
a scholarly presentation and that I have done no special research other
than look through some of the literature, particularly books and manuals
on teaching use of the library. In the main, what follows is based on

Farber, Evan Ira, "Catalog Dependency," *Library Journal*, Volume 109, Issue 3
(February 15, 1984), pages 325-328.

years of working with students and lecturing to them, as well as, along with my staff and other librarians, devising exercises and other devices for guiding students so that they can use the card catalog effectively. My focus, then, is on college students.

One of my assumptions is that the users have had some pre-college instruction in use of the card catalog and feel (usually without justification) fairly comfortable using the catalog they were acquainted with in high school or in the public library. There is, of course, a significant minority who never learned to use it at all, but I'm not considering them just now.

Alpha & omega tool

It seems that one of the biggest problems in bibliographic instruction has been to break student dependence on the card catalog. The typical response of freshmen coming into the college or university library for their first term paper is: "Oh, yeah, there's the card catalog and there's the *Readers' Guide*...so what's the big deal? I know how to use them..." Then they do just as they did in high school, considering the card catalog the sole tool for finding books—the beginning and the end of their search. Of course, if the assignment requires some periodical articles, they'll also use the *RG*.

Now, it's not too difficult to get students beyond the *RG*: the relevance, and the ease of use of other indexes—that is, the parallels with the *RG*—are easy to demonstrate. But to wean them from the card catalog? That's another story, a much more difficult task. Why?

First of all, there's the training they received in high school, where central importance is placed on the card catalog. Many of them learned to use it fairly well, at least for high school purposes, but it took them years to accomplish this. The card catalog, after all, is complicated, even esoteric. Gradually, students were initiated into its mysteries and learned how to use it with success and satisfaction. Are they about to give it up just because some librarian tells them they shouldn't depend so much on it? Hardly.

Not too long ago I was reading Irving Howe's recently published autobiography, *A Margin of Hope*. Howe talks about the attraction of Marxism for him and for so many or his friends in the early 1930s:

> What drew young people to the
> movement—I'm tempted to say, to almost any
> movement—was the sense that we had gained
> not merely a purpose in life but a coherent
> perspective upon anything happening in the
> world. The movement gave us a language of
> gesture and response. It felt good to "know."

67

That is, of course, the mind-set of the "true-believer." Perhaps there is some parallel with students who think of the card catalog as the foundation stone, the underpinning of an entire theoretical system—the structure of knowledge. "The movement," Howe goes on, "taught us to think," but along lines that were "too well defined." Students feel good because they "know" how to use the catalog along those well-defined lines. Taking it away from them would cause the whole system to fall, and they can't chance that. Moreover, citing the shortcomings of the catalog to them, shortcomings that are obvious to any reference librarian, is not going to do any good. Just as true believers don't want to hear about, and are likely to disregard—or rationalize away—inadequacies or contradictions in their belief system—and are certainly not about to act upon them—so undergraduates tend to ignore or dismiss these shortcomings.

Drawing a parallel between student attitudes toward the card catalog and those of true believers *may* be a bit extreme. Whatever the reason though, there's no question that it's very difficult to disabuse students of those attitudes. It is especially difficult to change that pattern of use when the pattern has led to success time and again.

That is probably the most important reason why it's so difficult to wean students from dependence on the card catalog. They may realize that the catalog is more complex than they'd like, but because they don't demand much from it, they can handle, or rather circumvent the complexities. As a result, they have only a limited view of what's really available in the library, and that's too bad; but even worse, that limited view is usually enough. If students find *something* on their topic, and that something is incorporated into a paper that's not only acceptable but gets a good grade, the need for no more than a limited view is reinforced. Every reference librarian has seen this happen time and again. The basic problem is not in the library or with the librarians, but with the nature of the assignment and/or instructor, neither of which demands the *best*, or maybe not even very good information. Even if the student can't find enough occasionally, there's always the reference librarian to ask for help.

We must recognize the dilemma: if we succeed initially in teaching students to use the card catalog fairly well, we may undermine the more important educational experience—the ability to research a topic systematically. We may be teaching just enough about using the library to make students think they don't need to know any more...

Catalog shortcomings
...A different and more difficult problem is finding information which is in a monograph but is not reflected in the subject headings for that book. A student doing a paper, say, on the history of Methodism

would never know that Thompson's *History of the English Working Class* has a superb section on that topic. There are, I suppose, two ways that we try to teach students to get to such materials. One is in the card catalog itself—using other subject headings, either those that cover larger areas of the subject matter, or by using tracings and other cross references, to get to related topics. The second way is outside the card catalog—using subject bibliographies that may refer to relevant parts of books...

The card catalog does not rank or rate materials as to quality or validity. In one sense, a catalog card does indicate the quality of a book—not intentionally, of course, but by implying that that book has been *selected* for the library. The trouble is that students tend to generalize, and think that simply because a book is in the Library it's valid. "Look," I tell them, "the library has lots of bad books—outdated, misguided. We've even bought some bad books because they're good examples of bad books." How can they tell one from the other in the card catalog? Evaluating books is not, of course, the job of the card catalog nor of the cataloger, but teaching that discrimination is an important part of the educational process. Are there ways of teaching students to use the card catalog to discriminate among books? We can point out publication dates, thus implying that more recent publications are generally more useful, but how would a student recognize that A. C. Bradley's *Shakespearean Tragedy,* though published in 1904, is still one of the most important interpretations of Hamlet, Othello, Lear, and Macbeth? We can point out that an Oxford or Harvard University Press imprint probably indicates something about a book's worth, but what about all those unrecognized imprints? All we can really do is indicate that one may be able to draw occasional inferences about a book's quality from the catalog card, but almost always one has to use other points of reference—reviews, bibliographies, histories of individual disciplines, etc.

This idea that books differ in quality, that some are better than others, that some are no good at all, is part of the process of teaching students to think critically, to understand that scholars can disagree—honestly, openly—indeed, that such disagreements are an essential part of the scholarly process. Since teaching this is one of the purposes of education, perhaps it ought to be left to the classroom teacher. BI librarians can devise assignments that help make this point and can indicate the usefulness of other means of selecting and discriminating, but I'm not sure that we can teach anything about the card catalog itself that accomplishes this, except to point out that it does *not* do it.

We want to show students that subject headings are far from perfect, and may not match the terms or phrases that a user has in mind, and even though cross references are provided, they don't always work.

"Why don't you have any books on Chinese art?," a student asked me. "Well, we have at least 30 or 40 books on Chinese art. What did you look under?" "Chinese art." Of course there is nothing under that subject and the subject heading book doesn't use the term, even as a "see from" reference. Probably the student should have thought about inverting the term, but for that individual, our instruction to the effect that one sometimes has to think creatively about finding the appropriate subject just didn't take. We try to get across the point that subject headings are devised by individuals who try to anticipate users' needs but aren't always successful. And so we try to teach them various ways of getting around the lack of ideal subject headings: begin with the most specific term and gradually broaden it; try related terms; see if there are book titles beginning with the term; and then use those tracings...

Accentuating the positive

Our approach, however, is *not* just negative. We *do* try to teach students something about the card catalog. Most of that teaching is in the context of particular course assignments for which we may prepare structured worksheets and/or handouts with suggested subject headings. In our lectures and on the handouts, we emphasize the use of the LC *Subject Headings* volumes, and the importance of the bibliography note and tracings on the catalog cards. We do not go into the filing rules or the many permutations of subject headings. We want students to know enough about the mechanics of the card catalog to cope, and then we expect them to learn how to sort through its complexities and deal with its idiosyncrasies as the occasions arise. That part of our instruction depends on individual help at the card catalog, and there is no better teaching/learning than that. Our primary thrust in teaching the card catalog is on *when* one should use it as part of a search strategy. We reiterate this time and again.

What's just as important, perhaps even more so, and certainly more difficult to teach than filing rules or form subdivisions, is using the card catalog at appropriate times: first, at the beginning of a search, in order to find useful reference works, especially guides to the literature, and bibliographies; and second, later on in the search, both to locate individual titles which have been identified in those reference works, and also to find additional materials through the informed and creative use of subject headings and tracings. How to teach that two-fold separate use, how to inhibit too early and too quick use, is difficult because it means retraining, revamping years of incorrect use and dependence.

Kenneth Boulding once wrote that effective learning results from making mistakes and correcting them. But with a card catalog, it's too easy for a user to make mistakes and *still* get some results, so there is no effective learning. We have to convince users that while it's easy to find *some* information on almost any topic, in order to find the best, most useful information one must develop a search strategy; and that entails using the card catalog not only in the right ways but at the right times. It seems to me that can only be done through the use of structured assignments and worksheets, with the results carefully checked so that only real success is rewarded.

Online implications

While I have tried not to let what little knowledge I have about online catalogs color my observations, I want to comment on one implication of teaching the use of the traditional catalog that pertains to teaching the use of online catalogs.

If, as I've claimed, it's true that students *are* too dependent on the card catalog—believing in its omnipotence in leading them to whatever kinds of information the library can provide—how much more impressed (and thus dependent) they will be by it when its intricacies are so much easier to manipulate through the magic of computerization! How could anything so responsive to their commands, so quick in sorting through so much data, so capable of manipulating so many concepts and terms, so impressive and powerful, have any shortcomings? There's a real danger that users will regard the catalog even more than they do now as the single key for unlocking the doors to the universe of information.

Yet some of those same limitations I have described will still exist. I suppose some, perhaps many, online catalogs will analyze the contents of many books. That, I guess, is relatively simple to design. I'm sure that the effective and even creative use of subject headings can be built in. But, can online catalogs be designed to encourage students to use an appropriate search strategy? To discourage them using the catalog too early? Can they help students to evaluate materials, not only by pointing out those books, say, on *Hamlet,* that are considered the most informative and reliable, but also by indicating which are appropriate for a beginner and which for an advanced student? Can they be designed to refer users to the documents collection or to the archives, or the map collection, or to the reference librarian at the right moment? And where will that reference librarian be? It has been pointed out to me that since access to online catalogs can come from so many isolated locations, immediate assistance from a reference librarian will be difficult if not impossible.

It seems to me that unless the online catalog, an incredibly useful tool in many, many ways, can overcome some of these limitations, it will be, in a sense, counterproductive in some small, but important ways. Solving that problem is a large, ambitious, and certainly difficult task. But if we want our libraries to fulfill their educational—not just their research—mission, it would be well worth the effort.

13

Alternatives to the Term Paper
(1984)

One of the points I used to make in many of my talks was that term papers were not necessarily the best assignment for teaching students how to make effective use of their libraries' collections. Too often, I suggested, students simply looked at a few easy to find sources, then, with a scissors-and-paste approach and some skillful writing, came up with a decent paper. That approach hardly added to their library expertise, and to avoid that tendency I had worked over the years with a number of Earlham faculty creating assignments that were more interesting for students as well as being better vehicles for teaching use of the library. So when Tom Kirk asked me to contribute a chapter on Alternatives to an issue of the periodical New Directions for Teaching and Learning *that he was editing, an issue titled* Increasing the Teaching Role of Academic Libraries, *I gladly agreed. Not only had I thought and talked about the subject so much that it would not be a lot of work, but since it would appear in print, that provided an incentive to delve a bit into the history of term papers, something that I was curious about and would be interesting, even fun, to investigate whereas it probably would not be very interesting in an oral presentation. So I added those findings as historical background.*

— Evan Ira Farber, 2006

Where or when the use of the term paper began would make an interesting study, perhaps even a good topic for a term paper in a history of education course. While the history of the term paper is not the topic of this chapter, it is safe to say that the term paper has been around a long time and that contention about its usefulness and arguments for and against its effectiveness as a teaching device have been around almost as long. In an article by Suzzallo in *A Cyclopedia of Education,* published between 1911 and 1914, he points out that the library method "…represents an extreme reaction from the slavish use of a class text, distinctly in the right direction. The teacher who relies largely upon one or more texts is very likely not to give the student power to investigate and develop a subject under the difficulties which would confront him, once he is removed from teachers and school facilities…The library method bears somewhat the same relation to the modern humanities as the laboratory method does to the modern natural sciences; it makes the pupil familiar with the materials and methods which would be used in the

Kirk, Thomas G., editor. *Increasing the Teaching Role of Academic Libraries.* San Francisco, Jossey-Bass, 1984. Pages 45-53.

more thoroughgoing field of research."[1] It is that last mentioned aspect of the term paper—familiarizing students with the materials and methods of research—that is the topic of this chapter.

The Term Paper as a Teaching Device

The term paper as a teaching device has been written about extensively (see Ford and others, 1982, which identifies over 200 articles, mostly in freshman composition courses).[2] Here, we are primarily concerned with assignments in courses beyond the level of most freshmen and so assume that the students who are given these assignments have already acquired some basic information about using the library.

Perhaps we should first ask why instructors use term papers so readily—what value do they see in them? If so many instructors use them as a standard assignment, why should they consider alternatives?

In discussing the purposes and shortcomings of term papers, one cannot do any better than consult an article written over forty years ago by Harry N. Rivlin (1942) that summarizes responses of faculty at Queens College, New York. The report was concerned "only with the preparation of a major term paper," for which faculty saw as objectives to be achieved: "to give able students an opportunity to do systematic, critical, or constructive work independently, under the guidance of the instructor; to supplement the student's knowledge of the field by wider reading and thinking," and "to enable the student to explore more fully some phase of the course in which he or she has a special interest...yet which should not take up too much time of the class."[3] It is interesting to note that while none of the faculty responses suggested improved library skills as an objective, a group of seniors who were asked to discuss term papers from the student's viewpoint "referred most often to the value of training in research procedures. Many of them mentioned the improvement in their ability to use the library effectively."[4]

The faculty members had a number of suggestions for improving the quality of term papers: schedule bibliographies and progress reports, restrict term paper assignments to advanced elective courses, use them only as an integral part of the course, and offer students a wide variety of

---

[1] H. Suzzallo, "Library Method." In P. Monroe (Ed.), *A Cyclopedia of Education*. New York: Macmillan, 1911-1914. Vol. 4, p. 23.

[2] J. Ford, S. Rees, and D. Wood, "Research Paper Instruction: Comprehensive Bibliography of Periodical Sources, 1923-1980," *Bulletin of Bibliography,* 34 (1982): 84-98.

[3] H. N. Rivlin, "The Writing of Term Papers," *Journal of Higher Education,* 13 (1942): 314-320. P. 314-315.

[4] Ibid., p. 316.

topics. All of these are, of course, useful suggestions, but later in the article Rivlin makes this salient point:

> More extensive use may be made of various substitutes for the term paper. In many instances the actual writing of the paper is the least valuable part of the entire undertaking…What the substitute assignment should be will depend almost entirely on the nature of the course, the composition of the class, and the special needs to be met by the assignment. If the assignment aims at introducing the student to bibliographic research, he may gain as much from the preparation of an annotated bibliography…All of us will admit that the term paper is sometimes used as a convenient and academically respected means of meeting a need that can be satisfied as well, and possibly better, by other types of assignments.[5]

His conclusion is that "the term paper is a worthwhile college assignment provided it is no *pro forma* assignment, but rather one that is carefully adjusted to attain specific aims and one that is reasonably supervised during its preparation." Every reference librarian could applaud this; the term paper can be a rewarding experience and of real educational significance, but, for the purposes of teaching students to make effective use of library materials or to improve their research skills, one has to acknowledge the common sense in Rivlin's recognition that other types of assignments may be better than the term paper.

Alternatives to the Term Paper

The crucial question, then, is: What kinds of assignments can be devised that have some of the acknowledged educational benefits of the term paper, avoid its disadvantages, and, at the same time, do a better job of extending students' knowledge of and skills in using library resources? The answer is, of course, that there's no limit to the variety of such assignments; they will, as Rivlin noted, "depend almost entirely on the nature of the course, the composition of the class, and the special needs to be met by the assignment." Surely one must add that they also depend on the flexibility of instructors' attitudes toward new kinds of assignments and, even more important, willingness to work with an

---

[5] Ibid., pp. 319-320.

instructional librarian in devising and implementing such assignments.

To illustrate this variety, a number of assignments that have been used in courses at Earlham College are discussed...All were devised by a librarian and the teaching faculty member working together.

The Annotated Bibliography. The annotated bibliography is hardly a novel assignment, and it is surely one of the most frequently used alternatives; the possible variations in its implementation are manifold. Here are three examples.

Example One. In a Shakespeare course at Earlham College, the class read nine of Shakespeare's plays during the term. For their final written assignment, the students first had to identify a critical problem in one of the plays and, using the bibliographical apparatus, come up with twenty articles, books, or essays that discussed that problem. From those twenty, students were to select six of the best sources that covered the full range of the problem and annotate these six.

The discussion between the librarian and the instructor began with the idea of doing an annotated bibliography, since all students had done at least one such bibliography in prior courses. The instructor felt that the students ought to be able to find twenty good sources, but the librarian felt that having to annotate all of them would take too much time. Since both instructor and librarian wanted the students to have to choose only the best sources and read those carefully, six sources seemed a reasonable number. The reason for asking for at least two recently published ones was so students would not depend only on standard undergraduate guides to Shakespeare but would have to look through indexes and annual bibliographies published since those guides.

Since the course consisted of upperclass students, all of whom presumably knew how to use the library well, the lecture was brief. The students were made aware of the vast number of publications on Shakespeare and the importance of using guides to the literature. The handouts consisted of an annotated listing of reference materials on Shakespeare, a two-page guide on how to write annotations, a few samples of good annotations taken from *Choice* magazine, and a standard annotated bibliography on Shakespeare's tragedies.

Example Two. In a political science course, American Foreign Policy, students were instructed as follows:

> Your assignment is to work in groups of
> three and to assemble and critically evaluate
> material from public and governmental
> information sources on a particular foreign

policy issue. At three different times during the term you will turn in a different part of the project, with the entire opus due on May 23. Accompanying your annotated bibliography at that time will be a fifteen-page interpretive essay that examines the ideological conflicts over the issue, a brief history of the issue, the actors involved in the policy formulation process, the other foreign policy issues to which your topic is linked, and a brief statement about the future of your foreign policy issue.

The reasons for assigning group projects were four: (1) it was a very large class, so the number of topics could be fewer; (2) the instructor believed that students should learn to work cooperatively; (3) the assignment was a large one, and division of labor might help reduce the amount of time spent on it; and (4) discussions within a group could provide a learning experience in itself.

The librarian's instruction to the class included the presentation of a search strategy and the use of government documents; handouts included an annotated listing of relevant reference materials and a two-page guide on how to write annotations.

Example Three. Another variation of the annotated bibliography assignment was made in an introduction to philosophy course which focused on sexual ethics. The students were asked to find several important articles on affirmative action and to make sure that the articles took different positions. They then annotated the two most important differing articles and related them to their own ethical theories. The librarian's presentation again was based on a sample search that used standard indexes the students should have been already familiar with; the *Philosopher's Index,* the *Encyclopedia of Philosophy,* and a few specialized bibliographies relevant for the topics were added.

The library aims in these assignments are obvious. Students learn a new range of reference materials and, thus, begin to understand that for every topic there is an appropriate body of reference works. Students also recognize that a major problem in searching for information on almost any topic is not one of finding enough information but of finding too much and being forced to select. They also learn that one of the most useful kinds of reference works is the one that helps sort out the important materials. Finally, students realize that even with these guides, one must apply certain criteria in making choices. The reason for using a sample search in most cases is to get students to understand that there is a systematic way of finding information.

From the instructor's viewpoint, the assignments meant that students investigated a specific topic in some depth, learned that there were varied or even conflicting interpretations, and, ultimately, because they need to decide which were most important, developed their own criteria on the subject.

The "Practical" Assignment. A very different kind of assignment is one that has a practical aspect. Obviously, such assignments are not appropriate in all courses, but for those where they are, there is a special appeal for students. Below are a few examples:

Example One. In a course in children's literature, each student was asked to describe a class they would like to teach—the grade, the socioeconomic level, and so on. Then they were asked to select $100 worth of children's books appropriate for that class. The library instruction introduced them to the bibliographies, indexes, and selection tools for children's literature, and the students had to justify each choice. The practical aspects are two: (1) the assignment posits a situation that a teacher might encounter; and (2) it introduces the students, all prospective teachers, to tools they can use in their careers.

Example Two. One of the most unusual practical assignments was given in a course on animal behavior for advanced biology and psychology majors. All of these students know how to use the material in their respective disciplines, but in this case they were asked to design an experiment in the field of animal behavior nutrition that would attempt to ask and answer a question so meaningful that a government agency or a research institute might want to fund it. They were asked to identify an appropriate funding agency, figure out the costs involved, and then submit a proposal describing their project along with a supporting annotated bibliography. Groups of students acted as reviewers for the proposals.

Since the students already know the reference literature in their disciplines, the library instruction was limited to showing them material on foundations and other sources of funding and material on the writing of proposals.

Example Three. An innovative and highly successful assignment was one called "Reasonable Patienthood." It has been given in a human biology course taken by students who were not biology majors but who had had an introductory course in biology. The class usually has about eighty students. The students were given a listing of about seventy-five diagnosed conditions and prescribed treatments, with examples ranging from the most common and trivial (jock itch—tolnaftate, sore throat—

77

Listerine) to the most serious (Parkinson's Disease—L-dopa, breast cancer—radical mastectomy). They were then instructed to, "as a responsible patient, investigate the nature of your diagnosed condition and the effectiveness of the prescribed treatment." In the end product, a two-page paper, the following items were to be covered: a description of the condition and its symptoms, the disease's etiology, its prognosis, evidence of the effectiveness of the prescribed treatment and its side effects and contraindications; and a comparison of the relative effectiveness of alternate treatments. In addition, each student was to give a ten-minute oral report on this paper.

The lab manual for the course included a chapter on this assignment. In that chapter was the list of diagnosed conditions and an annotated bibliography of sources for finding biological and medical information. Since the students had been instructed in an earlier course about using the biological literature, the librarian in this course simply reminded them about the materials and focused on the literature of medicine.

Not many assignments can have such personal, immediate interest to students as this one. Its results, though, are instructive. Even though the course is a demanding one and this assignment an intensive one, most students completed it readily and enthusiastically, and the comments on this assignment in the course evaluations were overwhelmingly positive.

In this case, the library objectives are minimal—simply getting students to be aware of another, very different body of reference materials.

Example Four. Students were asked in an advanced psychology course to select a specific topic that interested them (e.g. REM sleep) and that had been treated in a review article within the past five years or so. They were then asked to update the review of the literature in light of articles published since the earlier review was written.

The library instruction involved a sample search on an appropriate topic, beginning with the review article and then illustrating how to update it by using citation indexes and *Psychological Abstracts*. The lecture material during the session centered on the function of a review article, the rationale and mechanics of citation indexes, and the differences, in terms of their theory and structure, between citation indexes and traditional indexes and abstracting services. The practicality of the assignment was that it made students go through the same process a professional must go through before doing any experimental research.

Evaluating Scholarship. Surely an important part of teaching undergraduates is getting students to understand the process of scholarship. The foregoing assignments made students replicate part of that process. Other assignments described below focus on the way scholars examine and evaluate the materials of scholarship.

Example One. In an introductory course on United States history, the instructor asked students to examine primary materials on slave life or events of the abolition movement and compare them with the textbook's treatment of those subjects. The students were then to write their own brief accounts of those aspects or events. The librarian compiled a bibliography of guides to sources on slave life and the pre-Civil War period—biographical dictionaries and indexes, bibliographies of biographies and autobiographies, newspaper indexes, *Poole's Index,* and the *Index to the American Slave*—and the lecture consisted primarily of comments on these sources. This was a relatively simple assignment but a productive and interesting one for students. It made them look at primary sources, and then see how a text used or misused such sources. From the librarian's perspective, it helped show students, once again, that there are ways of finding materials—both through bibliographies or indexes and guides to the literature—that are more effective than just the card catalog.

Example Two. In a more advanced history course, one on East Asian history, students were given a list of books, all of which were significant contributions to the interpretation of major events or movements in East Asia. After having read any one of the books, each student was asked to get as much information about the author as possible, gather reactions to the book through book reviews, and then find information about the reviewers. The end product was to be a relatively short paper on the book's interpretation of the event, which would take into account all the information gathered. The handouts given to the students by the librarian included descriptions of the various book review indexes and biographical sources and a strategy for searching them.

Again, this was a relatively simple assignment but useful from both the instructor's and the librarian's viewpoints. Students were made to realize, perhaps for the first time, that scholars can disagree honestly and openly, and thus could understand the crucial role of reviews in the scholarly process. They also learned the importance of knowing the author's and the reviewer's credentials and perspectives and how to find information about these. A similar assignment has been used for other courses in history and political science.

Example Three. This final example from an American government course represents perhaps the ideal library-based assignment. It achieves both the objectives of the instructor and of the librarian, both sets of objectives being so integral to the assignment and to the course that they have a truly symbiotic relationship. The following is from the course syllabus:

> This project is designed to develop an understanding of the process of government in the United States through direct researching in the primary documents of that government. You will examine in detail the development of an idea or a proposal from its inception in Congress or the Executive [Branch] through its legislative career in both Houses of Congress...This study will be accompanied, of course, by the normal classroom lectures and discussion and by the reading of secondary texts.
>
> The final term paper will be a narrative that analyzes the particular aspects of the process that had significance in the outcome of the bill. It is hoped that this study will provide you with a more intimate and "firsthand" knowledge and "feel" for the governmental process than would be gleaned by the secondary sources only.
>
> Knowledge of the skills of information retrieval in these valuable sources can be a major research tool to students of political science. A second purpose of this term project, therefore, is to develop these skills in the discovery and use of government documents and relevant reference material in the library.

Students were divided into groups of four or five (in order to reduce the number of legislative items and to encourage them to share ideas), and, using a worksheet that provided spaces for all the necessary factual information, they then prepared a narrative account of the legislative history of the bill. They needed to find (and the library instruction showed them how) and use information in *CQ Weekly Report* and the Serial Set, and to use such indexes as the *Monthly Catalog* and *CIS,* that provide access to those sources.

From the instructor's viewpoint, the students gained insight into the political process by using these primary sources. Furthermore, the knowledge gained of government documents was useful in later courses. From the librarian's viewpoint, the government documents collection, consigned in many libraries to an obscure corner of the stacks or used primarily by graduate students and faculty, became an important part of the undergraduate collection, and its usefulness for other courses and other disciplines was easy to implement.

This was an assignment, then, planned to further both the instructor's and the librarian's sets of objectives, and those objectives were mutually reinforcing in the assignment's implementation. By learning about the process of government, students also learned about their source materials. By learning about the source materials, students saw the process of government at work. Such an assignment, however, could be devised only by the librarian and the instructor working together, each aware of and sympathetic to the objectives of the other.

Conclusion

It is important to reiterate that the term paper can be an appropriate and useful assignment, not only from the instructor's vantage point but from the librarian's. If it is to be appropriate and useful, however, the assignment must include five elements: (1) a staging of the process, so that students cannot use only a few sources just prior to writing the paper; (2) students must have sufficient expertise in the subject to permit them to evaluate materials they find in order for them to make valid inferences; (3) the requirements for the paper's length must be realistic; (4) the subjects chosen by the students need to be guided so that they are not too broad as to be unmanageable yet not so narrow as to be trivial or to lack material; and (5) the institution's library resources must be considered, not only their availability but also their accessibility by students at their particular level. If these elements can be addressed satisfactorily, then, the term paper can be worthwhile.

At the same time instructors should recognize that assignments other than the term paper may be more productive and educationally valid, particularly in improving the library skills of their students. Certainly assignments can be made more interesting to students for whom term papers have become something to be endured. What is needed are instructors with initiative, imagination, and the willingness to recognize that librarians have a real concern for their students' education and can help in devising and implementing new approaches to the teaching and learning process.

14

The Library in Undergraduate Education
(1985)

In August, 1984 I read a news release—I think in The Chronicle of Higher Education—*from the Carnegie Foundation for the Advancement of Teaching, stating that it was planning to do a book on college education.* "The new study, College: A Report on Undergraduate Education in America," *the release noted,* "involves a detailed, large-scale survey of faculty and students, extended visits to undergraduate institutions, and a thorough examination of statistical data and the professional literature." *The project was to be directed by Ernest L. Boyer, who, after a distinguished career in higher education, was head of the Foundation. Not incidentally—for me, anyway—he had served on Earlham's Board of Trustees, three of his children had gone to Earlham, and he had addressed the faculty several times; because of those factors I knew him well enough to call him Ernie and also knew that he was familiar with Earlham's library program. So I wrote to remind him to be sure to include something about the educational role of the library, noting that as far as I knew none of the many recent books on reforming undergraduate education did that.*

I got a quick response from him, saying that he appreciated my reminder and asked if I would do a background paper for the project on the role of the library in undergraduate education, and that there would be a generous honorarium. Of course I was delighted, not only by the opportunity it gave me to gather my thoughts on the subject, to speculate on future directions, and to do a bit of proselytizing at the same time, all this in a volume that I assumed would get national attention, but also by the honorarium (I think it was $1,000, which really did seem generous, although after the paper was finished, I estimated that came to about five dollars an hour). And so I answered him immediately—yes, of course I'd do a background paper for the project, and in February, 1985 I sent it off.

When the book came out in 1987 I was a bit disappointed that more of my paper wasn't used verbatim, though I was pleased that some of my concepts were alluded to in the text. For example, on page 165: "We further recommend that every undergraduate student be introduced carefully to the full range of resources for learning on campus. Students should be given bibliographic instruction and be encouraged to spend at least as much time in the library— using its wide range of resources—as they spend in classes." *Of course, I would have liked more attention to the rationale for and the process of bibliographic instruction, but as brief as it was, having the imprimatur, so to speak, of such a prestigious publication, was gratifying.*

Farber, Evan Ira. *The Library in Undergraduate Education.* Richmond, Indiana, Earlham College, March, 1985. An unpublished manuscript "Prepared for the Carnegie Foundation for the Advancement of Teaching."

BIBLIOGRAPHIC INSTRUCTION

Introduction

The idea of teaching students how to use the library has been around for a long time, well over a century. Only recently, however, has it become widespread, and the term most generally used for it now is bibliographic instruction. The rationale for BI (as it's generally referred to among librarians), is straightforward and is based on the fact that most students use libraries reluctantly and inadequately. That reluctance and that inability have long been evident, but now they're even more pronounced because the modern academic library seems so complicated and complex; unless students are taught its intricacies, learn the keys to its organization, recognize the various points of access to that mass of information, they will continue to use it inadequately and, because its seeming complexity is so daunting, only when they have to. Unfortunately, most teaching faculty don't realize how undergraduates feel when confronted, on the one hand, by a topic they know little about, and, on the other, by a mass of material and a complicated system of catalog cards and reference materials.

The purpose of bibliographic instruction, then, is to teach students to find information efficiently and effectively. "Efficiently," to save time: if a student wanders through the stacks long enough and looks through enough materials, with even an elementary knowledge of how library materials are organized, he or she will eventually find *some* material. But by learning to use the appropriate bibliographic tools—the catalogs, indexes, abstracting services, handbooks, subject bibliographies—one can find the information much more quickly. "Effectively," to get the best information: almost anyone can find *some* information on almost any topic—but is it the best? The most useful? Is it important, even valid? By learning how to use those bibliographic tools in the appropriate order—what librarians call "search strategy"— one can find better information as well as finding it more quickly. And, librarians have come to realize, search strategy can be taught, so that with a program of bibliographic instruction, students can indeed become more efficient and effective users of the library.

Such programs are important for several reasons, both in the short and long run. In the short run, they permit students to do better work, to get to materials they otherwise could not have, to go beyond the textbook, even beyond the instructor—to become, in other words, more independent learners. Bibliographic instruction similarly helps the teacher—the teacher is to some extent freed from the need to spoon-feed; assignments can be more varied, less restrictive, and expectations for student performance can be higher. Teaching can be more effective, more rewarding.

Another argument for bibliographic instruction is one that's important in the long run. It is based on the fact that in many ways our society is rapidly becoming—if, indeed, we're not already—an information-based one, and in such a society success or failure will increasingly be measured in terms of one's ability to find, organize and use information. We want our students to be able to cope with the increasing amounts of information available to—no, thrust upon—them. We want them to become more sophisticated, more discriminating users of information. Learning how to use a library effectively may not automatically bestow that ability, but it provides the impulse that will help attain it.

Early History

While the contemporary bibliographic instruction movement is really only about twenty years old, efforts to instruct students in use of the library began over a century ago. To understand the pattern of its methods and direction today, it's appropriate to look at some of the threads that have been woven into that pattern.[1]

Earlier, I alluded to the important developments in librarianship that took place in the final quarter of the nineteenth century. It was also during those years that the librarians began to write about their role as educators. In an 1880 government publication entitled "College Libraries as Aids to Instruction," Justin Winsor, the Harvard University Librarian, wrote that the college librarian should become "a teacher, not that mock substitute who is recited to; a teacher, not with a text book, but with a world of books." And, a little later: "We must build our libraries with class rooms annexed, and we must learn our ways through the wilderness of books...."[2] In that same government publication Otis

---

[1] For this look at the history of bibliographic instruction, I depended mainly on these sources: John Mark Tucker, "User Instruction in Academic Libraries: a Century in Retrospect," *Library Trends* 29(1): 9-28 (Summer, 1980); Frances L. Hopkins, "A Century of Bibliographic Instruction: The Historical Claim to Professional and Academic Legitimacy," *College and Research Libraries*, 43:192-198 (May, 1982); and the forthcoming book by Tucker, Larry Hardesty, and John Schmitt, *User Instruction in Academic Libraries: A Century of Selected Readings*, which Scarecrow Press expects to publish.

[2] *Circulars of Information of the Bureau of Education; No. 1-880* (Washington, D.C.: U. S. Government Printing Office, 1880) 7, 8.

Robinson, Librarian of the University of Rochester, wrote that it was no longer "the chief duty of a librarian...to collect books and preserve them. How to get them used most extensively, most intelligently, and at the same time carefully, is becoming his chief concern."[3]

Raymond Davis, Librarian at the University of Michigan from 1877 to 1905, was the first to give a credit course on bibliography; he described the course and the reasons for it in a paper given at the American Library Association conference in 1886. His reasons for it could have been written today:

> [Students'] knowledge of books of common
> reference was very limited; they did not know of
> the existence of special bibliographies, and of
> indexes to serials publication...In addition to
> this they made no effort, on coming into the
> library building for the first time, to learn what
> they might expect, or what was expected of
> them, or the whereabouts of anything. They
> were willing to leave all to chance.[4]

The librarians of many other institutions, including Cornell, Colorado, Oberlin and Bowdoin, offered courses or lectures on the use of libraries; a survey conducted by the U. S. Bureau of Education in 1914 found that about a fifth of the 446 colleges and universities and 56 percent of 166 normal schools provided instruction to their students in use of the library.[5]

The 1920s and 1930s

Over the next two decades, the movement seemed to have reached a plateau, though there were several important individual statements and efforts. Charles Shaw, Librarian at Swarthmore from 1927 to 1962, was a major figure in academic librarianship, especially known for his "Shaw list"— a list of about 14,000 titles that comprised the basis of an undergraduate collection, and was used by the Carnegie Corporation (which had initiated the compilation) in 1929 to provide grants of $5,000 to $25,000 to 81 colleges to strengthen their collections. Shaw proposed that colleges establish departments of bibliography which would give formal courses in the use of the library as well as on the

---

[3] Ibid., p. 15.

[4] "Teaching Bibliography in Colleges," *Library Journal* 11:289 (Sept., 1886).

[5] Henry R. Evans, comp., "Library Instruction in Universities, Colleges, and Normal Schools," *U.S. Bureau of Education Bulletin* no. 34 (1914) 3.

physical aspects of books. His proposal was never implemented, but his plea for the separate course and quality instruction provided material for later commentators.

Only a few years after that, a more significant step was taken when B. Lamar Johnson became Librarian and Dean of Instruction at Stephens College. That dual capacity permitted him to implement his ideas of the role a college library should play in the Stephens educational program, a program based to some extent on Alexander Meiklejohn's *The Experimental College.* In that work, Mieklejohn talked about the centrality of the book, a college's "chosen instrument." By "the use of books," he wrote, "minds shall be fed, and trained, and strengthened, and directed...The whole procedure points forward to a mode of life in which persons, by the aid of books...are trained to practice special forms of intelligence in which the use of books plays an essential point." To achieve this end, Johnson went on, the library program had three objectives:

> First, to teach students how to use books effectively; second, to lead students to love books and to engage in reading for recreation; and third, to make the library function as the center of the instructional program of the college. In short, we are attempting to make the library the heart of the college to the end that, as Mieklejohn says, the students may become intelligent readers.[6]

And then he went on to describe how the college administration had been reorganized to further implement that program: the dean-librarian is "responsible for changes in the curriculum and for the improvement of teaching methods."[7] In two later books, *Vitalizing a College Library* (1939) and *The Librarian and the Teacher in General Education: A Report of the Library-Instructional Activities at Stephens College* (1948), Johnson developed his ideas more fully and reported his experiences. However, his situation, especially his dual role, was unique, and so while his program created much interest and discussion, other librarians could hardly have the same influence in their institutions.

---

[6] B. Lamar Johnson, "Stephens College Library Experiment," *ALA Bulletin* 27:205 (May, 1933).
[7] Ibid., p. 205-6.

Changed Status of Librarians

But there were other reasons for that lack of influence. The status of the librarian had changed over the years. In the late 1800s the position of librarian was usually held by someone highly esteemed in the college or university, a person recognized as a scholar in one of the traditional disciplines; later the position of librarian was increasingly taken over by someone who had been trained as a librarian, whose responsibilities, as library procedures got more complex and staffs grew larger, became more administrative, more esoteric, less involved with academics. Harvie Branscomb, in a 1939 study for the Association of American Colleges, noted that college librarians were more and more technically trained and "were not qualified to take an active part in the discussion or execution of the educational program...A division of function was established which is still regulative: librarians were responsible for the care of books and faculty members for their use."[8]

In addition, the profession had become increasingly attractive to women. "Librarianship began with men in the majority but was fully established as a woman's profession by 1920," and by 1930, 91 percent of all librarians were women.[9] The predictably unfortunate consequence of this was lower salaries[10] and even further separation from male-dominated faculties. Thus the position of the college librarian, at one time highly esteemed and on a par with teaching faculty in status and compensation, became lower on both counts. There were, of course, exceptions, particularly institutions that were especially prestigious, or, like Stephens, where an unusual person gave the position prestige and influence.

Another factor may have been, paradoxically enough, the development of reference work as a standard aspect of academic librarianship. Frances Hopkins suggests this possibility: reference librarians in academic libraries were not highly regarded, and so stuck to the reference desk. Faculty fulfilled

---

[8] Harvie Branscomb, *Teaching With Books: A Study of College Libraries*, (Chicago: Association of American Colleges, American Library Association, 1940) p. 6.

[9] Anita R. Schiller, "Women in Librarianship," in *The Role of Women in Librarianship, 1876-1976; The Entry, Advancement and Struggle for Equality in One Profession*, by Kathleen Weibel and Kathleen M. Heim (Phoenix, Ariz.: Oryx Press, 1979) 222-256.

[10] Dee Garrison, "The Tender Technicians: The Feminization of Public Librarianship, 1876-1905," *Journal of Social History* 6:131-159 (Winter, 1972-73). However, whether or not lower salaries resulted from the predominance of women, or whether women predominated because salaries were low is still open to discussion. See Schiller, "Women in Librarianship," p. 240.

the main advisory role towards students, and the librarian's expertise in finding information had low prestige compared with the scholar's quest for knowledge... Any teaching beyond the basic-skills level invited faculty scrutiny, whereas reference desk work could be carried out in comparative privacy. For most librarians, imbued with the semiclerical values of the library school and ALA, the reference desk added sufficiently to their self-image as academic professionals without major budgetary changes and with little risk of exposing their limitations.[11]

Circumstances outside the profession, the academic and social environment, undoubtedly also contributed to the lack of progress in bibliographic instruction during the '20s and '30s. Educational reformers were trying new methods—honors courses, independent study, reserve readings, for example—methods to which the library had to adjust in terms of procedures or even organization, but which did not demand the librarians' involvement in the teaching process. Also, of course, the economic crisis of the '30s meant in many cases staff reductions or at least static budgets, so librarians were reluctant to take on additional responsibilities.

The University-Library Syndrome
Another possible factor was that, with the rapid growth of university libraries after 1900, and especially in the 1920s, professional concerns were increasingly tilted toward university library activities. That meant emphasis on those activities that supported graduate and faculty research—acquisitions, special collections, administrative theory and structure, etc.—rather than on those pertaining to the education of undergraduates, and reference service became more and more a resource for scholars rather than for students. As university librarians came to dominate academic librarianship, the career pattern for talented and ambitious library school graduates was increasingly seen in terms of university library work. College libraries simply did not attract any more the quality of personnel they once had.

---

[11] Frances L. Hopkins, "User Instruction in the College Library: Origins, Prospects, and a Practical Program," in *College Librarianship*, ed. by William Miller and D. Stephen Rockwood (Metuchen, N. J.: The Scarecrow Press, 1981) 176-77.

The domination of the profession by university libraries and librarians had an even more deleterious effect on college libraries. Increasingly, the faculties, the deans and presidents, even the staffs of college libraries came to regard them in terms of university libraries, and viewed the college library simply as a small university library. This view, the "university-library syndrome," as I've called it,[12] resulted from a number of factors, the dominance of university librarians in the profession perhaps not even the main one. Almost all faculty had their training in university libraries, and got used to the services and resources provided there. The librarian's role, according to this view, is "a passive one, one devoted to housekeeping, to getting materials quickly and making them accessible with dispatch and efficiency, and to being available when needed for answering questions, compiling bibliographies, or putting materials on reserve."[13] Presidents and deans also take this view, but primarily they want their librarians to run a tight ship. "Whether the college's students are really deriving much benefit from the library is rarely questioned. Lip service is paid to the library's being 'the heart of the college.' But as long as faculty members don't complain, as long as the size of the collection and other standards meet a level acceptable to accrediting agencies, the administration is happy to let the library alone."[14]

Nor have college librarians been immune from this syndrome. After all, the outlook of university librarians is constantly impressed upon them at meetings, in the associations, and in the professional literature. Moreover, almost all college librarians were trained in library schools which were associated with, if not located in, university libraries, and many of them began their careers in those libraries. Moreover, their course work in library schools did nothing to correct the view; on the contrary, they were taught that the function of a reference librarian was providing answers or information, not educating. Providing answers and information is important, of course, and it's tempting to stop there—it's satisfying, it's familiar, and it's comfortable. Taking an active, rather than responsive, role means seeking out faculty, even trespassing on their turf, assuming an unfamiliar, perhaps uncongenial role, a role that most university librarians would have disdained.

---

[12] Evan Ira Farber, "College Libraries and the University-Library Syndrome," in Evan Ira Farber and Ruth Walling, eds., *The Academic Library: Essays in Honor of Guy R. Lyle* (Metuchen, N. J.: The Scarecrow Press, 1974) 12-23.
[13] Ibid., p. 17.
[14] Ibid., p. 17.

So, for these various reasons, bibliographic instruction languished.

But if it was not gaining practitioners or converts during these years, its message was being promulgated in statements and studies such as Lamar Johnson's—statements and studies that would have a significant, though delayed, impact on the practical and conceptual development of the movement. Only a year after *Vitalizing a College Library* was published, Harvie Branscomb's *Teaching With Books* came out. Subtitled *A Study of College Libraries*, it was the outcome of the Association of American Colleges Library Project, which was funded by the Carnegie Corporation. The purpose of the project, Branscomb noted, was "a consideration of the extent to which the efforts of the college library are integrated with those of the institution as a whole. In other words, this project undertook to study the college library from the standpoint of its educational effectiveness."[15]

Branscomb had visited more than sixty college libraries, looking particularly at their circulation statistics. What he found, of course, was that the libraries were not used very much. Some of the fault he attributed to librarians, who, he felt, had come to place so much "more emphasis on acquisition and preservation of library materials than on the use." (p. 5). But most of his blame fell upon the faculty, who "are making only a very limited use of the library in their teaching work." (p. 37) The reason, then, that students use the library so little was simple: "They do not use the library's books because in a great deal of their work they do not have to; they can do quite acceptable work, in some cases possibly better work, without doing so." (p. 52) "A basic reason for this is

> the conception of the library as a depository of knowledge. Reservoirs of knowledge are highly needed and certain national and university libraries serve society greatly by performing this function. The college library can rarely and does not usually need to undertake this expensive role. Books in the library are useless unless they are used, and in a college this means primarily used for the teaching purpose for which the institution exists." (p.53)

---

[15] Branscomb, *Teaching with Books*, p. ix.

What could be done? He went on to talk about needed campus changes: getting a broadly educated librarian who understood and was interested in undergraduate education, who would be involved in campus matters and who could work with students and faculty; opening the stacks to students; creating browsing rooms; reforming the reserve book system; a number of other, minor suggestions, such as book collections in the dormitories, all aimed at improving the use of the book collection. He noted that there was too much emphasis on size, and reminded readers that the function of the college library was to build a collection primarily "for its teaching program and for the direct use of faculty members in study and research." (p. 167) While it might be impossible to agree on a figure for the proper size of a college library, several points seemed "undebatable": numerical goals, either as a maximum or minimum, are not appropriate; the collection must continually be weeded of books that "have ceased to be of value"; the collection should be expanded "only on the basis of need and actual use." (p. 175)

Finally, he recognized the need to teach students how to use the library, but he saw it in two parts—"introductory information and the more advanced work in the bibliography of special subjects." (p. 205) The librarians, he thought, should be responsible for the first, but the problem of more advanced instruction ought to be solved by "frequent and cooperative contacts between the library staff and the faculty." Perhaps the library staff might be used "by instructors for discussions with their classes of special library problems or materials." In no case, however, should the library "take over all responsibility for bibliography instruction." (p. 208) The key is "opening channels of communication, understanding and cooperation between the reading aspects of instruction and the classroom aspects." (p. 209)

In my opinion, Branscomb's real contribution to the development of bibliographic instruction was his recognition of and emphasis on so many practical aspects: the primacy of teaching, of the classroom process; the importance of a cooperative effort—of the politics of the relationship, really; the difference between the purposes, and thus the operational premises, of the college library and the university library.

The one shortcoming to his approach, I feel, was his trust that, once made aware of the problem, teaching faculty would work on a solution to it. He realized that cooperation between teachers and librarians was necessary, but his warning against "the library taking over all responsibility for bibliographic instruction" implied more reliance on faculty than is warranted in most cases.

Even with that flaw (by no means a minor one for the librarian trying to implement a bibliographic instruction program) as one reads Branscomb today one is struck by his insights, many of which are worth attention and acknowledgment not only by librarians, but by faculty and administrators as well. The book was reviewed widely and favorably, and the double imprimatur of the AAC and the Carnegie Corporation should have given it special credibility. One can't help but wonder what its impact might have been if it had appeared at any other time but on the eve of America's involvement in World War II.

The Library-College

As Branscomb provided a realistic appraisal of the need for teaching use of the library, so Louis Shores provided a visionary concept. Shores was director of the library school at George Peabody College for Teachers from 1933 to 1942, and later, from 1949 to 1967, at Florida State University. In an essay published in 1935,[16] he presented his idea of the "library arts college," in which he envisaged moving the teaching/learning process into the library. The librarian would be a teacher: "The positions of librarian and professor will merge." There would be no regular classes; students would have instead supervised reading periods and could ask for class meetings when they felt their readings needed discussion. The supervisors of the reading periods are library-trained subject matter teachers, and "all instructional quarters...are concentrated in the campus' one educational building — the library." (p. 113)

His "library-college" notion was idealistic, but vague conceptually and utterly impractical politically. Its idealism attracted a small but enthusiastic following, many of whom, however, drifted away from the movement as its dreams got more grandiose, its contact with the realities of campus life increasingly tenuous, and the many publications by its founder and his disciples less and less interesting or useful. While it had little impact on the mainstream development of bibliographic instruction, it served the movement in two ways: its emphasis on librarians as teachers got a number of librarians to think about that issue, and it provided a forum for those who became interested in pursuing the issue in more practical ways.

The Monteith Experiment

The writer who undoubtedly had the greatest impact on the practice and theory of bibliographic instruction was Patricia B. Knapp. She was responsible for a number of significant publications, including two monographs, *College Teaching and the College Library* (1959) which was based on her University of Chicago dissertation, and *The*

---

[16] Louis Shores, "The Library Arts College, A Possibility in 1954?," *School and Society* 41:110-114 (Jan. 26, 1935).

Monteith Library Experiment (1966), reporting the experiment she carried out there in 1960-61. But even before these appeared, Knapp had posited the rationale and method for bibliographic instruction. "Competence in library use," she noted in a 1956 article, is "a complex of knowledge, skills, and attitudes which must be developed over a period of time through repeated and varied experiences in the use of library resources."[17] Such experiences were best presented by the regular faculty "as an integrated part of content courses...throughout the four years of his college education...And they should provide sequence through increasing breadth and depth of the knowledge, skills and attitudes required." She went on to describe types of assignments, and then reiterated an important point: "The librarian must convince the faculty that library instruction is necessary; he must educate the faculty on the potential role of the library and assist it in planning instruction..." (pp. 230-1)

This gives the librarian a much more active and important role in a bibliographic instruction program, a role that assumes responsibility for the program's initiation and much of its implementation. A few years later, Monteith College was established as an experimental college within Wayne State University, and Knapp was made director of its Library Project. In that project, carefully designed and sequentially structured assignments got students to use a system of "ways" to get information, moving from one level of organization to another and from one subject field to another, with the constant objective of increasing the student's ability to work independently. The entire project was solidly based on learning theory and on the organization of knowledge, and integrated carefully into the curriculum.[18]

There's not much question that the Monteith experiment was the most significant attempt up to that time—and perhaps even since then—to attempt a total integration of bibliographic instruction with the curriculum. It was bold and creative in its conception, yet sensible and precise in its method. Unfortunately, however, it did not survive. Personality differences, disciplinary parochialism, and changing personnel all undermined the cooperative spirit which was evident at the program's inception and remained essential to its continuance. A library program that departed so far from the traditional role of the library could not easily be shaped to meet the practical demands—the politics, if you will—of the curriculum. What did survive from it, however, was

---

[17] Patricia B. Knapp, "A Suggested Program of College Instruction in the Use of the Library," *Library Quarterly* 26:224-231 (July, 1956).
[18] The project is described in detail in Patricia B. Knapp, *The Monteith College Library Experiment* (New York: The Scarecrow Press, 1966).

perhaps more important. Its thrust, its conceptual framework was looked to by instruction librarians as a paradigm, one that perhaps could not be repeated on another campus but could be looked to for guidance, even inspiration.

The 1960s

Surely, some model was necessary. In 1965 Barbara Phipps questioned 200 college librarians about their programs; of the 157 responses, 126 indicated that some form of library instruction was given, ranging from tours of the library to separate courses, some optional, a few required. No one program seemed to generate real enthusiasm. If they had anything in common, it was the feeling that instruction was very much needed, but that not nearly enough was being done, and that there was little cooperation on the part of faculty.[19]

Given this discreteness and this diversity of experience, and the lack of a vehicle for some common effort, it's difficult to say why bibliographic instruction began to take off in the 1960s. Perhaps it was a product of the experimentation and innovation taking place in higher education during that period; perhaps it was due to a new generation of reference librarians. In any case, there were a number of events in the late 1960s and early 1970s that seemed unrelated at the time, but in retrospect were obviously part of a movement.

Earlham College began its program of bibliographic instruction in 1964. Instruction was given in conjunction with regular course assignments, and such assignments were often designed with the possibility of bibliographic instruction in mind. The program, then, was built on cooperation between librarians and teaching faculty; moreover, it extended to many disciplines, including the sciences, and entailed some sequential instruction. In 1969, at a meeting of the College Library Section of the Association of College and Research Libraries, the purpose and methods of the Earlham program were described. The response, as recalled by the program chairman, was impressive:

> [We] expected the usual two- or three-hundred attenders...This was the first time, as far as we knew, that there was a public presentation on bibliographic instruction...To our surprise and delight, the room was overflowing, and there were, we estimated, at least eight hundred in the audience. Moreover,

---

[19] Barbara H. Phipps, "Library Instruction for the Undergraduate," *College & Research Libraries* 29:411-423 (Sept., 1968).

the response was tremendous. The obvious
enthusiasm, the questions we got there, and the
follow-up letters and inquiries all indicated that
there was an enormous reservoir of interest in
the subject.[20]

Shortly thereafter, the Ad Hoc Committee on Bibliographic
Instruction was formed within the Association of College and Research
Libraries. It quickly became obvious that there was enough interest on
the part of the Association membership for the group to get permanent
status, and in 1977 the Bibliographic Instruction Section of ACRL was
formed, a group that became central to national efforts.

Another important factor was the Council on Library Resources,
which had been founded in 1956 with funds from the Ford Foundation in
order to attack the various problems of libraries through research,
coordination of efforts, or other means. In 1969 it initiated two programs
that were to affect user education in academic libraries: a fellowship
program for mid-career librarians, and a College Library Program,
jointly sponsored with the National Endowment for the Humanities.[21]
Under the first program thirteen grant recipients focused on user
instruction, and several of their studies gained national attention. The
second program, the CLR-NEH College Library Program, was even
more influential. Based on Patricia Knapp's work, this program
"provided thirty-six institutions with grants to explore innovative ways
of enhancing the library's participation in the educational process."[22]
The programs ranged widely in many aspects—types of institutions,
methods, thrusts, degrees of success—but there seemed to be enough
progress to start yet another program in 1975, the Library Service
Enhancement Program. Under it twenty-five institutions were given the
equivalent of one librarian's salary to free one senior staff member to
work with faculty, administrators, and library staff members in
developing an instructional program.

In 1971, as a result of its CLR-NEH grant, Eastern Michigan
University held the first Annual Conference on Library Orientation for
Academic Libraries. The obvious enthusiasm shown by the participants
insured its continuance, and over the years it has served as a place for
librarians interested in bibliographic instruction to share ideas and

---

[20] Letter from Evan Farber to Larry Hardesty, April 8, 1981, quoted in Tucker,
Hardesty and Schmitt, "User Instruction in Academic Libraries," n.p.
[21] Nancy E. Gwinn, "Academic Libraries and Undergraduate Education: The
CLR Experience," *College & Research Libraries*, 41:5-16 (Jan., 1980).
[22] Ibid., p. 7.

experiences. At first, the participants were those who wanted to begin programs of instruction, and came for advice and encouragement; soon the participants consisted more of those who had programs under way, and were looking for ways to improve them. The need for an informational center was apparent and in 1972 LOEX (Library Orientation Exchange) was established with initial support from the Council on Library Resources. The members of LOEX are libraries and individual librarians, and for whom LOEX serves as a clearinghouse for materials and information.

There's no doubt that the Council's efforts had a major impact on the movement among librarians, but among faculty and administration not nearly as much as it had hoped. "Given the history of the adoption of innovations in higher education, one decade and a few million dollars are insufficient to alter the attitudes and practices developed over numerous decades regarding the role of the academic library in higher education."[23] Nevertheless, its support contributed to institutionalizing a number of programs, providing them and others with national exposure, and permitting an even larger number of individuals to get involved, many of whom became important to later developments.

Bibliographic Instruction Methods

Putting history aside for the moment, let's look at the ways in which bibliographic instruction has been implemented.

If there's one thing librarians have learned, it is that each program must be tailored to the educational context of its particular campus. That means that implementation takes a variety of forms. Most programs, however, have been patterned after one of four approaches, or may combine elements of them. These approaches are: the separate course, either required or optional, and if the latter, usually carrying academic credit; seminars and/or clinics; library skills manuals or workbooks; course-related or course-integrated instruction. After then looking at some recent developments, we'll look at the possibilities of computer-assisted instruction.[24]

---

[23] Tucker, Hardesty and Schmitt, "User Instruction in Academic Libraries," n.p.
[24] The number of books and articles on the methods of bibliographic instruction appearing in the last decade is overwhelming. A large proportion of them, especially the articles, are descriptions of individual programs or even just aspects of programs. *Bibliographic Instruction: A Handbook*, by Beverly Renford and Linnea Hendrickson (N. Y.: Neal-Schuman Publishers, 1980) summarizes the various methods. For those wanting to read more on the theory, I'd recommend beginning with *Educating the Library User* (N. Y.: Bowker, 1974) and *Progress in Educating the Library User* (N. Y.: Bowker, 1978), both edited by John Lubans, Jr. *Theories of Bibliographic Education: Designs for Teaching*, edited by Cerise Oberman and Katina Strauch (N. Y.: Bowker, 1982),

The *separate course* is probably the oldest method. Such courses, which vary greatly in content, in format, and in educational thrust, are appealing because the instructors—almost always members of the library staff—can have complete control over content and method. A course, then, can be consistent and effective in itself. Its disadvantage is that most undergraduates are not really interested in learning how to use a library for itself, and unless such a course is required or offered for credit, very few students will touch it—and they are the ones who, being highly motivated, probably need it least. Making it a requirement or even offering it for credit is not a simple solution, because then it becomes part of the continuing competition with other courses for a place in the curriculum and for enrollment. And because librarians don't have much political clout in curricular matters, the competition is probably not going to favor the library's interests. The separate course is perhaps most appropriate for advanced students, especially graduate students, whose motivation is strong, and for whom its high cost is justified.

Seminars and/or term paper clinics are just the more common types of small group, 'on-demand' instruction. The advantages of these are that they are easy and inexpensive to organize and that they meet particular learning needs. The main disadvantage is that most students will not take the trouble to attend them, probably not even realizing that they have a need for them. They reach, then, only a small number of students, primarily the highly motivated. For these reasons, such instruction works best on a graduate level, or for advanced students who have gotten more basic instruction prior to these small group sessions.

Another approach is *the library workbook, or manual*, which provides descriptions of library materials and procedures along with a series of questions relating to their applications. By answering the questions, students work through the manual at their own pace. Workbooks have been especially useful in large institutions where many students need instruction at a beginning level. They have long been used at the school level, but workbooks for college students began in 1969, when UCLA developed one to teach library skills to minority students. It worked so well that UCLA adapted it for all freshmen and soon a

---

does a good job of relating bibliographic instruction to educational theory. *Increasing the Teaching Role of Academic Libraries*, edited by Thomas G. Kirk, (New Directions for Teaching and Learning, No. 18, Jan., 1984) is a useful recent collection of essays. Its concluding piece provides a selective guide to additional materials. *User Education in Libraries*, by Nancy Fjallbrant and Ian Malley (2nd rev. ed.) (London: Clive Bingley, 1984), provides an excellent introduction to theory and practice. Its perspective is a bit different, since many of its examples are from Swedish and English experience.

number of other schools began to use it or a modified version. The University of Wisconsin, Parkside library staff bases its series of subject area workbooks (e.g., history, political science, sociology) on the UCLA model, but the thrust is on developing a search strategy and compiling a bibliography.

The advantage of the workbook approach is that there is a relatively small investment of staff time compared with other methods. The advantage to the student is that it is self-paced, thus allowing for individual differences and schedules. A major drawback is that a workbook needs to be planned very carefully, with a lot of lead time, and that revisions, necessitated by new reference works or changes in library procedures, are difficult. Another problem is fitting the workbook into the curriculum. Again, it may become subject to the politics of curricular planning. And, of course, it is static, and cannot take the place of a teacher.

Course-related bibliographic instruction is the approach used in the largest number of institutions. Generally, it is given in conjunction with courses for which there is some type of library assignment, e.g., a term paper. When the students are ready to begin working on their library assignment, the librarian gives a presentation to the class, usually showing how to find information for the assignment along with a handout describing specific reference works—encyclopedias, guides to the literature, bibliographies, indexes, etc. That session for the entire class supplies information about sources useful to most of them, enough information for them to get started. Reference librarians, then, instead of showing each student separately the basic sources, can focus on special materials for the individual topics.

Course-related instruction has several advantages. It capitalizes on what students are most interested in—the assignment at hand. It assumes the priority of the course and the teacher's role, with the librarian supporting the teacher and the course plan. It's flexible in several respects: instruction sessions can be as long or as short as necessary; the information can be shaped to meet the needs of the class— the students' level, the particular assignment, the size of the class. Moreover, it can incorporate new materials easily and can be worked up relatively quickly. Finally, it has the advantage of any good classroom situation—questions can be answered immediately, points clarified or emphasized, adaptations quickly made, all depending on student reactions and responses.

Its main disadvantage is that it requires a close and comfortable working relationship between teaching faculty and librarians, something that's not always easy to establish, and which may take a long time to develop. When a close working relationship does develop, however, the instruction can become "course-integrated," which is instruction at its

98

most effective. It is then a symbiotic system—the librarian's objectives (teaching students to use the library more effectively) and the teacher's objectives (giving students an understanding of the subject matter) are mutually reinforcing. When that symbiosis works well, students not only learn to use the library, but come to view it as intrinsic to their education. To this writer's way of thinking, it is the best approach to bibliographic instruction presently available.

Success of any of the above programs depends on a number of factors. First of all, because there is little inherent interest in learning to use a library, the program will fail if the material to be studied or the presentation of information is done badly. Second, there needs to be some follow-up, some implementation or reinforcement. This may come by fulfilling the assignment, by individual interviews at the reference desk, or by later instruction that builds on what's been learned and helps reinforce it. Third, a program needs the support of the library administration. Offering such a program is time consuming and personnel consuming, and the library will need to adjust its priorities. Finally, in most cases the success of the program will depend very much on faculty cooperation and support since most means of bibliographic instruction are more or less connected with regular courses. Teaching faculty need to understand that instruction in use of the library serves their ends—their students can do better work and can become more independent learners. Bibliographic instruction does not compete with classroom teaching; on the contrary, if done well, it enhances it.

Recent Developments

In the last decade, the interest in bibliographic instruction has continued to grow. Probably the most convincing evidence of its acceptance is that one rarely sees an advertisement for a reference or public services position in a college or university library that does not include some responsibility for bibliographic instruction. Courses on bibliographic instruction are now being offered in several library schools, there are countless conferences and workshops on a variety of aspects, and the number of publications continues to grow. All of these have helped improve methods and sharpened strategies. Progress, in other words, has been expressed both through the spread of bibliographic instruction to more campuses, and by the consolidation of gains on campuses where programs had gotten started. It has not, however, been accompanied by developments in theory. The Monteith paradigm still exercises a powerful hold. Frances Hopkins, for example, feels that "the most fruitful approach to understanding library research" is by investigating "the scholarly communication patterns that produce the literatures of the different disciplines and examination of the related bibliographic apparatuses." This will be abetted by faculty acceptance:

"As interaction between instruction librarians and regular faculty increases, new possibilities emerge for using library work to teach aspects of subject content that have eluded verbal explication."[25]

I'm not so sure. There's not much question that basing bibliographic instruction on the structure of the disciplines has real intellectual appeal. But it does seem to try to make bibliographic instruction into a discipline of its own, a discipline lying somewhere between epistemology and information science. Training in that discipline may help make a librarian more effective in teaching students how to use library resources, but teaching the discipline to students rather than *using* it to help them learn how to get to better information may not be effective and may lose the support of faculty.

It seems to me that if there are going to be any significant new developments, two things are necessary: more faculty support and more systematic evaluation.

Faculty support is greater than ever, but I'm quite sure that the number of undergraduate teachers who work with librarians is still a small proportion of the total—there are still many colleges and universities where bibliographic instruction is practically unknown. It will take more teachers who are process-oriented, who will work with librarians, who recognize the advantages of bibliographic instruction for their own teaching, and who most of all appreciate the contribution it can make to education's long-range goal of helping students learn how to learn.

Faculty support will also be useful in getting researchers in higher education to help librarians evaluate the process and results of bibliographic instruction. Does it make a difference in student learning and behavior? In what ways? What are its long-term effects? Every library that has begun a program of bibliographic instruction has seen an increase, often a dramatic one, in the use of books and periodicals. At a number of workshops and conferences, faculty whose classes received instruction in using the library have testified to the improvement in student performance and have talked about the various ways bibliographic instruction has aided their teaching. But most of this evidence, impressive as it may be, is anecdotal. Some convincing data have been reported, and there are a few experimental studies, but not nearly enough to answer the questions of skeptics.[26] Even Patricia

---

[25] Frances L. Hopkins, "User Instruction in the College Library: Origins, Prospects, and a Practical Program," in *College Librarianship*, ed. by William Miller and D. Stephen Rockwood (Metuchen, N. J.: The Scarecrow Press, 1981) 198.

[26] Richard Werking, "Evaluating Bibliographic Education, A Review and Critique," *Library Trends* 29:153-172 (Summer, 1980).

Knapp's Monteith College experiment, as carefully designed and implemented as it was, never really evaluated the results.

The testimonials of students and faculty may be enough for librarians and many faculty now, but only when the questions of skeptics begin to be answered satisfactorily can bibliographic instruction really be accepted as an integral part of higher education.

Computer-Assisted Instruction

Some attention should be given to computer-assisted instruction (CAI), not because it's used very much now, but because it undoubtedly will become an important way of teaching use of the library in the next decade.

There was a flurry of interest in CAI in libraries in the early 1970s, but then the interest waned. The decline in interest was due to several factors: the high cost of equipment and its rapid obsolescence; the time necessary for programming; the shift of attention to other uses of computers in libraries, especially for administration and processing; the burst of activity in more traditional approaches to bibliographic instruction. Now, with more librarians entering the field who feel comfortable using computers, with equipment accessible to students, and with the usefulness and presence of computers in libraries taken for granted, there is a renewed interest in CAI.[27]

The advantages are obvious: its accessibility—students can work at their own pace, whenever it's convenient, and perhaps in a convenient location; the "gee-whiz" factor—the user's marveling at what the computer can do—gives it an appeal that print doesn't have; feedback is immediate yet the terminal shows infinite patience for those slow to learn; there's a minimum of staff time involved; revisions of the program are relatively easy; record keeping can be built into the program. The disadvantage is primarily the time it takes to develop a program that does more than a printed workbook, particularly since the program should be tailored to the particular library. CAI seems eminently suited for basic library instruction; the more advanced the instruction, the more complicated the program, and the more important personal interaction becomes.

As more libraries move to automated catalogs, and as individual use of online data banks continues to grow, instruction for users of these systems will increasingly be built into their operation. In not very many years, even the most unsophisticated student will be able to use an automated catalog with better results than many veteran library users can

---

[27] Sidney Eng, "Computer Assisted Instruction and the Future of Bibliographic Instruction," *Catholic Library World* 55:441-444 (May/June, 1984).

get from today's card catalog. The programs that permit the kind of interaction with a catalog or data bank that a reference librarian offers today will be designed by the company that supplied the software for the catalog or the databank service.

What instructional needs will be left for the librarian?

First of all, there will still be many individual reference works — indexes, handbooks, encyclopedias, etc. — that will be in print form and will need explaining. But that's minor, and computer programs to do that can be designed by individual libraries.

One major job for librarians will be to provide individualized reference assistance, much as reference librarians do now, but on a more specialized level, since the basic instructional needs will be taken care of by computers. In a study of reference service at four libraries serving undergraduates, one of the findings was that a bibliographic instruction program affected the level of questions asked by students. The questions tended to be more sophisticated as a result of such instruction.[28] The role of reference librarian as teacher, when the one-to-one relationship between student and librarians permits the subtleties of searching for information and evaluating sources to be discussed, will be even more important than it is today. The reason is again the "gee-whiz" factor. That is, the mystique of the computer, its apparent infallibility, will cause students to be even more unquestioning about the information they get. One purpose of a liberal education is to teach an informed skepticism; an increasingly important role of college librarians will be to help achieve that purpose. Another job will be to teach patterns of search strategy: for particular areas of study or for particular kinds of questions, what strategy should one follow? That job, it seems to me, can still be done best in class sessions; the conceptual nature of the topic demands discussion and questioning, and an examination of the relationships within and among disciplines can make a real contribution to the educational experience. Here again, the role of the librarian as teacher will be more necessary and more common.

Gail Lawrence, of Ohio State University, in her essay on the computer as a device for bibliographic instruction, concluded that "the challenge of automation is a total redefinition of the role and function of library user education."[29] I think that conjecture may be based on a

---

[28] Billy R. Wilkinson, *Reference Services for Undergraduate Students: Four Case Studies* (Metuchen, N. J.: The Scarecrow Press, 1972).

[29] Gail Herndon Lawrence, "The Computer as an Instructional Device: New Directions for Library User Education," *Library Trends* 29(no. l):150 (July, 1980). Also, see Sidnay Eng, "CAI and the Future of Bibliographic Instruction." *Catholic Library World* 55:441-444 (May-June, 1984).

misconception of what "the role and function of library user education" has been—or should have been. Automation will change much of how bibliographic instruction operates, but not its basic purpose—to enhance the teaching/learning process, and may well help librarians do a better job of it...

Virtually unlimited access to materials

In the first part of this paper I pictured the college library in the year 2000, and the enormous amount of information that would be available to every student. For our students, that will provide some obvious benefits, but it also will present some real problems, especially that of overload. I likened it to today's student having access to the resources of the Library of Congress for their term papers. Where do they begin? How do they sort their way through all that material, how do they decide what's the most important, the most useful sources? For faculty, the advantages for their own research are obvious, and it will be interesting indeed to see what effect it has in this area. Veaner points out that it will

> "exercise a powerful leveling effect in academe...Specialist faculty, graduate students and teaching assistants, and academic librarians in the elite institutions may no longer constitute a premier, invisible academy of gatekeepers or pioneers at the frontiers of knowledge and research. Possibly electronic information systems can democratize aspects of research, bringing opportunity to the academic stars of lesser galaxies."[30]

But for their teaching, access to unlimited resources will create exciting new possibilities—and some problems. It will permit an entirely new kind of freedom for teaching—for access to lecture materials, for reserve materials (if, indeed, reserve materials will even be necessary), for materials students can read or use for papers. But what sorts of problems will it create for the teacher? Will teachers be able to give students guidance in using these materials? Should they limit the sources students can use? If not, how can they evaluate papers based on materials they never knew existed? These are problems teachers never had to think about before, and because the circumstances will be so different from what they are now will require an entirely new mind-set.

---

[30] Veaner, "1985-1995: The Next Decade...," p. 35-36.

The Role of the Librarian

Most experts on information technology feel that in the near future the general public will access many data bases directly, without entering a library. Will it happen on campuses? Undoubtedly—in fact, it already has. A number of faculty and other researchers consult data bases from their offices or laboratories. How general it will become on campuses, and what the role of the librarian will be are not so clear.

Samuel Dunn, a dean at Seattle Pacific University, predicted that "most students...will have their own personal computers [which] will be linked to university-wide networks that will allow students to call up most library materials and view them from their rooms or homes."[31] F. W. Lancaster, of the University of Illinois (and probably cited more often than any other expert on the future of libraries), wrote that, "as researchers become familiar and comfortable with the use of online data bases, the need for these researchers to visit libraries will rapidly diminish." On the other hand, he goes on to say that while "rapid growth of information resources in electronic form may greatly reduce the value of the library...it may increase the value of the librarian. The magnitude and diversity of the electronic resources available will put skilled information specialists in great demand."[32]

...This will be especially true for college libraries, it seems to me, where students will need help and guidance in order to make the availability of resources meaningful for them, to make the process of finding information an educational one.

How can we combine the new and the old? For many years libraries are going to have to combine the new technology, and all it implies, with traditional materials; library users, particularly in the humanities, are going to have to use both the traditional and the new, perhaps at the same time. And this must be done—for a long time, at least—in a building most likely designed before computers were even thought about.

Certainly libraries cannot continue "as they are," but that is not to say they will disappear, though there are those who talk about that as an eventuality. Again, we can quote F. W. Lancaster, who wrote about the disappearance of libraries as we know them. Because we are moving to "a paperless society," where almost all publishing will be in electronic

---

[31] Samuel Dunn, "The Changing University: Survival in the Information Society," *Futurist* 17(4):57 (August, 1983).

[32] F. Wilfrid Lancaster, "The Future of the Library," in *Telecommunications and Libraries: A Primer for Librarians and Information Managers* (White Plains, N. Y.: Knowledge Industry Publications, Inc., 1981) 150-1.

form, "the library as an institution will begin its inevitable decline."[33] But even he admits that "nonresearch libraries"—including college libraries, one assumes—

> "may be affected much less by the transition to electronics since…literature read for relaxation or inspiration is unlikely to be enhanced by display at a terminal and will continue to be available in paper form for some time."[34]

But one can make a more persuasive case for keeping the college library somewhat as it is now than simply "for relaxation or inspiration." First of all, there is material that will remain in print form, either for aesthetic reasons, or because no one has yet felt it necessary to computerize their contents. This material, and I suspect there will be much of it, will still need to be consulted in a library. The other reason is the need to keep the library as a place for study, for rumination, for the quiet exchange of ideas. Students like to study in libraries; surveys have shown that most students' time in libraries is spent studying their own books. They like to study in libraries not because there are materials there they need, but because of the atmosphere—the quiet, the comfort, the variety of study facilities, the possibility of privacy without isolation. Faculty also enjoy being in the library—as a library, not just as a means of finding information. The notion was well put by Paul Lacey, Professor of English at Earlham College, in his talk, "Views of a Luddite," to the Association of College and Research Libraries.

> I am not conceiving of the library as an information retrieval system primarily but as a social system, a teaching-learning milieu in which retrieval of information is only a part of the goal. Browsing, conversation, exchange of ideas, sharing and confirming values, supporting one another in the common enterprise of study, reflection, and publishing one's findings—these are extremely important to what a humanist, or any member of the scholarly community, does.

---

[33] Lancaster, "Future of the Library," p. 150-1. See also his *Libraries and Librarians in an Age of Electronics* (White Plains, N. Y.: Knowledge Industry Publications, 1982).

[34] Ibid., p. 151.

I am arguing that the library is not merely a place or a collection of functions but a living symbol of valuable and rich human relations...In our work as teachers and as researchers we know something of the joy of self-transcendence, being caught up in a text or a search that makes us forget ourselves, and we also know the joy of communion, of finding kindred spirits, dedicated scholars and writers who are a part of our human family. There must be places where such things can happen and be confirmed and memorialized. Universities and colleges are such places. So are libraries.[35]

Technology will have an incredible impact on what college libraries can do and how they do it. Users will look for and get information very differently, but the library as we know it today will—for a long time to come, at least—still also be a place to study, to browse, to think, to relax. "A library," Robert Frost said in 1963, "should be the place where the student has it out with himself." That function is too precious to give up...

Faculty and Administrative Attitudes

In the section on bibliographic instruction, one theme appears again and again: if the library is to take an active role in the teaching-learning process, faculty cooperation and support are essential. That cooperation and support has not been forthcoming very often. As Gresham Riley, President of Colorado College, told a national meeting of librarians last year: "Academic faculty are, for the most part, not predisposed as scholars to recognize and to acknowledge a legitimate educational role for the library and for librarians."[36]

Why not? Well, there are probably a number of reasons, but an important one is certainly an attitude towards librarians. Riley went on to say that "many (and probably most) faculty members" view librarians "not as equal partners in the teaching/learning process, but rather as on the same level as residence hall directors, counselors in the career

---

[35] Paul A. Lacey, "Views of a Luddite," *College & Research Libraries* 43:118 (March, 1982).

[36] Gresham Riley, "The College Viewpoint" in *Academic Libraries: Myths and Realities: Proceedings of the Third National Conference of the Association of College and Research Libraries, April 4-7, 1984, Seattle, Wash.* (Chicago: Association of College and Research Libraries, 1984) 12.

106

center, or athletic coaches." Will that change? Riley felt that faculty are "likely to be influenced by the local conditions which prevail at their college or university (in particular, the attitude of key administrators as to the role of the library)."[37]

Unfortunately, too many administrators hold the view that librarianship is a technique and that librarians are technicians. Guy Lyle, in his marvelously succinct and perceptive little book, *The President, the Professor, and the College Library*—a book still well worth reading— quoted Julian Boyd: "According to this view, held by too many presidents,...librarians are technicians, far below the rank of policy makers. They are to keep the machinery going, to chart its mileage per gallon, to change its tires, and to keep it ready-fueled, but not to touch the steering wheel." And, Lyle added, "this is a view frequently held by faculty members."[38]

That comment was made some twenty years ago, but attitudes have not changed that much. A few years ago William Moffett, Director of Libraries at Oberlin, surveyed a large number of academic librarians as to what they "expect of faculty and administrators and vice versa." The responses were not encouraging.

> It was disconcerting now to hear from a distinguished academic librarian in New England that "the most pervasive attitude toward the library that I've encountered is benign neglect. Nothing overtly subversive, nothing openly hostile, just a certain amount of indifference, impatience, and a lack of understanding of the complexity of library activity and of the importance of the library as a means for academic excellence." This experience was apparently shared by a California librarian who observed that academic administrators he had known often exhibited a set attitude that "reflects a hope that the library will not cause any trouble, that the library will not need any more funds than it currently receives, that somehow the library will manage to stay in the space it now occupies, and that it should manage to placate those irascible faculty

---

[37] Ibid., p. 13.

[38] Guy R. Lyle, *The President, the Professor, and the College Library*. (N. Y.: The H. W. Wilson Co., 1963) 22.

members." And from a Midwestern university a librarian wrote, "It has been my experience that the dean or vice president of academic administration who understands college and/or university libraries is a very rare specimen. I have encountered only one. The library's presence is accepted as a given, but it is not seen as a vital resource for the intellectual endeavors of the institution.[39]

Compare Riley's enlightened comment on the role of the library and librarians. "I believe," he noted,

"that the library and professional librarians have a major and equal role in meeting at least one of the objectives of a liberal arts and science education. The obvious basis for this belief is that the mastery of library search strategies is central to those skills which make possible life-long learning. Consequently, no matter what other functions and other people might be found at the center of the educational process, the library and librarians have a legitimate claim on that space."[40]

As other administrators begin to understand this, as they show more interest in the teaching-learning process and understand better what the library can mean to that process, their hands-off attitude, their view that "as long as faculty members don't complain, as long as the size of the collection and other standards meet a level acceptable to accreditation agencies,"[41] then let the library alone—that attitude will change.

Faculty attitudes are changing and will change even more. Certainly a factor will be the improving quality of librarians. Also, the impetus of the bibliographic instruction movement—its increasing recognition by the various disciplines and its demonstrated success on individual campuses—will make it a standard part of most college

---

[39] William A. Moffett, "What the Academic Librarian Wants from Administrators and Faculty," in *Priorities for Academic Libraries*, edited by Thomas J. Galvin and Beverly Lynch (New Directions for Higher Education, no. 39 Sept., 1982) 15.

[40] Ibid., p. 13.

[41] p. 16, above.

teachers' stock in trade, and they will be working more closely with librarians in constructive ways. The new library technology should change attitudes in several ways. A study of faculty perceptions showed that, for newer faculty, their most negative feelings about the library resulted from "their perception of adequacy of the collection in their areas."[42] When technology permits access to so much material, the cause for that negative attitude should disappear. In addition faculty will increasingly recognize the importance of instruction by librarians to help find and evaluate all the material available to them and their students.

The issue of faculty status for college librarians is relevant here, because the issue is closely tied to faculty (and administrative) attitudes toward librarians. The issue has been around a long time, and much has been written on the subject from a variety of points of view and with conflicting conclusions. A good recent summary of these conflicting views appeared in William Miller's essay, "Faculty Status in the College Library."[43] Miller feels that the desire for faculty status arose because academic librarians lack "respect for themselves and their work situations," and so they attempted "to model themselves on the teaching faculty as they searched for a satisfactory way to define themselves." (p. 121) But there's been no firm definition of what faculty status for librarians entails, and it varies considerably from campus to campus. For the librarians of even a closely related group of colleges, one can find just about every possible conformation insofar as tenure, rank, and other faculty appurtenances are concerned. Miller surveyed a group of college librarians to find out how they defined faculty status at their institutions. The results suggest "that it is defined and treated so variously that one would need an in-depth interview at every institution, and a lengthy written profile for each, simply to account adequately for the vagaries of each situation." (pp. 123-4)

Miller feels that "the most likely course of events is a continuation of the status quo, a somewhat demoralizing but nevertheless livable compromise in which the majority of college librarians have some form of academic status that they can, if they so choose, consider to be faculty status." (p. 129) He would prefer otherwise. The alternative he personally favors is "to seek recognition and status as librarians," (p. 131) though he fears this won't happen unless "some

---

[42] Jinnie Y. Davis and Stella Bentley, "Factors Affecting Faculty Perceptions of Academic Libraries," *College & Research Libraries* 40:531 (Nov., 1979).
[43] In Miller and Rockwood, *College Librarianship*, pp. 118-134. The most extensive treatment of the subject is Virgil F. Massman, *Faculty Status for Librarians* (Metuchen, N. J.: The Scarecrow Press, 1972).

strong wind sweeps through academia, giving them new direction in their quest for status and a sense of professional identity." (p. 133)

The two developments I've spent most space discussing above, bibliographic instruction and the new technology, may have the effect that Miller desires. Librarians will increasingly be regarded as partners in the teaching-learning process as well as experts in searching for information. They should feel quite comfortable with a new level of professional identity, whether their status on campus is formalized as faculty, library faculty, librarians, administrative faculty, or some other description that the institution feels most appropriate. Their role will be an important and respected one and their status on campus should be assured...

**

In a recent book review, Joseph Epstein, the essayist and editor of the *American Scholar*, observed caustically that a phrase in the book under review, "we are clearly living in an age of transition," was probably first used "by Adam to Eve as they were leaving Eden."[44] That observation makes me reluctant to use the phrase with reference to college libraries, but they *are* in an age of transition.

The next few years can make an enormous difference in what college libraries will do. Even though libraries' growth may be limited, by taking advantage of the new technology, and permitting librarians to use that technology to enhance the teaching-learning process, college administrators have the opportunity to make their libraries an important factor in undergraduate education. Despite what has been said in college publicity, or in administrators' speeches, the library is not the heart of the college. What is and has been the heart of the college is the teaching-learning process, and the role of the library is to enhance that process. That role has been realized too rarely, but now that realization is much more plausible. The potential is there, only the will is needed.

---

[44] Joseph Epstein, "Partisan Review & the Phillips Curve; Letter from New York," *Encounter* 64(1):73 (January, 1985).

15

College Libraries
(1986)

This piece first appeared as a chapter in Education for Professional
Librarians, *a book edited by Herbert S. White and published by Knowledge
Industry Publications in 1986. As the dean of a library school, White wanted to
see how the new information technology would—or should—affect the curricula
of library schools. Because the book treated many areas of librarianship I
thought that many readers might not be familiar with the world of college
libraries, and especially might not understand the differences between college
and university libraries, and so I felt the need to begin with some elementary
observations about the nature of college libraries, usually tying the observations
to the differences.*

*On reading the piece over, while I think most of it still is relevant, what
struck me—and will for most readers, I'm sure— is, in the sections on the
educational background and basic training of college librarians, the omission of
the need for some familiarity with the applications of computers. I don't mean
having some expertise with the technology, but at least some knowledge of and
interest in the potential of electronic information. Of course, the piece was
written in 1984, but even so I regret the omission.*

— Evan Ira Farber, 2006

To generalize about almost any aspect of college libraries is a
risky, even dubious exercise, simply because there is such diversity
within that group. There are college libraries in which one professional
librarian serves a few hundred students with a collection of less than
50,000 volumes. At the other end of the spectrum are the prestigious,
affluent colleges with sizable library staffs and substantial collections
approaching—some even surpassing—those of many university libraries.
And if one wants to include in the group the community college libraries,
a number of which serve as many as 25,000 students, the range is
stretched even further. The kinds of curricula, and thus the types of
collections, also vary widely. At one extreme, perhaps, is St. John's
College in Annapolis, MD, with a pristinely traditional liberal arts
curriculum; a community college can provide the other extreme, a
community college that offers many courses in a variety of applied fields
as well as in the more conventional academic disciplines.

White, Herbert S., editor. *Education for Professional Librarians.* White Plains,
New York, Knowledge Industry Publications, 1986. Pages 49-65.

If, then, college libraries are so diverse, how can one talk about them as a group? Is there any commonality that can be ascribed to them? There is one, I think, a very important one, and that is the fact that they all serve undergraduates—perhaps not exclusively, but primarily. The role, the programs, the thrust of college libraries is largely determined by this fact—and so, then, should be the kinds of librarians who work in those libraries.

Purpose

The role of the college library is very different from that of the university library. While a university library serves many purposes and types of clientele, its primary function is to support research, to build collections for the needs of scholars and graduate students. The reputations—indeed, the ranking—of university libraries are predicated on the size of their collections, or on their expenditures for acquisitions, or on a combination of quantitative factors. The purpose of a college library, on the other hand, is primarily to serve undergraduates and to do that by supporting the teaching/learning process. How well it does that, and not its size or its expenditures, should be the measure of a college library's success. There is some parallel with the difference between the roles of a university professor and a college professor. The former gains a reputation and gets tenure by research and publication; the latter, by the quality of his or her teaching, student evaluations of which have become increasingly important. Of course the difference is not that clear-cut, but it is a matter of emphasis, and there is no doubt that the emphasis of most colleges is on teaching. A college library may have as one of its objectives the support of faculty research, but the emphasis of its service will be on supporting the teaching/learning process.

This difference between the purposes of a university library and a college library ought to be clearly kept in mind by a college's faculty, administration and library staff. When any of these groups fails to recognize the distinction between the two, the library's ability to work toward its primary mission, support of the teaching/learning process, is probably doomed to failure. With its limited resources, a college library can do just so much; to try to emulate a university library's role or practices is foolhardy and simply leads to the college library fulfilling neither role: a small scale university library is almost a contradiction in terms, but in trying to be one the college library must sacrifice its real purpose and its true clientele, the students. This distinction, then, becomes important when considering almost any aspect of the college library's program, procedures or personnel. Yet, as important as the distinction is, too often it's ignored in the literature of academic

112

librarianship, including that on the recruitment and training of academic librarians. There are, to be sure, more similarities than differences between the qualities that applicants for positions in college libraries should have and those that applicants to university libraries should have. It may be even more a matter of degree than a matter of striking differences, but that matter of degree, or those differences in particular cases ought to be kept in mind. And the difference in the purposes of the two types of libraries is often the key factor.

Staff Size

Another characteristic of college libraries that must be considered in defining their personnel needs is staff size. Most college libraries have small professional staffs. The libraries in such colleges as Oberlin (with 17 professionals) or Smith (with 21) are few and far between, and hardly representative of college libraries. For example, Austin College surveyed 16 liberal arts colleges around the country a few years ago, colleges with which it wanted to compare itself. Though 11 of the 16 are considered selective colleges, the number of professional librarians averaged slightly less than 5.[1] Another example: a survey taken last year of 22 private college libraries in Indiana showed that while they averaged 4.2 professionals, 2 of the colleges had only 1 professional, and 10 had 2 or 3.[2] These minimal staffs are not at all unusual for what have been called the "invisible colleges," those small, private, often church-related colleges with limited resources that make up about a third of our four-year colleges.

ASPECTS OF COLLEGE LIBRARIANSHIP

The small number of professional librarians in most college libraries affects the work of the librarians in two important aspects: the style of work—the relative autonomy of the librarians; and the content of work—the need for college librarians to be generalists rather than specialists. Not only are these two aspects interrelated, each also reinforces the other.

In his recent essay, "1985 to 1995: The Next Decade in Academic Librarianship," Allen Veaner noted that "in smaller academic libraries, virtually all the major management responsibilities fall upon the

---

[1] "1981-82 Library Data for a Selected Group of Liberal Arts Colleges (900-1450 FTE)," compiled by Lisa Bailey and Dan Bedsole, Austin College, October 1983 (mimeographed).
[2] "Indiana Private College Library Survey, 1984-1985," collected by Larry Frye, Wabash College (mimeographed).

chief librarian," and then went on to say that although it had been pointed out "that the autonomous professional model is not the reality in the large research library, it could be highly functional in a college library or junior/community college library."[3]

The Autonomous Librarian

What Veaner is talking about here is the librarian's professional autonomy—the freedom, the independence of judgment that derives from not being a cog in a large organization. That is certainly true in the smaller library: there are many more opportunities for professionals' individual decisions, or at least for not having to check so many other professional opinions. To anyone who has worked in a large organization, especially one beset by bureaucratic procedures, that seems like a most appealing situation, but one must recognize certain limitations.

The first is that while there may be independence of other professional judgments, there is not always a similar independence from one's clientele and/or faculty colleagues. Many small colleges appeal to a special group, and so the small college community is usually a close knit one. Even those with a wider constituency, however, like to think of themselves as forming a community, and in such a community many voices, not always expert or even knowledgeable, often want to be heard when decisions affecting them in even the slightest way are made. The college librarian who insists on going his or her own way without listening to, or at least hearing, these voices jeopardizes the staff's working relationships, and, in the long run, the library's effectiveness. This of course does not mean that the librarians need to check every possible move with everyone; it does mean, however, that the librarians need to be aware of faculty, administration and student feelings and opinions on certain matters, and to take those into account when appropriate—and appropriate often means politically expedient. Knowing the faculty and students—their academic interests and needs, their concerns, even their likes and dislikes—is almost a requirement for running a successful library program at a small college.

The Isolated Librarian

A second limitation is the reverse side of "not having to check so many other professional opinions." That is, the disadvantage of not having many other professional opinions available, particularly in matters where specialized knowledge is needed.

---

[3] Allen B. Veaner, "1985 to 1995: The Next Decade in Academic Librarianship, Part II," *College & Research Libraries* 46 (July 1985): 295.

114

Because college librarians need to perform such a variety of tasks, to be such generalists (as described in the following paragraph), it is almost impossible for them to keep up with aspects of librarianship that are changing rapidly, almost any area where there is a need for much technical expertise. This disadvantage is exacerbated by the locations of many small colleges—distant from large cities or large libraries, even from each other, so that the opportunities to talk with specialists outside the college community are even more limited.

The Generalist Librarian

The third limitation is that the independence available to college librarians also demands that they be generalists. Charles Maurer, Director of the Library at Denison University, put it this way:

> In large organizations, including large libraries, the director has assistants for some or all of these [administrative] areas and in addition is insulated by the size of the operation from day-to-day concerns; department heads or section chiefs or area supervisors handle that...In any case, the [college library] director will sometimes be on reference, or circulation duty, and will not have personnel specialists or budget managers to take care of the details of those concerns. In an era of growing specialization this library head is one of the last generalists.[4]

William Moffett, Director of Libraries at Oberlin College, extended the generalist label to the rest of the college library staff as well. First, he asked that we think of the different types of academic librarians by considering them on a continuum. At one end are those "who see themselves as professional librarians employed in academia"— that is, those who work in large university libraries—and at the other, "those who tend to regard themselves as academics working in libraries"—the college librarians.

And so we have, on the one hand, professional specialists "whose first loyalties are to the values of the guild; and, on the other,

---

[4] Charles Maurer, "Close Encounters of Diverse Kinds: A Management Panorama for the Director of the Smaller College Library," in *College Librarianship*, ed. William Miller and D. Stephen Rockwood (Metuchen, N.J.: Scarecrow Press, 1981) 98.

generalists whose professional skills are clearly subordinate to the educational function to which they are committed."[5] Moffett did not mean to imply that all college librarians are committed to the educational function any more than he would insist that all university librarians see themselves only as professional specialists. He was simply pointing out the "different tendency" between the two—the tendency of professionals in large libraries to specialize, and the tendency of those in smaller libraries to be generalists.

The Teaching Librarian

Being a generalist extends to many areas for the college librarian. In his essay "A Paradigm for College Libraries," Peter Dollard, the Library Director at Alma College, wrote that "the college librarian should keep the managerial function clearly subordinated to the major goal of maximizing the laboratory potential of the library." He went on to say:

> This leads directly to another quality academic librarians must have: they must to a large extent see their role as that of a teacher. You do not answer reference questions, you demonstrate a research methodology…Technical services librarians in college libraries are commonly scheduled at the reference desk…A librarian supervising student assistants often teaches more than simply how to get a job done. It is not that teaching is a major activity of all college librarians, but that college librarians must enjoy teaching when the occasion arises.
>
> Related to the service ethic, but also very much related to a particular mind-set, is the way college librarians relate to all parts of the collection they are developing. You must have enough general knowledge and curiosity and be sincerely interested in a wide enough variety of subjects in order to pursue collection development with some vigor…You must have a real conviction that knowledge and learning

---

[5] William A. Moffett, "Reflections of a College Librarian: Looking for Life and Redemption This Side of ARL," *College & Research Libraries* 45:338-349 (September 1984): 344.

are valuable ends in themselves to be able to
develop your collection with zest.[6]

The Academic Librarian

Another aspect of being a generalist is closely related to
Moffett's view of college librarians as "academics working in libraries."
That is, at many small colleges, librarians play a variety of roles not
closely—perhaps not at all—related to the library.

There are a number of college librarians who, with their
additional subject backgrounds, teach courses in a variety of disciplines.
There are librarians who coach or help coach sports, librarians who serve
as academic advisers, and on many college campuses librarians who
participate in various aspects of the conduct of the college by serving on
special and standing committees. The point is, in a small college,
individuals may wear several hats because there are many more
responsibilities and opportunities for service than there are people to
meet those needs. As part of that small college community, the librarians
wear whichever hats fit and are appropriate to their talents or
inclinations.

Before going on to discuss the implications of these
characteristics for the preparation of college librarians, let's review them
briefly. First, college librarians are primarily concerned with
undergraduates, with supporting, even enhancing, their instruction.
Second, most college libraries have small professional staffs, leading to a
great deal of professional autonomy on the one hand, but on the other
some professional isolation. Third, college librarians usually work in a
community where there are close, sometimes inhibiting, working
relationships. Finally, also because of the small staffs, college librarians
need to be generalists within the library and often serve their colleges in
capacities outside the library.

THE PREPARATION OF COLLEGE LIBRARIANS

How should the preparation of librarians for positions in libraries
such as these differ from those for university or other research libraries?
Or, should there be a difference? It seems appropriate to see what recent
writings have had to say about the preparation of academic librarians.
There is of course a variety of opinions, but even with this variety, one
can come up with a consensus. The writings I've particularly looked at

---

[6] Peter Dollard, "A Paradigm for College Libraries," in *College Librarianship*,
ed. William Miller and D. Stephen Rockwood (Metuchen, N.J.: Scarecrow
Press, 1981) 42-43.

are those of Lester Asheim,[7] Patricia Battin,[8] Harold Borko,[9] John Budd,[10] Edward G. Holley,[11] Barbara Moran,[12] W. Boyd Rayward,[13] Robert Stueart,[14] Allen Veaner,[15] and reactions to Holley's paper by Irene Hoadley, Sheila Creth and Herbert White.[16] There's surely general agreement that while technical competence is important, it's no longer enough, that there needs to be more stress on theory and on research. Some feel that academic librarians need to know more about the field of higher education, even more particularly about the type of learning or institution in which one intends to spend a career. There was a continuing stress on the importance of communication, both oral and written, and on the ability to manage. Since Patricia Battin's list of qualifications for research librarians was quoted approvingly by at least four of the above authors, they should be mentioned:

1. A first-rate mind with problem solving abilities
2. A solid, rigorous undergraduate education
3. Concrete evidence of managerial abilities
4. An intellectual commitment to research libraries[17]

---

[7] Lester Asheim, *Library School Preparation for Academic and Research Librarianship; A Report Prepared for the Council on Library Resources* (Washington, D.C.: Council on Library Resources, 1983).

[8] Patricia Battin, "Developing University and Research Library Professionals: A Director's Perspective," *American Libraries* 14:22-25 (January 1983).

[9] Harold Borko, "Trends in Library and Information Science Education," *Journal of the Association for Information Science* 35:185-193 (May 1984).

[10] John Budd, "The Education of Academic Librarians," *College & Research Libraries* 45:15-24 (January 1984).

[11] Edward G. Holley, "Defining the Academic Librarian," *College & Research Libraries* 46:462-468 (November 1985).

[12] Barbara Moran, *Academic Libraries: The Changing Knowledge Centers of Colleges and Universities, ASHE-ERIC Higher Education Research Report, No.8,* 1984 (Washington, D.C.: Association for the Study of Higher Education, 1984), especially pp. 54-59 on The Preparation of Academic Librarians.

[13] W. Boyd Rayward, "Academic Librarianship: The Role of Library Schools," in *Issues in Academic Librarianship; Views and Case Studies for the 1980s and 1990s,* ed. Peter Spyers-Duran and Thomas W. Mann, Jr. (Westport, Conn.: Greenwood Press, 1985) 100-114.

[14] Robert D. Stueart, "The Education of Academic Librarians" in *Academic Librarianship: Yesterday, Today, and Tomorrow,* ed. by Robert Stueart (N.Y.: Neal-Schuman Publishers, 1982), pp. 231-245.

[15] Veaner, "1985 to 1995."

[16] Irene B. Hoadley, Sheila Creth, and Herbert S. White, "Reactions to 'Defining the Academic Librarian,'" *College & Research Libraries* 46:469-77 (November 1985).

[17] Battin, p. 23.

To make these even more generally applicable, Veaner suggested that one should "substitute any type-of-library adjective in place of 'research.' No academic librarian anywhere can afford to lack these requirements."[18] It would be hard to argue with any of this in spelling out the desirable preparation for a college librarian. Do college libraries want, then, their recruits to have the same training and qualifications as other academic librarians? The answer is—well, yes, but with some modifications.

Basic Training

Yes, of course college libraries need staff members who have good basic training, training based on that "identifiable 'core of knowledge' common to all types of librarians...that all students, no matter what their declared eventual career aspirations might be, should be exposed to."[19] This is especially important for college librarians because they have to be generalists; the smaller the staff, the more widely spread will the librarians' knowledge have to extend...

For similar reasons, it is just as important for college librarians to have a solid educational background, and that needn't be restricted to one's formal education. What we do want are traits that one associates with a broad, rigorous education—flexibility in thought, openness to opinions and experiences, intellectual competence, a sense of values and a breadth of interests and perspectives. Because the college librarian is ultimately responsible for building the collection—a collection that is not just to support the present curriculum but also to serve future generations of students, and, as Peter Dollard noted above, must "relate to all parts of the collection" and develop the collection "with zest"—a breadth of interests is essential. Likewise, in order to work more effectively with faculty—and thus to help integrate the library into the teaching/learning process—college librarians need to talk with, appreciate, support the interests of those faculty, whether they come from economics, music, biology or Afro-American studies.

Almost half a century ago, Harvie Branscomb, Director of Libraries at Duke University, wrote what is still one of the wisest commentaries on college libraries and librarians, *Teaching With Books, A Study of College Libraries.*[20] As opposed to a university librarian, he

---

[18] Veaner, p. 298.

[19] Stueart, p. 234.

[20] Harvie Branscomb, *Teaching With Books, A Study of College Libraries* (Chicago: Association of American Colleges [and] American Library Association, 1940).

wrote, "the position of college librarian demands more of the qualities of the teacher and educator...One can set out three main qualifications for the college librarian besides those general ones of intelligence and integrity which would be assumed. These are (a) a knowledge of the principles of library administration, (b) scholarly interests and understanding, with which is included an interest in the education of college undergraduates, and (c) an ability to work with students and to cooperate smoothly and efficiently with those sometimes difficult individuals, the faculty."[21]

The Context of Higher Education

College librarians, even more than university librarians, should have an understanding of the field of higher education, and especially the social and political context in which the particular library operates. Again, that need is so important to college librarians because of the various roles they play and because of the small size of their institutions. A successful college librarian is one who is going to be asked to do many things on campus. In order to serve on a campus curriculum committee or on an administrative council, one must know and appreciate the institution's educational mission, its academic and administrative idiosyncrasies, and the keys to interpersonal relationships that keep it going. And to work more closely with students, as an academic adviser or as an informal adviser, as many college librarians do, knowledge of the institution and the higher educational scene in general is surely important.

First-rate minds? Of course they should be required for all prospective librarians, but again, because college librarians work closely with students, often in a teaching capacity—to both individuals and classes—that quality is especially desirable. Furthermore, because of that close working relationship, college librarians can serve as models for students and can help recruit better applicants into librarianship. Since first-rate minds attract other first rate minds, the entire profession should benefit. Likewise, the ability to communicate is a crucial quality. The more frequent contact with faculty and students means that oral communication is especially important.

Professional Involvement

The importance of professional involvement can hardly be exaggerated for college librarians. As noted above, small libraries may be handicapped by their lack of expertise as well as by their geographical isolation, and they may not have "many other professional opinions

---

[21] Branscomb, pp. 86-87.

available, particularly in matters where specialized knowledge is needed." While state and regional networks have done a good bit to help overcome this disadvantage, the involvement in professional associations, the exchange of ideas and experiences at state and national meetings are invaluable.

Management Ability

As for management skills, because college librarians may have more autonomy than librarians in a university, they need to know how to manage. Most college librarians will not have to manage the numbers of subordinates or the amount of materials that many university librarians will. The type of management skills, then, may be quite different: in a college situation, interpersonal skills may be more important than sheer organizational ability. Also, in a college library, management may be more a shared responsibility—again, because one is required to serve in so many capacities.

An interesting development at Dickinson College, where true collegiate management has been instituted, could make this even more important. At Dickinson, where the library has a professional staff of eight, the role of library director—or chairperson, as the position is called there—rotates to a different librarian every four years. The system has been in effect for almost 10 years, and the staff reports individual satisfactions, even enthusiasm, as well as institutional advantages.[22] But for other institutions to make such a radical change from traditional administration it is probably too soon for a really convincing evaluation. If it does turn out to work well, and if it is emulated by other colleges, there will be a real demand for staff members who are capable managers as well as, say, fine reference librarians; an inept chairperson for four years could hinder a library's growth and blunt its effectiveness for a much longer period.

Commitment to Education

One of Pat Battin's requirements was "an intellectual commitment to research librarianship." For college librarians, the counterpart is a commitment to the process of undergraduate education and the role of the library in supporting that process. A college librarian

---

[22] Joan M. Bechtel, "Rotation Day Reflections," *College & Research Libraries News* 46:551-555 (November 1985). For a further discussion of the plan's rationale and background, see Dorothy H. Cieslicki, "A New Status Model for Academic Librarians," *Journal of Academic Librarianship* 8:76-81 (May 1982); and Joan Bechtel, "Academic Professional Status: An Alternative for Librarians," *Journal of Academic Librarianship* 11:289-292 (November 1985).

who is an expert on, say, government documents really doesn't belong in that library unless he or she is honestly interested in getting students to use those documents. "The college library has the same *raison d'etre* as the college of which it is a part," Harvie Branscomb wrote, "it exists for the sake of teaching or educating undergraduate students."[23] I've seen too many librarians, in colleges as well as in universities, who view their libraries as ends in themselves—the procedures, the organization of the collection as their *raison d'etre*. That's surely unfortunate in a university situation, but it becomes disastrous in a college, because undergraduates need librarians' help and encouragement. Without the staff's commitment to the process of undergraduate education, without an interest in helping young people grow intellectually and culturally, without the desire to help students learn how to learn, to show them how to find, evaluate and organize information for themselves so that they can, after their formal education is over, become more effective and creative members of society—without those aims as part of the staff ethos, a college library can easily become simply a warehouse, a place where information and materials are available to students if they want or need to use them, but not a library that plays an active role in the educational process.

Let's return to the question: should the preparation of college librarians be different from that of other academic librarians? We can see that neither the preparation nor the personal qualifications need to be very different. It is an oversimplification to say that one group is interested in working with scholars and/or scholarly materials while the other is interested in working with undergraduates, but to apply Moffett's usage of a continuum with somewhat different dimensions, one can say that each group tends toward one end or the other. Both interests are of course important, but for different agendas; there's no question that the styles of work, the measures of accomplishment, the kinds of satisfactions for each agenda are also different.

A parallel with academics is not inappropriate: there are those academics who are most interested in research and publication, either in doing their own or guiding others, or both. They are the recognized scholars, the leaders in their disciplines, who occupy major university positions. Then there are those academics who think that conveying their disciplines, contributing to the development of young people's appreciation and abilities is more important; for them, the college classroom, the teaching/learning process is the way to professional satisfaction. It is this group which college librarians identify with, this group which college librarians serve by supporting and by enhancing that

---

[23] Branscomb, p. 81.

teaching/learning process. There are other rewards, other satisfactions, other pleasures in being a college librarian, but none so great as making that contribution.

RECRUITMENT

Can library schools aid in recruiting or training for this role?

To some extent, yes, but the most effective recruiting needs to be done before then. Library schools, after all, no matter how good a job they do, can't make over the personalities or the talents of their students, and if we want candidates who are really empathetic with the purposes and processes of undergraduate education, the colleges themselves will have to be responsible for recruiting them.

Lawrence Clark Powell wrote years ago that "our profession does not automatically perpetuate itself. A good measure of a library...is the number of students or clericals it has recruited for librarianship...Every student who works for us is a potential librarian...The best recruits are those who are inspired by the librarians for whom they work."[24] Powell was addressing his own university library staff, but his words are even more appropriate for college librarians. To most university undergraduates, the library staff is unknown; college librarians, on the other hand, can and often do have a very different relationship with students. The student body at the small residential college is almost a captive audience; that, plus the close working relationship between students and librarians, should make recruiting efforts feasible.

Wheaton College in Illinois recently provided an example of what can be done. With the cooperation of the campus career development office, the library staff plus outside speakers held a well attended seminar for students, to publicize careers in library and information science.[25] Beyond the efforts of individual libraries or librarians, the library and the higher education associations and consortia ought to work together. Recruiting quality personnel for college libraries is, after all, in the interest of both groups. In his article, Moffett expressed the hope that "the Great Lakes Colleges Association (and perhaps other college consortia) can be persuaded to offer some internships in college library administration...By so doing we may be

---

[24] Lawrence Clark Powell, *A Passion for Books* (N.Y.: World Publishing, 1958) 125.
[25] Jonathan D. Lauer, "Recruiting for the Profession," *College & Research Libraries News* 45:388-390 (September 1984). I'm indebted to this article for reminding me of Powell's essay and the book it's in.

able to...counter some of that bias which discourages good people from seriously considering careers in smaller institutions."[26] Moffett was more interested in getting librarians to think about careers in college libraries; just as important is getting college students who are interested in higher education to think about college librarianship as a crucial and exciting aspect of higher education.

The Association of American Colleges, or the Council for the Advancement of Small Colleges, or any number of state or regional consortia, working with the Association of College and Research Libraries, or the College Libraries Section, or regional or state college library networks should begin planning such programs soon. The need for quality recruits for college librarianship was never more urgent. In the section "Qualifications of the Librarian" in his classic *The Administration of the College Library*, Guy R. Lyle quoted from Louis R. Wilson's "The Role of the Library in Higher Education." In that talk, Wilson spoke of the qualifications needed for the librarian who is to become a successful administrator, a wise counselor in the use of books, and a force in shaping college instructional policies. It insists that the librarian must be a person of imagination and initiative, that he must have a sound understanding of library administration and some subject field, and that he must know how to relate the use of the library to the educational program of the college.

Lyle then went on:

> One might add...he must be a person of character, integrity, and professional idealism...These ideals include an unshakable belief in the importance of books, an ambition to make them easily and conveniently available, and a faith in the ability of librarians to share with others their enthusiasm in bringing books to readers.[27]

Wilson's words were written almost a half-century ago; Lyle first added his comments less than a decade after that. With only minor modifications, that combination of qualifications would be quite appropriate today—and tomorrow. We ought to begin to find ways of making sure that the next generation of college librarians can assume the roles that a quality college education deserves.

---

[26] Moffett, p. 345.

[27] Guy R. Lyle, *The Administration of the College Library*, 4th ed. (N.Y.: H.W. Wilson, 1974) 136-137.

16

Reflections on Two Books
(1987)

This piece is from Leonard Kenworthy's book, Quaker Education: A Source Book, *published in 1987. Kenworthy, who died in 1991, was a highly respected authority and a prolific writer on Quakerism and on the international dimensions of education. He taught at Brooklyn College CUNY for many years and, when he retired, decided to do a book on Quaker education, a subject that nicely combined his two major interests. He asked me to write a few paragraphs for the book on the role of the library in a college, especially a Quaker college. He knew I wasn't a Quaker, but I think he also knew that having been at Earlham for twenty-five or so years I'd been thoroughly "Quakerized," as was the case of so many other long-term faculty members.*
— Evan Ira Farber, 2006

On occasion, and especially when I need to give some thought to the role of our library, I go back to two books on college libraries. One is *Teaching With Books: A Study of College Libraries*, by Harvie Branscomb. It was published in 1940 and looked at the question of why college libraries were not being used as effectively as they should have been (*plus ça change…*). The other is *The Administration of the College Library* by Guy R. Lyle. It first appeared in 1944, and a fourth edition came out in 1974. [A fifth edition appeared in 1992]. I have a special regard for it not only because it was the *vade mecum* for generations of young college librarians, but also because Guy Lyle was my mentor. It was under his guidance that much of my thinking about the role of the library in the college was shaped.

Guy Lyle was a superb administrator who stressed the importance of effective, responsible administration, giving special attention to the relationship of the library staff with the college administration and to the faculty. But he was also a real bookman. His love of and respect for the printed word comes through in many places in his textbook, especially with regard to the selection and acquisition of materials, and to "the encouragement of reading on the part of students in connection with their courses as well as for its own sake."

It was under his tutelage that I really became aware of the importance of building a good collection of books and periodicals, a collection not only to support the curriculum, but to permit—indeed,

Kenworthy, Leonard S. *Quaker Education: A Source Book.* Kennett Square, Pennsylvania, Quaker Publications, 1987. Pp. 200-203.

encourage—students to explore new ideas, to extend their interests, to pursue their fancies. To be sure, the main purpose of building a collection is to support the curriculum, but most curricula reflect only scattered aspects of our world. If one acquired materials for just curricular needs, the library would have almost no current fiction or poetry, would cover current events sporadically at best, and would probably ignore most of the non-Western, non-Christian societies around the world. It is, however, the library staff's responsibility to buy in those areas not treated in the curriculum, and in a college such as Earlham, where students are involved with current international issues, and interested in many lesser-known countries and cultures, that responsibility becomes especially important. While in college, students have an opportunity to discover and explore, to open up new worlds, an opportunity they may not have again for many years, if ever. The library should help them make the most of it. At the dedication of a college library years ago, Robert Frost said "a library should be a place where a student can have it out with himself." That time of reasoning, of reflecting, or even of musing, can be enormously important in a young person's intellectual and psychological development. It needs to be protected and fostered.

I come back to Branscomb because he has so many words of wisdom, but I especially appreciate his dictum that the college library "is not an end in itself. [It] has the same *raison d'être* as the college of which it is a part; it exists for the sake of teaching or educating undergraduate students." That sounds like an obvious, even trite statement, yet it is of critical importance in determining what a college library is and what it should do.

It is apparent to most observers that a college library must have a collection of material that supports the educational program. It is also apparent that the materials must be organized and made available to users. But the college library—as opposed to a research library—must go one step further. It must make sure that students know how to find and use the materials intelligently. That is the teaching function of the library and it entails a program of instruction that should extend through the entire educational program. Such instruction is important in the short run—so that students will make better use of the library, so that they do better work, so they become more independent learners, so that classroom teaching can be more effective—but it is just as important in the long run. Our society is increasingly dependent on information, and how well our society works will increasingly depend on its members' ability to find, organize and use information. Knowing how to use a library well may not guarantee that ability, but it can certainly help. Moreover, as individuals, we are in danger of being inundated by information. To add to the incredible number of publications—books,

126

newspapers, magazines, government documents, etc.—we are now encountering all sorts of new electronic information. To cope with all this, to make informed judgments about the direction of society about local issues, to make critical decisions about one's individual business or profession, about, indeed, one's own body, an individual needs to be able to find and evaluate information, to become a discriminating user of information. Again, learning how to use a library well may not guarantee this, but it can surely help. It is for these reasons that a college that is serious about preparing students for responsible roles in their local, national, or international communities must make sure its library plays an active role in the educational program.

With these two basic thrusts—first, a collection that supports the curriculum and also permits students to expand their horizons and explore new worlds, and, second, a library instruction program that insures that students can use that collection both efficiently and effectively—a college library will not just support the purposes of a good liberal arts education, but will actually enhance it.

17

The Educational Mission of the Library:
Librarian as Educator
(1988)

This talk was given at a conference of the Librarians Association of the University of North Carolina's School of Library and Information Science. I am an alumnus of the School (when it was just the School of Library Science) and at this meeting received a Distinguished Alumnus Award. I can't remember the audience's reaction to the talk, but reading it over recently, I can see that it was too long, almost fifteen pages of typescript, mercifully shortened in print here by the editor. I should have realized by that stage of my career that a talk shouldn't go on for more than twenty minutes—at the most half an hour—that is, ten to twelve typewritten pages. After that, the attention of many in the audience begins to flag. If that was true in this case, it would have been too bad: there are some points in the talk that I think were insightful, provocative and even prescient. For example, my comments on the continuing importance of BI in an information-based society—which, relatively speaking, was still in its infancy—are still relevant as are the comments on the art and appeal of teaching students.

— Evan Ira Farber, 2006

What I want to suggest in this talk is that there are many ways for the librarian to be an educator. I *am* going to talk primarily about college librarians. I do that not because college librarians are the only librarians who educate, but because it's what they do that I know best—that's what I am. Now, though I will focus on college librarians, that does not mean that what I have to say does not apply to other librarians. Not *all* of what I have to say, of course—a college library is different in many ways—but it seems to me there are enough commonalities with other libraries to make some of my observations pertinent to librarians in other areas of academe, indeed outside of academe.

Some years ago, while serving on our college's personnel committee, I read the self-evaluation written by one of our faculty members who was coming up for tenure. In it, he described his approach to and excitement with teaching.

Student comments, insights from the

Talk given at the 1988 Spring Conference of the Librarians Association at The University of North Carolina at Chapel Hill, "What Is a Librarian? Exploring Roles and Relationships," March 7, 1988.

instructor, an appropriate example someone came up with, a metaphor the class had been developing over time, a new connection between two authors, a developing diagram on the board, all fall together into a compelling synthesis, and students can see and feel themselves participate as individuals in one of the noblest experiences academic work makes possible—the birth of an idea, of a fresh perspective on the world or one's society or one's self.

That experience is a kind of epiphany, the essence of the teaching/learning process, the kind of interaction that can happen occasionally in the classroom, in faculty offices, perhaps even over coffee cups. As with other epiphanic experiences, it probably doesn't happen very often, and to hope it might happen in every class, or even every day, would be unreasonable. But it does happen—and often enough to make teaching worthwhile.

Librarians, however, don't have the luxury of extended, long-term contact with students, the time, the room to develop ideas and concepts gradually—so we're not able to experience that exhilaration, certainly not in the same way as my colleague (who, incidentally, got tenure) described it. To be sure, a reference librarian, a reader's advisor, can feel enormous satisfaction when the library user is connected with the book, the article, or the information that serves as the perfect source in a report or a term paper. But as gratifying as that experience is, as rewarded one feels by the user's appreciation, that is not really education.

But there are ways in which librarians are educators. Some of those ways are fairly direct and immediate, direct in that librarians are in personal contact with students, and immediate in that those students learn something new or change their behavior or intellectual attitude. Other ways are indirect, and while their impact on students may not be as obvious, they may be just as important in the long run.

Whether direct or indirect, whether of crucial importance or simply adding a jot to a student's education, all these ways should spring from the same basic source, the librarian's commitment to education—in this case, to higher education. A commitment, that is, not to the library as an end in itself, not to the materials, the procedures, the intellectual rigor—as challenging or as interesting as these may be—but to the library as an instrument of education, an instrument for helping young people to grow intellectually and culturally. Again, to promote, to enhance the teaching/learning process.

The most obvious direct way of educating students is

bibliographic instruction. The original purpose of BI was simply to permit students to make better use of their libraries so that they could do better work. That is, of course, *still* an important aspect of BI, and it has become even more important as libraries have become more complex, as the tools have grown more numerous, more specialized, diverse, and sometimes complicated. Those factors alone would be enough to justify BI. But, it seems to me, as we see more and more clearly the impact of the information age on society, we can also see the increasing importance of BI in preparing students to enter that society.

One writer has noted that "in an information-based, society, success and failure will increasingly be measured in terms of one's ability to find, organize and use information." One can, of course, think of "success" in narrow terms—that is, contributing to one's career. In those terms, certainly one of the things BI should do is teach particular informational tools that will be useful for a career or in preparation for a career. Teaching the prospective chemist how to use *Chem Abstracts* in print and online, or the business major how to find financial data using CD-ROMS, for example, does help prepare them for successful careers and the librarians who do that do meet the description—to some extent—of being educators.

But, important as that may be, it is a limited application of BI. I would rather think of BI's educational contribution as preparing our students in a more basic way, a way that has broader, more important implications—that is, in helping them cope, to be effective in society, particularly in an information-based society.

Nevitt Sanford, the educational psychologist, wrote three influential books in the 1960s—*The American College* (1962), *Self and Society: Social Change and Individual Development* (1966), and *Where Colleges Fail* (1966). His main theme—and it was a somewhat radical idea twenty years ago—was that the primary goal of higher education was the individual development of each student—a development that entailed new ways of thinking and the ability to deal with an even more complex world. It is a view that has been accepted by many educators. One important step in learning to deal with that complex world is the individual's intellectual movement from a simplistic, categorical view of the world (described in such unqualified terms as we-they, right-wrong and good-bad) to a realization of the contingent nature of knowledge and relative values. It is the movement from a student's attitude that his or her role is to learn "the right answer," answers which are the domain of established authorities, to move from there to a position that there are many points of view, all perhaps equally valid—after all, "anyone has a right to an opinion" and "you can't judge opinion"—and then, finally, to the position that there are ways of deciding among opinions, of evaluating different viewpoints.

130

A parallel in the library is the beginning student's use of the collection—where simply because something appears in print, between covers—and especially because it is in the library—it's treated as gospel. How do we get students from one stage to the next in terms of sources of information? How do we get them to recognize that all sources of information are not equally valid? A possible first step is through book reviews. Here, when seeing reviews with divergent interpretations of the same book in, let's say, the *Book Review Digest*, a student will realize that authorities can disagree, openly, honestly. Another step could be showing a student a variety of perspectives on a controversial issue, perspectives represented by, on the one hand, the *National Review* or the *American Spectator,* and on the other by the *Nation* or *In These Times.* Perhaps that's simplistic—but my point is that by introducing students to conflicting sources of information and showing ways of evaluating those sources, we can help move these students from the categorical view of the world to a relativistic one, one in which they can see the need to evaluate their own ideas as well as those of others. One of the Carnegie Commission's reports mentioned that a major purpose of higher education is to teach "organized skepticism." And librarians can, I think, make an important contribution to this end...

Another means of contributing to the teaching/learning process is teaching the teachers. This can include a number of activities. First of all, it should include notifying faculty of new items—books, articles, documents—that could help them in their scholarship or relate to their courses. That, of course, implies learning what individual faculty members are teaching or what their current research projects are. That's not always easy to find out, but there are ways. Second, it should include making sure the library gets current materials on teaching, on student development, and on higher education in general—and makes faculty aware of them. Most teachers in higher education are unaware of—and, I'm afraid, not very interested in—the literature of higher education, yet much of it can be enormously helpful in improving the quality of teaching. I think of just one minor example. There's a little monthly newsletter, *The Teaching Professor*, that has superb short items on teaching and would be useful to any dedicated teacher. Yet I dare say not one in a hundred faculty have ever heard of it, much less read it...

The encouragement of reading. Years ago, the library literature carried many articles on college students' reading. Now, one rarely sees an article on the subject. It is not, I'm sure, that librarians think students do enough reading, but the matter is pretty well left to the faculty and, besides, most librarians have enough other, more interesting, more "professional" things to do. There are, of course, still librarians who do things to encourage reading. The design of the library can help. Providing an attractive and comfortable area for browsing—an area in a prominent place, so attractive and so inviting that students will be *drawn* into it. Scheduling author talks, literary exhibits, highlighting new periodical subscriptions or special new books, contributing book reviews or notes to campus publications. There are any number of ways, none of them terribly profound, and certainly not expensive, but all motivated by the recognition of the library's educational role. Guy Lyle's words, written fifteen years ago, are still worth noting. "The college library should stimulate and encourage general reading because the formal processes of college are not the whole of college, and reading for its own sake is an essential attribute of culture. In a technological society, reading carries on the humane tradition. It is the college library's function to provide every opportunity for its development."

Building the collection. It hardly seems necessary to mention this as an educational mission. I cite Guy Lyle again: "One cannot have a first-rate library without a systematic, enlightened program of book selection and acquisitions. Library materials are the core around which sound teaching and learning take place in the college." Making sure that the collection can support the curriculum, meet present student needs and anticipate future needs, provide cultural and recreational materials— these are prime responsibilities. More and more, though, the administrator has got to realize that *access*, not acquisition, is the key. There are not many libraries that can meet with materials on site the increasingly diverse needs of students and faculty. What these libraries can provide, however, is access to the materials—access through whatever means are possible—and access to almost any material, anywhere is not very far down the road.

If a librarian takes it upon himself or herself to carry out one of the roles of the librarian/educator—teaching students how to find information and how to evaluate information—it is incumbent upon that librarian also to provide access to that information. If he or she doesn't, it seems to me the instruction will almost be counterproductive because it leads to frustration.

Finally, there is one other role for the librarian as educator. And that is, to set the tone for the library and the library staff. To speak and act as an educator, so that the library is perceived as an important component in the educational program. No—not just perceived, but becomes an important component.

I often begin a talk to faculty or administrators from other institutions by saying that though it may seem heretical coming from a librarian—and despite what the institution's publicity says—the library is not the heart of the college. What *is*, is the teaching/learning process, and the library's role is to enhance that process. Of course, an administrator must administer, but no decision should be made and no action taken without considering the educational implications.

A recent issue of the quarterly, *New Directions for Teaching and Learning*, was devoted to interviews with outstanding college teachers. One of the questions they responded to was, "Why is college teaching the right profession for you?" One of them answered—in part—this way:

> During these four years, girls become women and boys become men. Through these men and women, I may make some small contribution toward achieving a better world, a world in which all persons live in dignity. These men and women are destined to make decisions that determine whether basic human needs are met, whether unjust social and economic inequalities are removed, and whether people are in control of their own destinies.

Noble sentiments, indeed. No less noble is the desire to help that teacher make that "small contribution." Those men and women will need more than character development to make decisions, to improve conditions. They'll also need to have a knowledge base and an information retrieval system. That's our job...

18

Turning Students into Readers:
Librarians and Teachers Cooperating
(1988)

*I wish I could remember how the audience, almost all members of the
International Reading Association, responded to this talk. Now, on reading it
over, it seemed to me one of my better pieces, nicely phrased and delivered in a
relatively informal and conversational tone—though perhaps for this group the
subject was not the foremost of their concerns. For librarians, however, though
much of the content is what they may have heard Farber say many times, there
was something new: and that is my point that for academic librarians the
importance of encouraging recreational reading, a long time professional
responsibility, had been ignored in practice and in the literature for many years,
certainly in recent ones.*

*The disappearance of responsibility for promoting recreational reading
is a great loss, but is that of any concern to today's academic librarians? I'm
afraid not, so this piece, while maybe good reading, may only be of interest to
historians of the profession.*

— Evan Ira Farber, 2006

I'm going to focus on college students. Not because the issues
are more important with them. I'm going to focus on them because
they're what I know best—for most of my adult life I've advised college
students, taught them, and worked with them both as an administrator
and as a reference librarian. To be sure, some of what I say is applicable
only to college students and perhaps of interest only to those working
with them, but I think that some, perhaps much of what I say can
certainly be related to adult learners and to secondary school students,
and, to a somewhat lesser extent, I'm sure, to elementary school students.
But my reference point will be the undergraduate, the 18 to 21-year-old
who is fairly serious about his or her college education.

Why don't such students use libraries for reading? Of course,
some do, but their number is, I'm afraid, quite small. And I don't mean
reading for courses. Certainly students use the library for *that*—for
reading books on reserve, or using the library as simply a quiet,
comfortable place to read their own textbooks. And certainly a fair

Farber, Evan Ira. "Turning Students Into Readers: Librarians and Teachers
    Cooperating." Paper presented at the Annual Meeting of the
    International Reading Association (33ed, Toronto, Canada, May 5,
    1988). ERIC ED 302807.

number of students come into the library to read the daily newspapers or their favorite magazines. But reading Charles Dickens or James Dickey? Or the latest *Paris Review* or *Antaeus*? Or other good recent novels, or short stories, or—perish the thought—some contemporary poetry? Not likely. Maybe Stephen King, or, more likely, the latest Rosemary Rogers or Sidney Sheldon—but "good" reading? Unless it's related to a course, very probably not.

Why not? Is it lack of time? Lack of interest? Simply a continuation of personality traits shaped during the pre-college years? Surely these reasons can account for several, perhaps many, of the students who don't read. But what about those others who *did* use their public libraries, who *were* regular, if not avid readers since they were weaned on Dr. Seuss and A. A. Milne? What happened to *them* in college?

I suggest two possible reasons. One is that recreational reading is not encouraged in academic libraries. No, not just "not encouraged" (excuse the proliferation of negatives, please)—not just not encouraged, but hardly given a chance. The other results from a syndrome known as "library anxiety." It's a syndrome which may not be endemic to college students, but is certainly common among them. It's a syndrome that causes students to—if not actually avoid libraries—at best use them as little as possible. I'll come back to this later. I certainly don't mean to imply that these two reasons are the only ones student don't read for pleasure. But I do say that they're not insignificant and, furthermore, that they're easy to correct, and much of what I have to say will be on ways of correcting them.

Years ago—many, many years ago—before World War II, encouraging the reading habit was widely regarded as one of the important functions of the college librarian. One has only to look at the early volumes of *Library Literature*, the index to articles and books in the field of library science, to see the many articles on the subject. Or to look at the floor plans of college libraries in the 1920s and '30s to see that a browsing room was an almost standard feature. But as higher education became more and more concerned with independent study, with "research," less attention was given to extra-curricular reading. What may have been the finishing touch—for a while, at least—was a very influential book published in 1940, *Teaching With Books: A Study of College Libraries*, by Harvie Branscomb, at the time Director of Duke University Libraries, and later Chancellor of Vanderbilt University. Branscomb, for a project sponsored jointly by the Association of American Colleges and the American Library Association, was investigating the very limited role of libraries in undergraduate education, and, in particular, the underutilization of book collections by students. An admirable study in almost every other way, but unfortunate in Branscomb's opinion that if students take their studies seriously "there will be little time for outside reading...The college library, it can be argued, needs to take it own task more seriously, not to attempt the role of the public library, the great concern of which with recreational reading is itself questionable."

I said that Branscomb may have given "the finishing touch" to the de-emphasizing of recreational reading. That's probably not fair. It's more likely that he was reflecting a changing attitude. But in any case, there's not much doubt that the encouragement of extra-curricular reading has been given much less attention than formerly, and, again, I only need to point to the decreasing number of items on it in the professional literature, or the changing design of libraries.

There were, of course, major exceptions. My mentor, Guy R. Lyle, was not only a distinguished college and university librarian, but also the author of the standard text, *The Administration of the College Library*, which went through five editions, from 1944 to 1992, and was used by college librarians across the country as their *vade mecum*s. In each of the five editions, a chapter was devoted to encouraging recreational reading. But as much influence as that book had, the portion on recreational reading was hardly heeded. In 1981, *College Librarianship*, a collection of essays edited by William Miller and D. Stephen Rockwood, was published, and though most of it related to aspects of the college library's collection, there is only passing reference to recreational reading.

I know I was very much influenced by Guy Lyle, under whom I worked for seven years. Whether it was my own love of books, or my happy experiences with public libraries, or my working under Guy Lyle—probably a combination of these and other factors—I have felt it an important part of my role as college librarian to encourage, in whatever way I can, students' reading and love of the printed word. Indeed, some of the most satisfying encounters with students are about recreational reading—a student saying how much he or she enjoyed a particular book or recommending that we buy a new work by a favorite author. Just the other day, I was talking to a couple of prospective students about the library's role in the college. (The Admissions Office makes it a point to have prospectives and their parents see the library and for me to talk briefly with them.) One of them, a young woman from the San Francisco area, asked whether or not the library has much current fiction. I showed her our collection, which is not just substantial, but is prominently displayed, and then said to her that I was delighted to have her ask—that it was the first time I'd been asked that question by a prospective student—and wondered why she asked. "Well," she responded, "The Admissions Office told me there weren't any really good bookstores in town, and I like to keep up with new fiction." Now, she is undoubtedly an unusual student, but I cite the incident not only because it gave me such pleasure that I wanted to repeat it, but primarily to show that there still are such students.

How *do* we get students to read?

A number of writers on the subject have suggested that it's up to the faculty to do the job. That, however, is a forlorn hope. There are very few college faculty members who will encourage students to read outside of their courses. Certainly a professor of history will suggest that his or her students read some other works than those assigned, and an English teacher may even recommend some novels—but probably only those novels that have become part of the professional canon—which means those they encountered during their graduate studies. I'm exaggerating, of course, but for the most part it's true; faculty do not encourage extra-curricular reading. It is, I think, very much up to librarians.

First, librarians needed to provide the materials. This seems simple, being merely a matter of selection. That in itself is not simple, because it means knowing the audience and then making a judicious selection from the many, many titles available. It's a time-consuming task, though from my experience, a most interesting and pleasurable one, one of the really "fun" things to do. But for most librarians, that procedure is complicated by the budgeting aspects. That is, there is just so much in our budgets for acquisitions, and if some of it is going to be spent on current fiction and poetry, or on periodicals which contain good creative writing, some departmental budgets will be reduced accordingly. In these times of limited budgets, when most of us don't really have enough funds for what many faculty might consider "frivolous" purchases, such purchases could have negative political impact. There are ways of responding, but it takes a strong library director whose status is secure.

Then, the materials not only need to be acquired, but they need to be made available. That means not just stowing them on shelves somewhere, but displaying them attractively in a prominent place, so that passers-by will be enticed to browse. Few academic libraries keep dust jackets on books purchased. What a waste! Those jackets are designed (often by top-notch designers) to attract readers, and librarians ought to capitalize on that.

There are many other things libraries can do to promote reading. Exhibits, author talks, contributing book reviews or notes to campus publications, highlighting new subscriptions or new books of particular interest. All of these are impelled by recognition of the library's educational role. Guy Lyle's words, written fifteen years ago, are still worth noting. "The college library should stimulate and encourage general reading because the formal processes of college are not the whole of college, and reading for its own sake is an essential attribute of culture. In a technological society, reading carries on the human tradition. It is the college library's function to provide every opportunity for its development." There are any number of ways of providing these opportunities, none of them terribly profound, but surely important.

I suggested earlier that another deterrent to student recreational reading is a syndrome known as "library anxiety." I think every college and university librarian has known—or at least suspected—that students, especially first-year students, don't feel especially comfortable in using the library. That suspicion was confirmed a couple of years ago by a study done at one of the medium-sized state university libraries. Freshmen taking a beginning composition course were asked to keep a journal in which they recorded their feelings when they first had to use the university library. How were those feelings expressed? In such words as "anxious, scared, confused." *Of course* that was their response. Here were students mostly from small towns, from rural areas, who had used local public and high school libraries—libraries with a few thousand volumes, with simple card catalogs—and suddenly they were faced with a library of hundreds of thousands of volumes, a massive card catalog with complex headings, a variety of service points, unfamiliar terms, strange surroundings and busy workers…Of course they were "anxious, scared, confused."

And the result?

Avoidance. Using the library only when they had to, and then not very effectively. Such students are hardly apt to be enticed by exhibits, by book notes, by publishing, by book displays no matter how attractive, how appealing. The library, for them, is a place to be avoided.

How do we overcome this?

First, by design, by making the library an attractive, comfortable place; by having a staff that is friendly and helpful; by keeping bureaucratic indicators and procedures to a minimum.

These, however, are going to change perceptions and practices only slightly. What libraries should do is to make students feel comfortable, feel in control of their environment. People avoid a situation because they don't feel at ease in it, feel out of place.

How to do this?

To my mind, and to many other librarians, the most effective way is by teaching students how to use libraries, so that they can view the card catalog as a source of information, the indexes and bibliographies as aids—all of them easy to use if one knows how. Once they understand, even very imperfectly, that all these are key to the organization of information, and that they can use these keys—albeit somewhat inexpertly—they'll feel much better about the library.

138

Ah, but how to teach them? There's the rub, because it's not easy. It sounds easy—why not just offer a course in using the library—but that's deceptive. Not because it's not easy, but because it's not very effective—for two reasons. First of all, unless it's a required course, very few students will take it—and those that do will be the highly motivated ones, the ones that would probably learn how to use the library in any case. Secondly, even if it is required, it will most certainly be not very exciting—to say the least—and merely confirm students' negative feelings about libraries—and librarians. Most students, after all, are not really interested in learning how to use the library. *I'm* interested—*you* may he. But not most students. At least not until *they need to use the library. Then,* they'll listen, will implement what they're taught, and thus learn by doing—always the most effective way of learning.

The only way of teaching students how to use libraries is through their regular courses. It's the course, after all, that's the coin of the realm, and that's what we must trade with. Students are primarily interested in getting better grades, or saving time, and if we can show them how to fulfill their assignments more efficiently and effectively so that they can save time, can do better work, then they will listen.

Library instruction should be built into the course—not just in English courses, but in all subjects where finding information is important—in psychology, in biology, in art history, in business, in chemistry, etc., etc. Students then come to expect that instruction, expect librarians to come in and show them how to find the information they'll need.

That all sounds fine so far, doesn't it? Then where's the rub? It's in that phrase: "library instruction is built into the course." Because the course—all courses—are in the hands of the teaching faculty. It takes, then, cooperation, a fairly close working relationship between librarians and teaching faculty. Most teaching faculty, however, are used to independence in planning courses and implementing them. Moreover, very few faculty are aware of how inept students are in their use of the library, nor can they see what a difference it can make in their teaching effectiveness and in their students' performance for those students to learn how to use the library.

Working with teaching faculty, then, takes patience, perseverance and diplomacy. It's not easy, in other words, but there's no question that the results are worth it. This is not the place to talk about strategies for eliciting cooperation, or about types of assignments that can be devised. I should say, though, that when that cooperation has been achieved and interesting productive assignments have been devised, the result is a symbiotic relationship between the teacher's objectives and the librarian's. That is, the assignment will not only promulgate the teacher's objectives (the subject matter and/or methodology of sociology,

139

literature, chemistry, or whatever) and also the librarian's (how to find information about sociology, literature, chemistry, or whatever), but the two sets of objectives will be mutually reinforcing. When that happens, real learning takes place. Also, when that happens, students' use of and positive attitude towards the library will increase substantially. That's been the experience of every school, college, or university where there's been an effective program of library instruction. Again, it's a lot of work, but the results are worth it.

In a sense, what I'm saying is that such a program will make students appreciate, even enjoy the library. *Then* one can begin talking to those students about reading. Luxurious buildings, great collections, huge budgets may impress faculty, administrators and other librarians. But students will only be impressed by them if they can use them for their own purposes. And they cannot—most of them, anyway—until they are taught to do so. Only then, when they feel comfortable, enjoy the library, will they turn into the readers we want them to be.

19

On or Off Campus:
The Prospects for Bibliographic Instruction
(1989)

It's too late to do anything about it, but I now realize that this talk at the Off Campus Library Services Group Conference in Charleston in 1988 related only tangentially to the group's founding purpose, the establishment and provision of services to branch or adjunct campus libraries. I suppose that I didn't have any expertise—or even, I'm ashamed to say—much interest in those topics, and perhaps because I assumed even small branch libraries would need to offer instruction, that my ideas on the future of BI would be of interest. In any case I don't find any mention of the other issues peculiar to that group. However, I was interested to see how prescient I was about the future of BI. The verdict: just so-so.

In this talk I predicted the following: "[T]eaching users to find information...will be taken over by technology...We will not be teaching classes—machines can do it better..." Really? I don't think that's happened and as far as I know most classes are still being given by individual librarians. Perhaps that's due—partly, anyway—to the fact that changes in access to databases and the constant proliferation of new databases replacing and/or supplementing previous ones happen so quickly that instructional technology can't keep up. Or, in assuming technology could do the job, was I, horribilis dictum, *guilty of "technological idolatry," something I often warned others about?*

Also, I wondered about the permanence of "library anxiety." I have no doubt that it was a real phenomenon in 1988 and instruction librarians needed to be aware of it. Indeed, I spoke more than a few times about the importance of getting beginning students over that hurdle. But now, twenty years later, I think most undergraduates, as soon as they see a keyboard and a terminal, feel perfectly comfortable coming into a new library and using its terminals. Is there any anxiety? Perhaps I'm wrong about their attitude, but now I think the problem is probably more overconfidence than anxiety. If that's so, how should that problem be addressed? Maybe we should plan to increase their anxiety so they'll listen to instruction? That's a bit extreme, I know, but even if we should, how to do it? Oh well...I still find the problems and potential of instruction fascinating but I'll have to leave all that to others.

— Evan Ira Farber, 2006

Lessin, Barton M. (Ed.) *The Off-Campus Library Services Conference Proceedings: Charleston, South Carolina, October 20-21, 1988.* Mount Pleasant, Michigan, Central Michigan University, 1989. Pages 91-100.

...We have these marvelous developments in technology, in these various areas—computers, telecommunications, storage technology, and artificial intelligence, or expert systems. What is the impact on libraries, and in particular, on the student? Let's assume that academic life continues pretty much as it is—semesters, hour-long classes, lectures, exams, term papers, etc. That's probably not unreasonable—not for the next decade, anyway—since the wheels of higher education turn very slowly, and changes in curriculum, in teaching styles and class formats—if they come at all—are very gradual, much behind events and developments outside academe.

What will have changed on campus is the library's ability to provide information. Almost literally, students will have access to any information—in print or electronic form practically instantaneously. Libraries will provide information on site—mostly in electronic form— but will provide access to much more information elsewhere.[1]

We have, then, this possibility: students who may be faced with a dilemma: either they use a very superficial approach to searching for information—an approach on the level of the *Readers' Guide,* or *Infotrac*—that is, access to information that is quick and easy to get—or, by making use of the new information technology, they'll be overwhelmed by material the student doesn't have time to read, nor the expertise to cull it or evaluate it and absorb it.

In a sense, that's not much different from what we have now. At one end of the spectrum we now have students who either don't like libraries or don't know how to use them—in both cases, they stay away from libraries—and at the other end of the spectrum we have students who want to use libraries, know enough how to get materials—lots of materials—but who exhibit little sense of discrimination—who don't understand that all books and articles are *not* of equal worth—who don't know how to evaluate sources of information. Today, we spend most of our efforts with the lower end of the spectrum, those students who really don't know how to find information.

Increasingly, that kind of instruction will be taken over by machines. Students won't have any trouble learning how to find information, or learning how to use even the most complex library tools. All that will be built in. Artificial intelligence, expert systems, hypertext could do a better job of that than we can today. Remember, the computer has infinite patience, doesn't take coffee breaks, can be very versatile in its responses and can adapt to individual needs and requests—and requests not just typed out, but spoken (speech, after all, can also be

---

[1] W. D. Penniman, "Tomorrow's Library Today," *Annual Review of OCLC Research July 1987-June 1988,* 59-60.

transposed into binary units).[2]

If we won't be teaching what and how we do now, what will we do? That is, will there still be a job for BI—even for reference librarians? The October issue of *C&RL News* contains the proceedings of a panel discussion on "The Future of Reference Service."[3] It is a very interesting, even provocative discussion, with many questions raised and a number of new directions suggested. There was, however, no resolution—and I guess I would have been surprised if there was. Reference service means such different things in different situations. I don't think there's much doubt, however, that reference librarians will be offering much more specialized reference assistance. Basic reference will be taken care of by computers, but the role of the reference librarian as teacher will be ever more important. Only the one-to-one relationship between student and librarian permits the subtleties of searching for information and evaluating sources. The conceptual nature of those topics demands discussion and questions, interactions that can only be carried on usefully, instructively, in a teacher/student relationship—in this case, a reference librarian/library user relationship.

Or, describing it another way, specialized knowledge may increasingly be accessible through machines, while human librarians are trained to be generalists in the best sense, able to integrate different points of views.

In *Library Hi Tech* last year, two scientists speculated that "librarian-knowledge workers" will personalize information and provide knowledge in the context of the recipients' interests. The librarian will have to be a specialist in devising expert systems for individual needs.[4]

Fred Kilgour, founder of OCLC, suggests that librarians will know what the information needs of individuals are, and could make available information that those individuals didn't even know they needed! Putting it in an academic setting, we would have individual students as clients, and would be aware of their information needs, just as we do now with some faculty.

But what about the BI librarian? As I said, the main occupation of today's BI librarians—teaching users how to find information—will be taken over by technology. And the other function—helping users

---

[2] W.Y. Arms, M. K. Kibbey, T. J. Michalak, J. H. Morris, D. S. Scott, M. A. Sirbu, M. Dillon, & M. J. McGill, " Mercury: An Electronic Library," *Annual Review of OCLC Research July 1987-June* 1988, 36-37.

[3] "The Future of Reference Service: A Panel Discussion". (1988). *College and Research Libraries News,* 49(9), 578-589.

[4] L. E. Murr, J. B Williams, "The Roles of the Future Library," *Library Hi Tech,* 5(3), 7-23.

shape their searches, showing them how to evaluate information, will increasingly become the librarian's role. We will not be teaching classes—machines will do that better—they can do it in a less structured, more individualized way. But we will be supplementing that machine teaching. The art of creating expert systems now has real limitations. As one authority says: "Applications that have been successful have all tended to involve problem domains that are narrow, discrete, homogeneous, and with a limited number of entities and relations." Much of reference work fits that, but much of it doesn't and it's the latter kind of reference work we'll be doing more of. One writer has suggested it means going back to the role of "reader's advisor." That's not a bad label—better than "information expert" as another writer suggests, but the idea is very much the same.

But it seems to me there's another reason for working hard at what we're doing now. The application of artificial intelligence concepts—the use of expert systems—remember, is one of the keys to the new technology. But the basis of expert systems is, of course, expert advice. That is, the way in which an expert responds to a query or solves a problem, or performs an operation is translated into a program for a computer.

So an expert system is no better than the advice of the experts it is based upon. If, then, we expect those machines to do really expert jobs, we need to keep improving our methods, systematizing them, so that they can be translated into steps a computer can follow.

There are other reasons to keep at it. In one of the papers delivered to this group at the 1982 St. Louis meeting, Angela Weyhaupt of Barat College, made the comment that "the bottom line of BI is not merely knowledge but behavior."[5] That is a simple observation, but a very important one, I think. It leads me to observe that no matter how much technology changes what we do and how we do it, one thing that will stay the same is the importance of changing behavior, and the behavior I'm especially thinking of is "library anxiety."

Now, most of you have read about that syndrome, but all of you—if you've ever worked at a reference desk or other public service point—have seen it. It's that syndrome that was described so well by Connie Mellon in *College & Research Libraries* a few years ago.[6] That

---

[5] Angela Weyhaupt, "Behavioral Bibliographic Instruction: Merging Feelings and Facts," in B. M. Lessin (Ed.), *Proceedings of the Off-Campus Library Services Conference* (pp. 182-190). Mt. Pleasant, Michigan: Central Michigan University Press.

[6] C. A. Mellon, "Library Anxiety: A grounded Theory and Its Development," *College and Research Libraries,* 47(2), 160-165.

article, you may remember, told about a project in which students in freshman composition were asked to keep a journal of their initial reactions to using the library. Their responses? "Scared, bewildered, confused, anxious" and other such descriptors. I was greatly impressed by that article. I'd sensed this was the case, but having it documented, described, interpreted so well really impressed me, and helped reshape my approach to BI.

Those students were scared, anxious, because they were in an unfamiliar situation—they were, in other words, not in control. And when one is faced with an unfamiliar situation, is not in control of a situation, one is tempted to avoid it. Sure, they were students in a particular library but they were pretty typical—not just of freshmen, but of library users anywhere. My inference from thinking about that was this: that one of the most important things we can do in BI is make students feel comfortable, feel in control. So, for example, our workbook for freshmen is much simpler and briefer than it used to be. Sure, part of its purpose is to teach students a few things about search strategy and aspects of the library. But mostly it's to make sure they have a successful search for information, so that when, later, they come to work on their own topics, they have a certain amount of confidence. It seems to me that's especially important for the adult learner.

Now, one might argue that coming generations of students who, after all, will have grown up with computers, may not be so anxious about using online catalogs, CD-ROMs, videodiscs, or whatever the new technology creates. But it seems to me that much of the searching for information, information which after all, is going to expand as fast as— or faster than—the devices that provide access to it, can never be simple and straightforward. I'm not talking about facts, but information, which may entail opinion, perspectives, evaluations. That kind of search has no automatic logic, no necessary closure. There will always be the need to frame questions, to shape a topic, to interact. There will always be a certain amount of anxiety, of dealing with the unfamiliar.

Moreover, there's going to be an increasing need for socializing, for personal contact. As computers become an increasingly standard aspect of our working lives, we'll seek ways of finding personal meetings. No matter how sophisticated the new information technology, it can't completely replace that human contact.

I remember the President of Earlham College saying—oh, about twenty years ago—that it would be foolish to invest in the airlines. His logic made sense: a large proportion of air travel is by businessmen to attend meetings and since videoconferencing was already feasible technologically, it was just a matter of time before businessmen would meet by video rather than travel to meetings. Well, he was a marvelous college president, but in this case not much of a seer. As you've undoubtedly observed, business travel hasn't declined—on the contrary—and anyone who's taken part in a teleconference or videoconference knows how unsatisfying it is. My point is this: there is no substitute for personal, face-to-face interaction, and in reference or readers' advisor positions, with sources and types of information becoming increasingly numerous and complex, that interaction will continue to be essential, perhaps even more so than now.

One of my colleagues, who teaches English at Earlham College, spoke to the ACRL Conference in Minneapolis some years ago. His talk was titled "Views of a Luddite," but it was not so much a skeptical look at library technology as a humanist's view of the role of the library in an academic setting.[7]

"I am not conceiving of the library as an information retrieval system, but as a social system, a teaching-learning milieu in which retrieval of information is only part of the goal. The library is not merely a place or a collection of functions, but a living symbol of valuable and rich human resources." Similarly, I make a case for the BI librarian as efficient and knowledgeable. Even as user-friendly as the new information technology will get, those incredible devices cannot provide the eye contact, the personal reassurance, the friendly advice, the encouraging words that students will always need. Our tools will change much of what we do with change, but some of that human personal factor will always be important.

---

[7] P. A. Lacey, "Views of a Luddite," *College and Research Libraries*, 43(2), 110-118.

20

The New Frontier:
Homesteading in a Wilderness of Information
(1991)

The following piece is the Foreword in Teaching & Technology: The Impact of Unlimited Information Access on Classroom Teaching *(Pierian Press Ann Arbor, Michigan, 1991). That modest volume contains the edited proceedings of a national forum held at Earlham College in 1990. While working on my 1983 talk to the conference on Educating Users of Public Access Online Card Catalogs I thought about the potential additional impact of electronic information on student use of the library—not on just their use of the OPAC, but on their use of other library resources. How would almost unlimited, easily accessed information at their fingertips affect their library habits and attitudes? And because I'd become so interested in classroom teaching—and especially the different styles of teachers and the effectiveness of library-based assignments—it was a natural segue to thinking about the same development's affect on teaching, on lectures, on assignments. No one, as far as I could find, had looked at this. Those thoughts led—eventually, as noted below—to a two-day forum on Teaching and Technology in which about 80 people participated: teaching faculty, administrators, and librarians, as well as a few representatives of organizations interested in higher education. The volume contains a list of the participants as well as the proceedings.*

In reading it over I would make one important change. I implied that the problems of unlimited access to information—that is, the problems related to the teaching/learning process—occurred to me while writing the background paper for the Carnegie Foundation for the Advancement of Teaching. I think that a hint of that notion can be detected in my talk on Catalog Dependency *in which, while alluding to the prospect of electronic sources of information, I warned about the possibility that students will regard the OPAC—and I had no idea of how central and wide-ranging it would become—as the "single key for unlocking the doors to the universe of information." It was not long after that, when reading Theodore Roszak's* The Cult of Information *if I recall correctly, I chanced upon the phrase "technological idolatry," which seemed to me the perfect shorthand for the uncritical attitude most students exhibit in looking for information, and probably in other situations as well.*

Did the forum succeed? I really can't say, even though the responses, both immediately after and later, were positive. If it had any effect, it encouraged people to think about the issue. I should have written five or even ten years later to all the individuals who participated, asking them what effect, if any, the forum had on them, but I didn't. Perhaps some historian will.

— Evan Ira Farber, 2006

Teaching and Technology: The Impact of Unlimited Information Access on Classroom Teaching; Proceedings of a National Forum at Earlham College. Ann Arbor, Michigan, The Pierian Press, 1991.

In recent years technological developments in information science have revolutionized the ways in which information is stored, manipulated, distributed and used. In a few years information from almost any location, using any source, and on almost any topic will be easily and quickly accessible. The concern will no longer be "How can we get enough information?" on any subject but rather "How can we sort through all that information to find what we really need?"

The effects these developments in information technology have had and will continue to have on libraries—on their administration, their finances, their personnel, indeed, on their very role in academe—have been discussed at length. Their effects on aspects of college and university administration—on the design and construction of buildings, on campus communication systems, on financial administration, for example—have also been discussed widely, both in the professional literature and at conferences. The impact of this information revolution on scholarly research and publishing has also received a good bit of attention, but what has not been discussed very much are the implications for what goes on in college classrooms, for the teaching/learning process.

This omission in academic speculation is surely curious, not just because the teaching/learning process is common to all institutions of higher education, nor because what goes on in classrooms should be of paramount interest, but also because it is really that teaching/learning process which provides the *raison d'etre* for all the other aspects of higher education, even—perhaps especially—the college library. That omission struck me as I was writing a background paper for the Carnegie Foundation for the Advancement of Teaching. The paper was on the role of the library in undergraduate education, and among the many topics I discussed was, of course, the new information technology. Within ten or fifteen years, I speculated, any library would have the potential to provide unlimited, almost immediate access to practically any information in print or electronic form. That might be a slight exaggeration, I granted, but even if my time frame was wrong, or if my estimate of the amount of information that would be available was too high, still it seemed obvious that there were many, and important, implications for the role of the library and for the role of librarians. Those I discussed at length, but then—almost as an aside—I raised a number of questions about what this easy access to information will mean for the classroom teacher.

On the one hand, it will permit an entirely new kind of freedom for teaching—for providing lecture materials, for materials students can read or use for papers. But what sorts of problems will it create for the teacher? Will teachers be able to give students guidance in using these materials? After all, students will have, in a sense, the entire Library of

Congress on their desktops. Will teachers have to limit the sources students can use? If not, how can they evaluate papers based on materials the teachers not only had not read but didn't even know existed. Now, when a teacher designs a course or makes up a syllabus, or devises an assignment, he or she usually has in mind a particular library the students will use; at least a teacher has a sense of the sources students can find. But with the new technology, it's wide open. Term papers may even cease to be a viable assignment because of those problems, and because plagiarism will become so easy—and undetectable. These are problems teachers never had to think about before, and will require an entirely new mind-set.

I spoke with some of my teaching colleagues at Earlham about these speculations. They suggested other possibilities and submitted more problems; indeed, they thought the issues were not only important enough for all college teachers to think about but also raised so many provocative questions that a more public discussion seemed appropriate, and so we began thinking about a conference. We found out there were all sorts of conferences on the implications of information technology for science, or for business, but not for undergraduate teaching. And there were even more seminars and meetings on computers and education, but they were primarily concerned with hardware, or software, or computer-assisted instruction. No one, it seemed, was concerned about the impact on classroom teaching of this incredible availability of information—at least, not concerned enough to discuss it in a public forum.

In June, 1987 the Lilly Endowment gave us a small grant to begin planning such a conference. Their contribution was significant: not only did it give us the wherewithal to continue, but it also confirmed our sense of the topic's interest and significance. With that assistance and encouragement we invited some outside consultants to help us decide on a format and suggest possible speakers. Then, with those plans, we began looking for major funding. Some support came from OCLC and from ABC-Clio, and in September, 1988 the Pew Charitable Trusts funded our proposal and permitted us to make the conference a reality.

The Forum on Teaching and Technology was held in Richmond, Indiana, February 26-28, 1989, with approximately 80 participants attending. Most of them were a select group of faculty and administrators from colleges and universities across the nation—institutions known for their commitment to teaching.

The focus of the forum was on the changes in the ways people learn and the ways faculty teach, looking at how faculty from several disciplines have been and will be affected by the developing information technology. Then speakers addressed the institutional implications of the issues raised—matters of organization, resource allocation, and personnel response to change. Readers should bear in mind that the speakers were not asked to present scholarly addresses, but rather to speak from their experience and about their approaches to teaching—personal statements which would provoke discussion and encourage speculation. (A list of "Forum Issues"—suggested questions, really—that might be addressed had been sent to each invited speaker.) The proceedings were taped, then transcribed and all speakers' remarks returned to them for their corrections and/or additions...

Was the forum a success? Certainly it was if one needed a demonstration of faculty concern for what goes on in the classroom. The speakers' commitment to their roles of classroom teachers is very obvious, reflecting an extraordinary thoughtfulness about their disciplines and means of teaching them effectively, and a sincere, affecting concern for their students. Certainly it was a success if the reactions of the participants can serve as a measure; they enjoyed it and thought it stimulating, and enough found it sufficiently provocative to want to continue the discussion, either at another conference, or on their own campuses. It was also successful in the many questions that were raised, some of which were addressed during the forum, but most of which simply pointed to the need for further exploration.

Why, then, do I even need ask whether or not it was a success? I suppose because we wanted everyone to come away from the forum fully comprehending the magnitude of this ongoing revolution and its impact on the teaching/learning process. We were interested, as Peter Suber said at one point in our planning, "in the effects on teaching of quick and easy access to boundless information, *not* in technology *per se,* not in CAI...or software." Or, we wanted the participants to understand the implications of what Gordon Thompson said of his English literature students and apply his concerns to their own classes: "Right now, we sometimes help students decide what 90 percent of the commentary on a work to ignore. Soon, we will have to help them decide what 99.9 percent of the available commentary to ignore." But we were not at all sure that most of the participants came away with the sense of urgency we felt.

That sense of urgency can perhaps best come from working with students in a library, helping them find information, showing them some of the newer technology, watching them trying to sort through the mass of material they collect, and then, realizing how much more material they'll get in a few years with the technology that's almost upon us. One has to comprehend the power of this new technology and, at the same time, see how students can be lost in today's wilderness of information, a wilderness that only faintly foreshadows the one the next generation of students will face. This is not a situation familiar to most faculty.

The next step, then, it seemed to us, was to get faculty familiar with this situation.   That is a step we're now taking at Earlham College. The Forum, however, provided the stimulus, the intellectual rationale for that step and for raising many related questions among a substantial group of faculty and administrators. If it only did this it was a success, but we hope this publication of its proceedings will stimulate a wider audience to think about the impact of the information revolution on the teaching/learning process.

21

Bibliographic Instruction and Collection Development in the College Library
(1991)

After reading this over I wondered if today's college librarians are as interested in collection development as my generation of college librarians was. We were concerned with meeting those three criteria that I paraphrased from Guy Lyle's Administration of the College Library: *A college library should have "...a collection of cultural and recreational materials...[A] good basic collection that will meet their curricular needs; and, third, a good reference collection that will serve as a key to the immediate library, and to resources elsewhere." But that was in 1975, before the electronic revolution in information, or perhaps just as librarians began to recognize some of the implications for their libraries.*

Now, I assumed, with so much attention given to electronic sources of information, most of that attention is given to the selection of databases, access to them, and related matters. I would further assume that the selection of books and periodicals, and certainly the criteria underlying that selection process, are given little notice. I don't have a file of Library Literature *handy but I'd be willing to bet that the number of entries under Collection Development—College Libraries (if that's the heading I mean) in the volumes before 1980 greatly outnumber those in volumes ten years later. I'd be delighted if someone would confirm or dispute my assumptions.*

However, even if those criteria are not as applicable as they once were, an important point of the piece, that a BI program (or whatever term is now accepted even though the objectives are the same) can be enormously helpful in promoting working relationships between librarians and teaching faculty. Once it was by providing students with the ability to gain access to information from printed materials; now it's providing students (and faculty) with the ability to access information in electronic form as well as print.

— Evan Ira Farber, 2006

In discussing the relationship of collection development and bibliographic instruction, it's appropriate to begin with some basic working statements. My concept of what a college library collection should be really first occurred to me shortly after I came to Earlham College in 1962 and began to see how different the purposes of a university library, from which I had just come, were from those of a

Hill, Joanne Schneider, William E. Hannaford Jr., and Ronald H. Epp, Editors. *Collection Development in College Libraries.* Chicago, American Library Association, 1991. Pages 64-70.

college library, at which I had recently arrived. Those differences in purpose and their implications for administration and services, and especially for the collection, became increasingly obvious to me over the next few years; a decade or so later, that concept of a college library collection had taken shape, and in 1975 I wrote,

> the needs of college undergraduates have to be determined by different criteria than those used for university students. A college library must have, first of all, a collection of cultural and recreational materials that can expand students' horizons; second, a good basic collection that will meet their curricular needs; and, third, a good reference collection that will serve as a key to the immediate library, and to resources elsewhere. Only after these three needs are met should we think about a collection to fill the occasional research need.[1]

I still feel those are the basic criteria by which college libraries should be guided and I will use that concept of a collection in this discussion.

When I refer to bibliographic instruction, I have in mind only course-related (or, even better, course-integrated) instruction. The other method of teaching use of the library (as a separate course) is used in a number of institutions, but is not nearly as widespread in practice as course-related instruction. While a few of the points below are somewhat applicable to the separate course approach, that approach has much less relevance for collection development. The reasons for that should become apparent.

The first of the criteria in my 1975 statement—that a college library must have "a collection of cultural and recreational materials that can expand students' horizons"—is one that is probably affected only minimally by the presence or absence of a bibliographic instruction program. That is, no matter what the curriculum, a respectable college library should have certain standard works representing the ideas and work that constitute our cultural and intellectual heritage. Of course, the definition of what is included in that rather nebulous concept will change

---

[1] Evan Ira Farber, "Limiting College Library Growth: Bane or Boon?" in *Farewell to Alexandria: Solutions to Space, Growth, and Performance Problems of Libraries*, ed. Daniel Gore (Westport, Conn.: Greenwood Press, 1976) 39.

over time. Such a collection should now certainly include works, for example, by certain significant Asian and African writers, whereas some years ago those authors would be found in only the more sophisticated college library collections, if even there. The nature of that conceptual change, however, will be shaped almost as much by the content of higher education in general as by the context of an individual institution. Insofar as recreational reading materials are concerned, their selection will be affected somewhat by the existence of a bibliographic instruction program for reasons that I believe will become apparent later.

How the second criterion of an undergraduate collection—the support of curricular needs—helps shape that collection is subject to wide variation from library to library. Yet there is no doubt that it is the criterion most central to our discussion. Any particular curriculum, after all, is simply a structure, a framework, sometimes logical, more often—and more cynically—an accretion of courses established by tradition, by faculty politics, by administrative fiat, by student demand, by departmental need, or by individual faculty preference—or by any combination of these. What we are interested in, however, are those activities that add substance to the structure, form to the framework, and permit that conformation to result in an effective undergraduate education. They are the activities that constitute the teaching/learning process, and librarians are interested in them here because of that second criterion, support of the curriculum. If the basic purpose of building a library collection is to support the curriculum or the teaching/learning process, and the primary purpose of bibliographic instruction is to enhance that process, then the relationship between the two should result in a symbiosis, in which both not only support and enhance the teaching/learning process but also reinforce each other. It is my contention—my major premise, really—that a bibliographic instruction program, by promoting closer working relationships between librarians and classroom teachers, and between librarians and students, makes the job of developing the collection easier and results in a collection that better meets the needs of students and teachers.

"Closer ties" is the key. Let us first discuss those ties with the faculty. Cooperation between teaching faculty and librarians is a hallmark of practically any bibliographic instruction program and, simply as a factor of cause and effect, results in closer ties. Cooperation takes place at several points during the process. It takes place first at the initial contact, when an instructor decides to have library instruction in conjunction with an assignment. It occurs next when the teacher and the librarian talk over the instruction. Third, cooperation takes place during the instruction itself, which usually is given in the classroom or in the library, and, finally, it occurs during the follow-up, either immediately following the session or later on, in planning a repeat session. Each of

154

those steps entails working together, at times briefly, at other times, more extensively. The first step, the initial contact, is simply based on acquaintance: on the teacher's part, acquaintance with the purposes of bibliographic instruction and, to some extent, the procedures; and on the librarian's part, acquaintance with the course and, just as important, with the teacher's academic interests and working style. The second step, planning the instruction, incorporates and builds on some of the interactions of the first, and involves detailing the assignment—its purpose, content, and timing, and the instructions to students. This stage of the process provides the best opportunity for establishing closer ties. Classroom teaching is for the most part an autonomous affair, and it can be a lonely one. Instructors often do not have (or don't choose to take) the opportunity to talk over with colleagues their class assignments, even though those assignments are central to what concerns them most—being successful teachers.[2] Having someone to talk with about the assignment, especially someone who's interested in helping make it a success and, moreover, someone who poses no threat (as a department head or even another instructor might), can be very welcome, and on such an occasion the librarian can take the opportunity to become more familiar with the instructor's academic and other interests. In the third step, implementation, the students see the librarian and the instructor working together, and that's important for students' perceptions of the librarian's main role—helping them fulfill their assignments. The final step, follow-up, or evaluation, builds on and can strengthen the ties already established.

The reason for describing this process in somewhat more detail than may seem necessary is simply to show the working relationship between the librarian and the instructor, a working relationship that enlightens the librarian about the content and purpose of the instructor's courses and at the same time increases the instructor's awareness of the librarian's role in the teaching/learning process, and how that role can

---

[2] "Colleagues don't talk much to each other about teaching. In 1978, Jerry Gaff surveyed 1,680 faculty at 145 institutions and found that 42% of them said that *never* during their entire career had anyone talked with [them] in detail about [their] teaching and helped [them] clarify course objectives, devise effective student evaluation, or develop a more effective approach for certain kinds of students. Only 25% said that discussions on these topics had taken place more than once...To talk openly about teaching at many of our institutions implies one has a problem. One talks because things aren't going well. But if one knows the content well enough, one can teach it...The reasons why dialogue about teaching does not occur are less important than the reasons why it should. *Colleagues could be better teachers if they talked to each other about what they do and why they* do *it.*" See *The Teaching Professor* 1 (July 1987): 1.

help the instructor achieve his or her course objectives.

Now, how does that working relationship, those closer ties, affect collection development? As noted earlier, those ties make the job of developing the collection easier and thus result in a better collection that meets the needs of students and faculty. A lot has been written about that job, and, while commentators have differed on how much weight should be given to the faculty or to the librarians for developing the collection, the importance of cooperation in carrying out that responsibility has been recognized by all. Yet most of us have seen or at least heard of situations where there was a certain amount of rancor over book selection. Those situations, it seems to me, mostly stem from an adversarial relationship, a "we-they" feeling between the two groups, a feeling that might have been obviated or certainly ameliorated if the individuals had worked together in planning instruction. That process of working together in planning bibliographic instruction provides the ideal opportunity for appreciating each other's contribution.

A colleague has characterized bibliographic instruction in this regard as a "political lubricant." Not a very subtle term, to be sure, nor, as far as I know, one generally used in academe; it is, however, apt. Let's face it—administrative decisions and curricular policies *are* often determined by "political" relationships and considerations. Budgetary allocations and personnel decisions, both of which directly affect the library's ability to build and/or maintain a collection, are, if not shaped, certainly affected by such political considerations. There are, of course, many other activities, devices, and actions that also help promote more cordial relationships between teaching faculty and librarians. Any of these—receptions, parties, social occasions—can work to the library's political advantage, but as effective as anyone might be at a particular time, none of them makes an inherent contribution to the educational process.

Working closely with faculty in planning instruction can create another opportunity for enhancing personal relationships. As noted previously, early in the planning process the librarian should become acquainted with the instructor's academic interests. That is, to be sure, most important for the instruction itself, but it can also be helpful in book selection and useful in informing the instructor about items (articles, publication announcements, etc.) that may lead to book requests. Even if the items are not of immediate use or significance, the librarian's thoughtfulness will be recognized and appreciated. Having a book on order or, even better, on the shelf when a faculty member sees a review can do marvelous things for improving relationships. There are few better ways of knowing what faculty members want or need than by talking to them about their courses. My observation that teaching is at times a lonely affair is not, I think, fully appreciated by librarians. This is particularly true in colleges, where individual faculty members may be the only ones in their specialties and so have no colleagues or even graduate students with whom to share their interests. Thus, when a librarian anticipates a need or sends an item reflecting that interest, it is particularly appreciated.

The preceding has emphasized the importance for collection development of close librarian-faculty working relationships. Those relationships tend to create a favorable political environment that gives librarians more freedom to develop the collection than they otherwise might have. Equally as important is the knowledge librarians gain about the content of courses, about the topics on which students will be writing papers, even about the subject matter and the discipline itself, which may go far beyond the course. That knowledge permits and even encourages librarians to look for and add to the collection materials that will support the courses and assignments. Combined with the freedom created by the favorable political climate, this knowledge can lead to active and effective collection development.[3]

So far, we've not really discussed the students' contribution to the bibliographic instruction-collection development equation, except insofar as they are the ones being taught or helped. Although that role is important, my assumption here is that, when students receive bibliographic instruction, their perception of the librarian changes: the librarian is now seen as a *colleague* of the teacher, someone who knows the course, the assignment, and ways to find information for that assignment. In other words, the librarian can help shape the topic as well as find information on it. Because of that consultative relationship, students and librarians work together more closely, more candidly; librarians come to know students' interests and needs much better, thus enhancing their ability to select appropriate items for the collection.

If there were such a thing as a perfect job of collection development, it would mean meeting every user's need or demand with

---

[3] At various times during the writing of this paper, I went through several current issues of *Publishers Weekly,* selecting items in the Forecasts section for ordering. I do this regularly, but with these particular issues I tried to be aware of which items I selected because of our bibliographic instruction program—that is, because I had given instruction in certain courses. Of course, I have to ask myself, would I have chosen those same items simply because I knew our curriculum and collection, or did I choose them because I worked with certain instructors and students? Certainly, it's not easy to ascribe any single action to a particular experience. I do know, however, that I felt much more certain about my selections because of my contact with the instructors and their students. Indeed, there were several items I would have overlooked were it not for that contact.

the items on hand, by either having added them to the collection or having already borrowed them from elsewhere. Librarians are not clairvoyant, however, and can base their book selection only on what they anticipate will be needed. The standard advice for college library collection development officers is simple and straightforward: As Guy Lyle put it many years ago, the "most important influence upon the book stock of the college library will be the nature of the curriculum."[4] That's basic, sound advice, but it provides only general guidance. We can anticipate the needs of students and faculty more accurately, more precisely, by working closely with them through bibliographic instruction than by simply knowing the curriculum, no matter how accurate or thorough that knowledge is.

Knowing students' interests and needs more intimately may have another effect on collection development. Librarians, along with most faculty members, tend to be traditional in their ideas of curriculum content and other academic matters. Book selection for most libraries is based primarily on reviews in scholarly or other mainstream journals, or on *Choice,* or on publishers' mailings, or on other standard sources. These sources, however, may not reflect changes in student attitudes and styles (e.g., the recent growth of interest in Central America, in South Africa, in animal rights, in the Palestinians' cause, in homophobia). Some of those interests, such as the Palestinians' cause, were created as a result of particular courses or programs at this college and we might have predicted the demand for materials in those areas. It's not likely, however, that we would have predicted the enduring strength of those interests or the sudden interest in such topics as animal rights. Although we could meet almost any student's need with some adequacy, we were able to respond in greater depth because students felt comfortable enough to talk with the librarians about their interests and to request materials.

Even with all the prescience humanly possible, however, even with the best possible working relationships with faculty and students, no library can hope to meet all student and/or faculty needs, and it must depend on filling those needs with materials from other libraries. Richard Werking has described interlibrary borrowing as a function of collection development when a library's administrative viewpoint shifts from being "collection-centered" to being "client-centered." When that shift occurs, interlibrary borrowing "becomes an important part of a library's collection development and acquisition processes, one that is undertaken in response to a demand that is expressed rather than

---

[4] Guy R. Lyle, *The Administration of* the *College Library,* 3d ed. (New York: H. W. Wilson, 1961), 234.

presumed."[5] It is appropriate, then, to discuss briefly the relationship between bibliographic instruction and interlibrary lending.

The most obvious relationship in a small library is a simple quantitative one: Teaching students how to find materials will result in an increased demand for materials outside the library. That then raises an important policy question: How much of the library's (probably limited) resources should be given to meeting that demand? The only valid response is "as much as is needed." One really can't (or shouldn't) teach students how to use the library effectively, how to find information they can use for their papers and reports, and then say to them, "Sorry, but we don't have any of those items." In principle, that seems wrong, but aside from that, it will simply frustrate students and be counterproductive to the success of the bibliographic instruction program.

If, then, we agree to provide as many resources for interlibrary lending as are needed, those resources have to come from somewhere, and unless the college administration is willing to supplement the library's budget accordingly, they will have to come from a redistribution of the library's existing budget—very possibly from acquisitions. Such a redistribution, unless it cuts into the heart of the collection program, that is, into really essential items, is justifiable— improving interlibrary lending service will increase the availability of materials much more than would a limited number of added volumes.

Previously, I discussed the contribution of bibliographic instruction to librarians' increased knowledge of students' interests and needs. An expanded interlibrary lending service can also contribute to that knowledge. Materials requested from other libraries can provide clues to students' interests and needs; likewise, records of periodicals from which articles are requested can pinpoint titles that the library should acquire.

Finally, the process of providing support for curricular needs very much affects the processes of building a collection of cultural and recreational materials and a good reference collection. That is, by participating in bibliographic instruction, librarians can have a better reading of, a better feeling for, student and faculty needs and interests. In turn, this should help librarians build collections that reflect those

---

[5] Richard Hume Werking, "Some Thoughts on Interlibrary Sending and a Resource-Sharing System for Academic Libraries in Texas," a memorandum distributed to the members of the AMIGOS Interlibrary Loan Policy Review Committee, December 13, 1988, 1-2. Werking prefers the phrase "interlibrary sending" to "interlibrary lending" or "interlibrary borrowing" since most transactions are not loans or borrowings but one-way transmissions of reproduced items.

needs and interests. Similarly, those same librarians should have a better sense of faculty and student interests in recreational reading materials as well as a better sense of the reference works needed. All areas of building a college library's collection, then, can benefit from the library staff's involvement in bibliographic instruction.

22

Teachers as Learners: The Application of BI
(1992)

This piece was published in 1992 as one of the papers given at the 19ᵗʰ
LOEX conference. The thrust of that conference, as well as part of its full title,
was "Working with Faculty in the New Electronic Library..." I can see now
that I missed the boat—I focused on the first three words of that title, and
ignored the "New Electronic Library." What I did was to repeat much of what
I'd said many times before on ways of getting to work with faculty, the only new
wrinkle was a brief reference to many (most?) faculty members' reluctance to
talk about their teaching, according to the survey noted in footnote 3. I'm
surprised no one in the audience came up to me later and said something like
"Haven't I heard this before?" Deference to my age probably caused that
hesitation.

I regret not having addressed the new scenario in which librarians not
only were "Working with Faculty in the New Electronic Library..." but were
teaching many faculty how to find their ways through the various electronic
databases as well as showing them how to make use of them in their teaching.
In other words, teachers were learners. It's a bit ironic that I missed that in this
talk, because we were doing just that at Earlham. It didn't take me much longer
to recognize that the relationship of librarians to classroom faculty was
changing and in a 1999 article, "College Libraries and the Teaching/Learning
Process: A 25-Year Reflection," (chapter 28 in this volume) I noted several
examples such as the one reporting that "on many campuses librarians have
been asked to take on an instructional role to the faculty."

And in one of my last talks I suggested that if we look at the history of
the relationship of librarians to classroom faculty we might picture it on a
triptych: in the first frame, say until the 1960s or 70s, librarians played a
passive role, acting as helpmates of the faculty; in the second frame, from the
1960s until recently, librarians acted more as colleagues, working with faculty
on improving their teaching and students' learning; in the third frame, from the
1990s to the present, and into the future, faculty recognizing librarians, as an
Earlham colleague put it, as sort of faculty's rangers in the wilderness of
information. Of course, there's a good bit of overlap among the three periods,
and I've admittedly indulged in some carefree generalizations, but so be it.

— Evan Ira Farber, 2006

Shirato, Linda, Editor. *Working with Faculty in the New Electronic Library:*
Papers and Session Materials Presented at the Nineteenth National
LOEX Library Instruction Conference Held at Eastern Michigan
University 10 to 11 May 1991, and Related Resource Materials
Gathered by the LOEX Clearinghouse. Ann Arbor, Michigan, Pierian
Press, 1992. Pages 1-5.

Before I get to the body of my talk, I should point out that it's based on two major premises. Both are working, not just theoretical, premises and both are fundamental to my approach to BI in the undergraduate library. (Keep in mind that throughout this work I'm talking about undergraduate education. Some of what I say may apply to graduate education, or to BI in schools or public libraries, but if it is relevant for those situations, it's purely accidental—my experience, my expertise lies in undergraduate education.)

The first premise is my belief (it's more than a belief—it's a basic working principle for administering my library) that BI should be the focus, the common denominator of the library's programs and policies, of almost everything that goes on in the library. And when I talk about BI, unless noted otherwise, I'm talking about course-related or course-integrated instruction, not separate courses. In one of my first pieces on BI, in John Lubans' book, *Educating the Library User,* which was published in 1974 (one of the first books on BI), I almost apologized for taking that approach: "Given the realities of the situation…one must come to the conclusion (regretfully, perhaps) that only by working through the courses, and that means through individual faculty members, can the objectives of library instruction presently be achieved…Working with faculty, then, becomes a given." I felt, in other words, that course-related instruction was based on political necessity, not on educational desirability. I've changed my view and dropped the "regretfully." Now I think that course-related instruction has more advantages than the separate course.

My second premise is the paramount importance of the teaching/learning process. This premise really has two parts. The first is something I say in almost every talk I give; and that is, of course, that the library is not an end in itself—(it is not "the heart of the college")—but exists to support, to promote, to *enhance* what is the heart of the college—the teaching/learning process—those interactions between faculty and students that go on in classrooms, in laboratories, in tutorials, over cups of coffee, wherever—interactions that contribute to students' intellectual and critical skills, disciplinary and interdisciplinary knowledge, cultural and cross cultural awareness—all those outcomes we hope for in an undergraduate education. It's by how well the library supports and enhances those interactions that it should be evaluated, not by its size or budget. Those quantitative measures are important only insofar as they contribute to the library's role in the teaching/learning process. That's one part of my second premise.

The other part is a long-time interest in, experience with, and reading about classroom teaching, and particularly the improvement of classroom teaching. Part of my commitment to BI comes from my interest in undergraduate education: effective teaching is surely the most

162

important component of that education and BI can make a real contribution to that. I also believe that most teachers are interested in improving, in becoming good teachers. Kenneth Eble is one of the most prolific and respected writers on college and university teaching (we have 18 books written or edited by him). In his 1983 book, *The Aims of College Teaching,* he talks about this interest in improving. The particular chapter focusing on that is titled "Teachers as Learners," and that's what I'm going to talk about, but primarily with relation to BI. If BI can make teaching more effective (as I believe and think you believe), faculty—who are interested in being better teachers—should be open to working with us. But too many are still not, and we need to look at them as learners.

Let me expand a bit on my first premise, BI as the focus of a library's program. I think I didn't realize how true this had become in my own case until about five years ago, when I was asked to give a talk at a conference on the integration of library services; my assignment of course was to approach that topic from the perspective of BI. As I thought about that I began to see that from almost every aspect of administration and service, our BI program was in mind—sometimes in the background, but much more often on the table—when we made decisions or had to choose among options: personnel selection, even aspects of furnishings and building. "BI, though it began because of some other perceived needs, and then seen as an important end in and of itself, soon became the focus, the common denominator of most of our efforts. There are very few decisions made about programs or practices that don't take it into account." It's tempting for me to go into this even more, but that's not part of our agenda today. But I think you need to understand how basic it is in my approach to library administration.

Let me get to our present agenda, the teaching faculty and building relationships with them. In 1978 I gave a paper on library-faculty communication techniques. The thrust of that paper was not so different from this one—that is, if BI is so good, and can make such an important contribution to student learning and to teaching effectiveness, why is there so much resistance to it by teaching faculty? And how can that resistance be overcome? Well, since I wrote that paper 13 years have gone by. During these years I have looked at many other situations, talked to lots of librarians and teaching faculty around the country, done a lot of reading on the subject, and have 13 years more experience of working with and observing faculty, not just in a BI context, but in 10 of those years as a member of the college's personnel committee. In that committee I looked over scores of faculty members' self-evaluations, gaining insights into their abilities, shortcomings, attitudes, concerns, frustrations, and aspirations.

What's changed since then? Well, for one thing, the BI

163

movement has grown steadily, perhaps dramatically. In 1978 the BI librarians had just established their own section in ACRL, and it's now the largest activity section of that organization, with over 4,000 members. Whereas LOEX provided one of the few conferences on BI and was one of the few places that gathered materials, now there are many conferences and a number of centers. Now there's a periodical, *Research Strategies,* devoted to BI, and articles on BI appear in just about every other library periodical with some frequency (though there still aren't enough in the disciplinary journals). The number of advertised library positions that stress or include BI as a responsibility has grown enormously. To my way of thinking, however, one of the most significant events came in 1987 when one of the most important recent books on undergraduate education, *College: The Undergraduate Experience,* by Ernest Boyer was published. It is especially important for us because it's the first major publication on undergraduate education that not only mentioned but promoted BI. "The college library must be viewed as a vital part of the undergraduate experience...The library staff should be considered as important to teaching as are classroom teachers...We further recommend that every undergraduate student be introduced carefully to the full range of resources for learning on campus. Students should be given bibliographic instruction and be encouraged to spend at least as much time in the library—using its wide range of resources—as they spend in classes."[1]

That's very significant, not just because, as I noted, it's the first major work to mention BI, but also because the study was sponsored by the prestigious Carnegie Foundation for the Advancement of Teaching. Even more significantly, perhaps, certainly from a practical viewpoint, two regional accrediting associations, Middle States and Southern, now include BI as part of their criteria for libraries.

That may not seem like a lot in 13 years, but remember—the wheels of change in education move very slowly.

But there's still resistance. Why? Well, again let me go back to 1978. I thought then there were two major explanations for the resistance. The first was simply that BI was an innovation, and faculty almost always respond to innovation cautiously, but if they do at all they do according to the risks and rewards involved with accepting that innovation. In other words, if an institution rewards innovation, its faculty will respond more readily. But 13 years ago most institutions did not reward good teaching—they rewarded publication, and BI is not only no help in getting published, it takes time away from it. Has this

---

[1] Ernest L. Boyer, *College: The Undergraduate Experience* (New York: Harper and Row, 1988) 164-165.

changed? Not entirely. But it is changing. There's much more attention now to improving classroom teaching. One has only to look at the spate of books on the subject (one publisher, Jossey-Bass, devotes practically its entire list to it), or the number of conferences and workshops on teaching, or the increase in the number of institutions where teaching is evaluated by students and help for improving teaching has been institutionalized. So the arena we work in should be friendlier.

The other major factor I addressed was that of personality. "Many teachers have fragile egos, and because someone wants to work with their students—someone who can point out materials and methods with which they may be unfamiliar—it is easy for them to infer that others think them inadequate...Further, most teaching faculty have never met librarians serving in a teaching capacity, and cannot think of librarians as peers with whom one can share the responsibility of teaching."

Was I too severe? I think not, though I might change the "fragile egos" phrase. (Although I do know a number of faculty with very fragile egos.) In her recent book, *Improving College Teaching,* Maryellen Weimer says it this way:

"Many faculty members respond to attempts to encourage them to better teaching with open resistance...What is it about instructional improvement that brings out this overtly negative faculty reaction? Quite simply, faculty feel threatened when attention is directed toward their teaching."[2] That's not quite the same as fragile egos. But I have come to realize how possessive faculty feel about their classes. They are in charge—it's their territory. As Professor Weimer says: "Teachers occupy positions of power in the classroom. They are supposed to know, to be the learned experts, to manage the classroom...If they do not or have not and find that out, from their position of power, they have far to fall."

A few years ago I was visiting one of the California universities. At dinner my host introduced me to one of her faculty, a guy in the drama department. When she introduced us, she commented on how much she enjoyed giving BI to his classes and what a pleasure he was to work with. "That's interesting," I said. "I love to work with our drama people, too. Why do you suppose they're so easy to work with?" He thought a moment, then gave what I think was a very useful insight: "It's probably because theater people are used to working with others." Of course! Directors don't run the whole show; they have to work with scenic designers, lighting technicians, a stage crew, and others. So

---

[2] Maryellen Weimer, *Improving College Teaching* (San Francisco: Jossey-Bass, 1990) 16-17.

they're used to sharing the platform. As I said, that was a useful insight, and it made me even more aware of the problem of the classroom as personal territory.

That problem is still with us. Many faculty members are still unwilling to share their classrooms, to give up some control over their classes. Does the changing constituency of the professoriat affect this? That is, now with a younger, more liberal group of faculty? Are they less defensive, less possessive, more willing to share? I think so, but I can't say for sure. How about the increase in the number of women faculty members? Are women easier to work with? I think so, and here I feel more certain. I wonder if anyone has done any comparative studies.

Another obstacle to working with faculty is their lack of time, and really, the better the teacher, the less time he or she has. Early on, I didn't even consider this—after all, I knew that BI would improve almost any course, so certainly every conscientious instructor would be glad to give me time. Well, an experience some years later caused me to now give it some weight. I was teaching one section of a humanities course— a course that all first-year students had to take. Mine was one of 15 or so sections, but I was not only teaching my section but giving BI to all the other sections. Now, I was very careful to get in touch with each of the other instructors and meet with their students, but I completely neglected to give my own section any BI. When I reflected on this later I realized that I had been so busy with the everyday business of the course— reading the assignments, making notes for lectures, thinking about tests, meeting with individual students, choosing and ordering texts for the following term—I was so busy with that that I forgot about the BI. The lesson for me? Teaching—good teaching—requires lots of time, and we just can't expect BI to be the major concern of a good teacher. It's up to us to take the initiative, to get in touch with individual faculty members. Sure, occasionally a faculty member I've worked with over the years will call me first, but I'm always pleasantly surprised when that happens.

Another part of that reluctance to work with us is due to faculty members' inability to see us as colleagues, persons with whom they're willing to share the responsibility for teaching their classes. There are several reasons for this, some of them quite obvious, but all, I think, possible to respond to.

First, we need to gain their respect for what we're supposed to do—that is, what we're traditionally supposed to do: in my own case, be a good administrator, keep up the book collection...For many of you, it probably would be being a good reference librarian. (That's one reason I say, if you're looking for another position, try to get one where the person you replace was a dud, a failure—then you automatically look good—at least, you have a honeymoon period.) But of course, doing our traditional job well is just the beginning.

166

I have another device for making inroads with new faculty. (This device is much easier in smaller institutions, but it's worth mentioning.) Find out the names of faculty who have been hired for the coming year. Write them, tell them how glad you are that they're coming, and ask if there's anything you can do for them before their arrival—check their bibliographies, see about ordering items, and the like. You have no idea how pleased these people are to get such a note. If they respond, fine, but even if they don't, you've established contact. Most of the time, however, the need is to establish a working relationship with faculty members already there. Now, this is an important thing to do, not only from the BI perspective, but from the wider administrative perspective. That is, a good working relationship with faculty members not only permits better service to students, but it helps gain support for the library—moral as well as financial support—from the faculty, and through the faculty, from the administration.

The most effective way of establishing a working relationship is by indicating a shared interest in the faculty member's courses. Most faculty love to talk about their teaching. That's natural, isn't it? Yet they're often reluctant to talk to faculty colleagues—there is, after all, a certain sense of competition among faculty, within departments, even between departments. If you doubt this, let me quote from an item in *The Teaching Professor:* "Colleagues don't talk much to each other about teaching...[a researcher] surveyed 1680 faculty at 14 institutions and found that 42 percent of them said that *never* during their entire career had anyone talked with them in detail about their teaching...Only 25 percent said that discussions on [teaching] had taken place more than once...To talk openly about teaching...implies one has a problem."[3]

Preparing for BI provides an ideal opportunity to talk about one's teaching with an interested but non-threatening figure, the BI librarian. How to encourage this? Well, the letter to new faculty. For faculty already there, by sending him or her material that might be useful for the course: notices of new books, articles they might not see (not from journals they would be expected to see), then by setting up a time to talk about the course. We're seen, then, as someone who's interested in what the course is trying to do and how it does it, and maybe even having suggestions for improving it. Then, by talking with the instructor, we can find out more about the faculty member's interests, and later, after the course is over, talk about how it went. Did the BI take? Should it have been done differently? How can it be improved next time? Thus, you've built a working relationship that will be enhanced by using the same devices over the years.

---

[3] *The Teaching Professor* (July 1987).

I've really just touched on a few ways of working with faculty. I could go on and on—and I often do. But each of us has to work out his/her approaches, depending on a variety of factors—the institutional context, administrative support, the nature and size of the faculty, our individual personalities, interests and talents, and so forth.

There are times when *you* may get discouraged, when the resistance to your best efforts, to all that *you* believe is right, seems impenetrable. Think of the parallel with classroom teachers and their students, especially those I see in junior high school. How do they manage to keep going, with so much working against them: the problems, the anti-intellectualism of pre-adolescents, uncooperative parents, unsympathetic administrators? They do keep going, and I think what does keep them going are the successes, those kids for whom education has become a means of growth, of intellectual and psychological and social development. In other words, those for whom education has made a real difference in their lives, for whom the mission of education has had some validity.

Well, we believe in the validity of BI, that it can make a difference in higher education, in the effectiveness of the teaching/learning process. We have an advantage over those junior high school teachers. Their learners are going to leave and they'll have to start all over again with a new group. Our learners, the teaching faculty, will stay—most of them, anyway, for a while—and we can continue working on them—or better, working with them…perfecting that working relationship. Then we can use *them* as change agents, helping to carry our message to their colleagues.

Sure, we'll continue to have failures, but let's look rather at our successes, at the students we've helped, who because of us have done better work, saved time, gotten better grades, and feel better about using libraries. Let's look at those professors, who, having learned from us, are more effective teachers and enjoy teaching more. Let's learn from our failures, to be sure, and continually improve our methods, but let's keep in mind and feel good about our successes—if our objectives are worthy, as you and I believe they are.

23

Bibliographic Instruction at Earlham College
(1993)

It was probably in 1969, at an ALA Conference, that Earlham's bibliographic instruction program first came to the attention of academic librarians. In the next few years, as the program's reputation grew, an increasing number of librarians visited the library to get a first-hand view of it. The flow of visitors, although flattering, became somewhat of a burden and so in 1977 we hosted a conference that not only explained but also demonstrated the program. The positive response by that small group of about thirty encouraged us to host another...and then another...so that over the decade we hosted eight conferences with altogether about 400 attendees, librarians and teaching faculty from almost all 50 states—and even a few from abroad. In 1984 I suggested to Larry Hardesty, then library director at Eckerd College in St. Petersburg, Florida, that we hold one of our conferences there. Florida in February! How could it fail? It not only didn't fail but was so successful we held four more there. The following piece is an edited and shortened transcription of my opening remarks at the last of those conferences.

Readers should understand that the unique feature of these conferences—and I'm sure a major reason for their success—was the presentations not only by Earlham librarians but by a few members of Earlham's teaching faculty (usually three, one each from the sciences, the social sciences, and the humanities) speaking about their introduction to bibliographic instruction, their uses of it in their courses, and the effects of using it on their teaching and on their students.

While the audience consisted mostly of librarians, a number of teaching faculty and even a few academic administrators also attended. Their presence was the reason a good portion of my talk was very basic: I could assume that the librarians knew something about bibliographic instruction, but that was not necessarily true of classroom teachers or administrators.

— Evan Ira Farber, 2006

The premise that underlies all our library's activities, especially our bibliographic instruction program, is, at first, one that may seem heretical coming from a librarian. You eventually, however, will see it

---

Hardesty, Larry, Jamie Hastreiter and David Henderson, Editors. *Bibliographic Instruction in Practice: A Tribute to the Legacy of Evan Ira Farber; Based on the 5th Earlham College-Eckerd College Bibliographic Instruction Conference February 5-7, 1992.* Ann Arbor, Michigan, The Pierian Press, 1993. Pages 1-14.

makes sense. The premise is this: the library is not the heart of the college—despite what your catalog says, or what your president states when addressing visiting librarians. What is the heart of the institution? The teaching/learning process, of course. This process consists primarily of those interactions that go on between faculty and students—in classrooms, in laboratories and offices, and over coffee cups or beer mugs. It is the process that leads to students' intellectual development and acquisition of learning skills, to improvements in their critical judgment, and to advances in their disciplinary and interdisciplinary knowledge.

What is the library's role in this process? Primarily, it is to enhance the teaching/learning process. Of course, it has other functions: to build a collection, to organize and distribute materials, to provide a study hall, to collect archival materials, to provide recreational and browsing materials, and to be a social place for students and faculty. The main purpose of the library is, however, to enhance the teaching/learning process. How well it does that is the standard by which we should evaluate a library. What is important is not how big its budget is, not how many volumes it has, not the size of its staff, not how many subscriptions it receives. All of those factors are significant, to be sure, but only insofar as we use them to promote the teaching/learning process. That is the reason for bringing along the teaching faculty to discuss bibliographic instruction with you. Even if you do believe what I have to say about the effectiveness of our bibliographic instruction program, my opinion is a secondary source. What our teachers have to say, how they view bibliographic instruction's impact on the teaching/learning process—that is firsthand evidence. They offer a more valid, undeniably more convincing argument.

Let me talk a moment about our target audience—our students. Many students, perhaps even most, do not especially like libraries—or librarians. They base some of that antipathy, unfortunately, on experience. Some they base on the stereotype of librarians. Mostly, however, they base it on feelings of inadequacy in using libraries. Many of you are familiar with the term "library anxiety" and you may have read the article that appeared in *College & Research Libraries* some time ago about the phenomenon of library anxiety. For those of you who have not read it or do not remember it, it involved a library project at a small state university, an institution with seven or eight thousand students. All freshmen took a required English course in which, "Instructors required students to keep search journals. These were diary-like entries that described the search process and the students' feelings about it...It was found that 75 to 85 percent of students in each class described their initial response to the library in terms of fear or anxiety.

170

Terms like scary, overpowering, lost, helpless, confused and fear of the unknown appeared again and again..."[1]

What is the result when students feel that way? What is one's reaction to a situation when one feels helpless, anxious, unfamiliar, or not in control of a situation? One avoids it, of course. It is a natural response that many students will avoid the library unless an assignment absolutely forces them to use it to check out reserve materials or do an assignment—and they come in only at the last moment. We face the phenomenon of library anxiety, a fear that so many students, particularly beginning students, have.

Even students who like libraries often do not use them well. They come into the college or university library and see the *Readers' Guide* and card catalog, or now the automated catalog, and think, well, I know how to use these things. I have it made. They do not realize that academic libraries are much more complex than their high school or public libraries. Most importantly, they do not know there are myriad indexes, bibliographies, abstracting services, and guides to information. The library contains an enormous amount of information, and to the uninitiated it must be terribly complex. What those uninitiated do not know, however, is there are also tools to help individuals sort their way through this complexity to find particular items of information and there is a systematic way of using those tools. They have not learned that browsing may not be the best way of finding what they need. Nor, most important perhaps, have they discovered that a reference librarian can be a friend, or, as one of our faculty put it, a forest ranger in a wilderness of information.

What you have, then, are students who are afraid of libraries and do not like to use them. You also have students who may like libraries but really do not know how to use them. Compounding the problem, most library assignments do not demand effective use of materials. Therefore, they do not encourage students to improve library skills. They can get by with their very limited knowledge about using a library. A bright student taught in elementary or high school how to use the library can usually find a few references in the *Readers' Guide* and a few books through the catalog and can put together a decent paper.

Too many library assignments do not really teach much about using the library. For example, the "treasure hunt" assignment reinforces the belief that the best way of finding information is to just look through the collection. Some assignments are unreasonable, at least for students' abilities, because most faculty members assume that students know a lot

---

[1] Constance A. Mellon, "Library Anxiety: A Grounded Theory and its Development," *College & Research Libraries* 47 (March 1986): 160-165.

more than they do about libraries. (Never underestimate the library ignorance of students, especially those who claim they know.) Remember, and here I am speaking to faculty members, how inadequate you were when you first encountered your college or university library.

Well, why does all of this happen? Why is so much lacking? Why these negative results? Mostly, it is because librarians and teaching faculty do not work together. My contention is that a good bibliographic instruction program, one in which teaching faculty and librarians cooperate, can respond to these inadequacies—and more.

What does that mean? What can it mean for all of the constituencies concerned with the role of the library? For administrators it means better use of the collection. I cannot understand why a dean or a college president—who would be terribly upset if the money invested in a new gymnasium was wasted because that gymnasium was not used, or underused—is hardly bothered by a library on which hundreds of thousands, perhaps millions, of dollars have been spent over the years in building a collection that sits on the shelves greatly underused. There is not much question that every library which has begun a bibliographic instruction program has seen the use of the collection increase, particularly the use of the periodicals. For administrators, bibliographic instruction will mean better use of the resources that librarians and the institution have spent years developing.

For students, it means doing better work and getting better grades. They can do their work in less time because they can be more efficient. It also means that they can begin to enjoy using the library. Library use may not be fun, but at least it need not be so onerous. For students who are going on to graduate or professional schools, learning how to use a library is especially important. I have received many comments from Earlham graduates who have reported they were way ahead of their graduate or professional school colleagues. They felt comfortable about going into any research library in the country because of the confidence and expertise they had gained from their library instruction at Earlham.

For reference librarians, and other members of the staff, it means that students and teaching faculty perceive us differently. Students see us more as part of the teaching process. Teaching faculty see us more as colleagues. We know more about the curriculum and have a better handle on student and faculty bibliographic needs. One of my responsibilities is to make sure our collection reflects the needs of our curriculum. I have a better feel for what teachers and students need and more confidence in selecting materials because I work with teaching faculty in implementing their syllabi. Because I have spoken to their classes about their assignments, students usually feel free to talk with me about their individual topics.

What does a bibliographic instruction program mean for the teaching faculty? It means that their students become more independent learners, and independent learners are interesting to teach. One's teaching can be more effective and even more enjoyable. I think my colleagues will attest to these assertions later on. If they forget, I hope you will ask them about my remarks.

These are some positive results of a bibliographic instruction program for the different groups in a college. Important and beneficial as they are, they are only the immediate, short-term results. There are, in addition, long-term advantages to bibliographic instruction. It is becoming increasingly important for students to learn how to learn, to be able to go beyond the professor, and beyond the textbook. Much of what we teach undergraduates will be outdated in a few years.

When they are out in the working world, they will need to be information-literate, to find information on developments in their fields, their professions, on matters pertinent to their civic responsibilities, and even to their personal lives. Most of them will be changing occupations sooner or later, and will need to become familiar with new ways of finding information. We are without question moving into becoming—indeed, we already are in—an information-based society. In such a society, success and failure will increasingly be measured by one's ability to find, organize, and use information. By use, I mean find and evaluate the best information. Bibliographic instruction may not guarantee all of that, but it can unquestionably help.

Let me assume, for now, that I have made the case for bibliographic instruction. How does it work? As Larry Hardesty noted earlier, bibliographic instruction is nothing new; it goes back into the nineteenth century, though under different names—library instruction, user education, and others. Perhaps the most common device has been the library tour. The tour is one of my pet peeves. I do not really consider it bibliographic instruction, no more than a tour of the White House is political science. It teaches very little. Indeed, it is ineffective. More than ineffective, it is counter-productive. Such tours are almost always given in the first couple of weeks of the school year, maybe the first week that new students are on campus. Are students really interested in learning about the library at this stage? Of course not. They are interested in their new courses, in getting along with new roommates, paying for their tuition—and all those other matters that concern adolescents and post-adolescents. Here we are, trying to tell them about libraries. They could not care less. It only reinforces the stereotype of libraries as boring places and librarians as mere custodians. There may be libraries—or parts of libraries—in which it is so difficult to find one's way around that tours may be necessary. Even they will be much more effective when combined with some real need for using the library. With minor exceptions, then, I do not advocate library tours.

Another method for bibliographic instruction is the separate course, called, perhaps, "Introduction to Library Research." Offering such a course has some real benefits and advantages that make it a very tempting means of teaching use of the library. Such a course can delve more deeply into the intricacies of the bibliographic system and can make it intellectually interesting and challenging. Another reason it is so tempting is the teacher—in this case the librarian—has control over the thrust of the course, the materials, the students. One can almost teach it as a discipline.

The disadvantages, however, should discourage the temptation. Learning how to use the library does not really impress most students until they need it for a particular course or a particular assignment. Unless it is a required course the only students who are going to take it are those highly motivated students. They are the ones who need it least. They are going to learn how to use the library anyway. The students who do not ask for help really need the instruction and, unless required, they are not going to take such a course.

There is another real disadvantage—a realpolitik disadvantage, if you will—with a required separate course. If it is built into the curriculum, it is politically vulnerable. In times of retrenchment when the institution is looking to cut back—or, indeed, any time when the curriculum is reexamined—that course is likely to be scuttled, or at least reduced in scale, because it does not have a real power base on campus. What then? If the library was dependent on that course for its bibliographic instruction foundation, it will be in a bad way. It has no foundation, no regimen, no tested procedures, and has to start from scratch. As I will say several times during this workshop, it takes time to build a program. That library will have wasted a lot of time and energy that could have been used more productively.

The approach I advocate—the one we use at Earlham—is course-related instruction. That is, we give library instruction only with particular course assignments—with one exception, which I will discuss later. The purpose of the instruction is to help students find information for that assignment. Usually, this is a research paper of some kind, but it can be an assignment for which students need information: a book review, material for a speech, an annotated bibliography, all kinds of assignments. The instruction, then, becomes relevant for the students. It takes advantage of students' real interests: getting better grades and saving time. At more advanced junior and senior levels, it provides students the means to emulate their faculty mentors, to be junior professionals. It enables them to do research on their own.

174

24

Plus ça Change...
(1995)

This piece appeared in the Fall, 1995 issue of Library Trends, *an issue devoted to "The Library and Undergraduate Education." I have no recollection of conversations nor any correspondence relating to my inclusion in the volume, though the topic was of course one about which I'd done a lot of writing and speaking.*

It was probably while writing the piece that I announced my retirement as College Librarian and so there must have been many things occupying my mind and my time. So now, it seems to me that the article is more a summation of points I'd made over the years. Perhaps its purpose was to point out the increasing importance of reference librarians as teaching agents to guide students through the proliferating wilderness of electronic information.

— Evan Ira Farber, 2006

One of the few advantages of achieving the status of an elder statesman is the license it gives to reflect or reminisce and still have those reflections or reminiscences listened to or read with a good bit of tolerance, even perhaps with interest—albeit a bemused interest. It is tempting to indulge in these reminiscences—too tempting to resist, probably, but they will be kept to a minimum. This article will encompass some reflections—reflections that take advantage of the experience garnered over thirty years of working with undergraduates, and reflections that look at both some of the changes as well as some of the constants of implementing a successful program of bibliographic instruction. I will then reflect on how those changes—rather, *if* those changes—will help provide some direction in the years to come.

The title, *Plus ça Change,* is, of course, only half of the aphorism, loosely translated: "The more things change, the more they are the same." The latter half, *Plus c'est la même chose,* is the more intriguing part of the saying. In examining library use instruction over the past thirty years, it is easy enough to point to those factors that have changed; all, or certainly almost all, the changes relate to computer technology. Thirty years ago, those in bibliographic instruction (it was not called "BI" then but "library orientation" or "library use instruction";

Farber, Evan Ira. "Plus Ca Change...," *Library Trends*, Volume 44, No. 2 (Fall 1995), pages 430-438.

the first use of the term "bibliographic instruction" in *Library Literature* seems to have appeared in 1974) were concerned with teaching only a few tools such as the Library of Congress subject heading volumes, a few specialized encyclopedias, some Wilson indexes, other disciplinary indexes or abstracting services, and the use of printed bibliographies. Some introduced students to the Library of Congress classification or reminded them of Dewey's mnemonic devices. Those who worked in libraries that were government documents depositories may have explained the SuDocs classification. One looks at the simplicity of our early handouts with some yearning—but surely that same simplicity would seem almost laughable to younger bibliographic instruction librarians now. Today there are not only many more specialized reference works in print—i.e., encyclopedias, handbooks, and bibliographies—but also students have to be shown the idiosyncrasies of our individual systems' OPACs and introduce them to the proliferation of electronic databases available on standalone CD-ROMs or through the OPACs. And most recently—and prominently—we must cope with the Internet and what sorts of information—bibliographic, numeric, and other—are increasingly available through it. These decades, and especially the last few years, have seen an enormous change, or rather a series of changes, in the content of what we feel is necessary to convey to students; we have constantly scrambled to keep up with those changes—or felt very guilty for not giving students the latest and the best. What factors have remained constant? The faculty, first of all, has remained constant.

In the late 1960s, the bibliographic instruction program at Earlham had achieved a widespread reputation: we were working with faculty members in almost all disciplines, reaching a substantial proportion of our students, and the staff's excitement and enthusiasm about the program's successes were obvious. At the same time, we were still frustrated by the fact that we were not working with the other faculty members (more than just a few) whose classes had library-based assignments. It was puzzling. We knew that most faculty were dedicated and conscientious, and really concerned about their students' learning. We thought that they must know that bibliographic instruction would enhance learning, would make students' papers more interesting, and their teaching more fun. With even longer experience, I had begun to understand—not excuse—them and, a few years later, I characterized faculty who resisted our overtures as people who thought they could not spare the time either to talk about instruction or to implement it; were territorial—that is, reluctant to share their classes with anyone; were mostly taught the way *they* were taught; had fragile egos so that it was risky to criticize their library assignments or even to make suggestions; and they could not think of librarians as peers with whom they could share their students.[1] All of these, and probably others that I have overlooked, were obstacles to working with faculty. And yet if, as I said, those same faculty were dedicated and conscientious—and there is no question that most of them were—there had to be a way of convincing them that librarians could help their students' learning and their teaching. The key, it seemed, was to take advantage of that dedication while keeping the obstacles in mind and working around them. It took time, patience, perseverance, and more than a bit of politicking, but most faculty were eventually won over.

Has that analysis of faculty resistance changed? To some extent, yes. It is a different generation of faculty—they are more open, more democratic, less defensive. And because library technology has changed things so much since many of these faculty were in graduate school, they know librarians can find information they cannot; in a sense, they have gained a new respect for librarians. But they still exhibit some reluctance to share the classroom or to take the time to plan library instruction, still overestimate students' abilities to use library resources, and still do not really understand how improving that ability can help make students more independent, more interested, and more interesting, and thus more rewarding to teach.

However, things are changing, if slowly. First of all, the ubiquity of bibliographic instruction has meant that many younger teaching faculty have some familiarity with it, perhaps when they were students. Or they may come to teach at an institution where a bibliographic instruction program exists and, in a sense, be socialized into the uses of that program. A second, and more important, factor is the impact of the new information technology. In the past, one obstacle bibliographic instruction librarians faced was that so many faculty taught just as they were taught. Now, however, faculty recognize that their teaching toolkits must include the Internet, or Dialog, or whatever electronic sources are appropriate for their courses. Because librarians are the ones to show their students how to gain access to these sources and to demonstrate what they provide, faculty members are much more willing to accept librarians as teaching colleagues—not fully accepted in all cases, but at least colleagues to consult and work with.

How about students? When meeting with groups of alumni, one question almost always asked is "What are Earlham students like now?" My typical response is, "Well, their tastes have changed—and, in music, for the worse. They are much more comfortable with the opposite sex,

---

[1] E. I. Farber, "Teachers as Learners—The Application of BI," in L. Shirato (Ed.), *Working with Faculty in the New Electronic Library* (pp. 1-5). Ann Arbor, MI: Pierian Press. Pp. 3-4.

and their dress and hairstyles are much more varied…but as for their social concerns, their interests, their study habits, they are pretty much like you were twenty (or thirty) years ago." Groups of alumni are not particularly interested in hearing about the problems of teaching students how to use library resources. I do not say that students—at the beginning level, anyway—still have little understanding of the range, the richness, the usefulness of the resources of an academic library and again, initially, usually depend on a few things they can find easily in the catalog, be it printed or electronic. First-year students especially underestimate the complexity of finding information, and they also are unaware that there are many tools to help work through that complexity. That is, they bring to the college library the same habits they learned in their high schools—if indeed, they learned any there.

Another characteristic today's students share with those of a generation ago is an inability to discriminate among sources. Rarely have we seen a student who questioned the validity, or even the usefulness, of a book in the library. If a book was in the library, students seemed to infer that its content was reliable, that the information in it must be valid. To help correct this misconception, to encourage students to be more critical in their search for information, we used to point out to them that not only were there books in the library that were not authoritative, but that we even acquired some books because they were good examples of bad books. For example, we would explain that there was at least a shelf of books in the collection which seems to prove that Shakespeare never wrote any of the plays most people attribute to him—i.e., they must have been written by someone with a much better education and background. These books are disparaged by the teachers of courses on Shakespeare, yet the library had purchased them, cataloged them, and they looked very much like any one of the authoritative works written by the most eminent Shakespearean scholars. Why had we bought them? Because, though the books were not products of good scholarship, they represented a significant aspect of Shakespearean studies.

Are today's students less naive? Certainly about some things, though "cynical" might be a more appropriate word than "naive." Students do not believe what they see in the supermarket tabloids or other sensationalist magazines one finds at a checkout counter. They are skeptical about much of what they read in newspapers about politics and not without good reason. But they do believe almost anything that comes from a computerized source. It results, I think, from what Theodore Roszak, professor of history at California State University, Hayward, called "technological idolatry" in his book, *The Cult of*

Information.[2] That attitude of students, the belief that whatever appears on the terminal or whatever comes from the printer is true, is a much greater danger today than, say, the danger of students not knowing about the claims to the authorship of Shakespeare's plays or not recognizing that books published by certain special interest groups are hardly reliable guides to American political history. Why is the danger so much greater now? Most obviously, perhaps, because of the proliferation of available sources. The example of students' lack of library skills one used in earlier days was that of a beginning student coming into the university library, going to the card catalog, and finding dozens, maybe hundreds, of items on her topic, not having the vaguest idea of which ones were most important or useful, so probably ending up by just checking out the first few items. Today it is worse; a student can easily get into the library's electronic catalog and through it to other libraries' catalogs and perhaps several or more other relevant databases. Confused and overwhelmed by the multiplicity of references, the student turns to some quick simplistic way of getting the information. Not only has the student probably missed much better sources of information, but the quick and precise responses at the terminal give her a sense of accomplishment, of a job well done.

But there is yet another, even greater, danger. Earlier I mentioned students' finding books that denied Shakespeare's authorship. There are, of course, ways of evaluating such books, even if one is not an expert in the field and one tries to teach students some of those ways — the use of reviews, the author's and publisher's credentials. Those are some of the filters that scholars use. But on the Internet? A delightful cartoon in the *New Yorker* a couple of years ago encapsulated the problem nicely. The cartoon shows two dogs conversing, one seated at a computer, the other on the floor. The one seated at the computer says to the other dog who's looking up at him: "On the Internet, nobody knows you're a dog." That is true, of course. Nobody knows whether you are a dog, or a Nobel Prize winner, or a flake. Unless one is an expert — someone who knows the field and the players — one really cannot tell anything about the validity, the usefulness of the source. It all looks very much the same. Even experts cannot always tell. Fortunately, academics are beginning to recognize the problem, and a group of librarians recently began to make an effort to solve it. An article in *The Chronicle of Higher Education* describing the effort points out that what is needed is a project "to impose some structure and standards" on the Internet, that "students and faculty members...need authoritative 'subject access' — a

---

[2] T. Roszak, *The Cult of Information: The Folklore of Computers and the True Art of Thinking* (New York: Pantheon Books, 1986).

single place on the Net where they can be referred to resources that experts consider worthwhile..."[3] But it goes on to mention some of the problems such a project will encounter—problems of support, cooperation, bureaucracy, to say nothing of the fact that the Internet is a moving target, constantly growing and changing. It will be, one must recognize, a long time before students will derive any benefits from the application of "structure and standards" to the Internet.

What we have now, then, are students who are using (or perhaps one should say abusing) the new technology and are overwhelmed by material they do not know how to evaluate; faced with so much to read, confused by the multiplicity of sources and conflicting views, they choose to settle for a quick superficial approach. Could we expect anything else? It is not really that they choose to settle for this quick superficial approach, but that they are forced to settle for less. That is not really very different from the students who used to be faced with hundreds of card catalog trays and very little guidance to their contents.

Given this situation, how will bibliographic instruction change? As far as beginning instruction is concerned, unquestionably it will more and more be computer directed. Students will not have any trouble learning how to find information or learning how to use even the most complex tools. All of that will be built into students' queries on the terminal. Artificial intelligence and expert systems can do a better job of instruction than we do today. For example, the use of workbooks has been shown to be one of the most effective methods for introductory levels of bibliographic instruction; there are, however, some inherent problems in administering their use: they are time-consuming and thus expensive to construct, distribute, and grade, and they invite plagiarism unless they are individualized (which can make them even more expensive). Computerizing them can solve some of those problems and make their applications even more effective (The Ohio State University Library's Gateway to Information system is a good example. See Virginia Tiefel's article in this issue of *Library Trends*). A computer has infinite patience, no time constraints, does not take coffee breaks or fail to show up on weekends, and it can adapt to individual needs and requests. And soon it will not be just typed-in requests that computers can respond to but spoken ones. Even today there are computers that can understand single-word commands or short phrases with reasonable reliability. Later, when more sophisticated programs using artificial intelligence and natural language technology are plugged in, even the

---

[3] R. L. Jacobson, "Taming the Internet: Librarians Seek Better Indexing, Subject by Subject, But Task Is Daunting," *Chronicle of Higher Education,* 41 (April 21, 1995), A29-A31. P. A29.

most computer-phobic users should have no problems with using them effectively.

There is also no question that computer-based assistance will go far beyond beginning instruction, that so-called intelligent agents will find and assemble information for users. Some years ago, Apple Computers produced a video showing the Knowledge Navigator, sort of an information valet or what some are now calling a knowbot (knowledge + robot) that is, an automated valet or maid that knows not only its client's informational needs but also the client's personal qualities to shape the package of information.

If this capability is on the horizon, what is the role of the librarian in teaching students how to find information? Will we, indeed, have a role? If the existence of that role is in doubt, one can legitimately ask: Does it make sense to spend a lot of our time and effort improving the bibliographic instruction we give now? Why try to tune an antiquated model? Why not just mark time and wait for the new model? It seems that there are three possible responses.

The first response is the very obvious one. As service-minded professionals, we are obligated to improve what we do. If we do not improve, we are letting down all those who prepared the way for us and those who follow us, not to mention those with whom, and for whom, we work now. If we do not continually try to improve, we cannot really claim to be professionals.

The second response is more speculative, perhaps, but also more pragmatic. Those knowbots, or information valets, or however those automated retrievers of information will be known, of course entail the use of expert systems; expert systems, in turn, are based on the advice of experts—the ways in which experts respond to queries, or solve a problem, or perform a particular operation. If, then, we expect machines to do really expert jobs, we need to keep improving our models, even systematizing them, so that they can be translated into a computer program. Here again, one can point to the Ohio State University Library's Gateway to Information system that was very much based on the ways librarians provide bibliographic instruction.

The third response, though, is the one most easily overlooked. For example, a piece in *Internet World* last year speculated that: "[I]ntelligent agents and filters will be developed to reduce the problems of information overload by providing easy, customized access to information sources"[4] The writer of that piece was identified only as Chief Technical Officer of the International Internet Association, but one

---

[4] D. Miller, "The Many Faces of the Internet," *Internet World,* 5(7), 34-38. P. 38.

can be sure he has never been a reference librarian since what he either ignores or is unaware of is the critical role of the reference librarian. Workbooks, as mentioned earlier, have been perhaps the most effective means of giving students some self-instruction in using library resources, and computerized workbooks (e.g., the Gateway to Information system again) are the next logical step. But every workbook, printed or computerized, should be constructed so that one of the steps in it requires meeting a reference librarian. Why? Every public services librarian has seen students come into the library and begin looking around without any idea of what to do or where to go first…and then giving up in frustration, for some reason refusing to ask the reference librarian for help. Was it fear, embarrassment, or the male syndrome of reluctance to ask for directions? Whatever it is, the lack of recognition of a reference librarian's helpfulness is sad and terribly unfortunate.

If there was just one skill, one step, that librarians who are concerned by student (and public) ineffectiveness in using libraries should try to inculcate in those seeking information, it should be: Ask the reference librarian. In constructing a printed or computerized workbook, somewhere in its structure the individual ought to be required to talk to a reference librarian—just to answer a simple question or, better, to approve a particular choice. The purpose, of course, is to ensure that the person doing the workbook recognizes that a reference librarian is approachable and, indeed, is interested in one's information needs. Certainly, such an encounter is not needed at every step; as mentioned earlier, expert systems will be able to do a lot of what we do now in bibliographic instruction and in basic reference work. One encounter should be enough to overcome that hesitation, that reluctance that prevents so many students from asking for the help they need.

The reason for a reference librarian's intercession with a student at a critical juncture in his or her search is simply that it can result in making a small but significant contribution to that student's education, to that student's ability to evaluate information. The "teachable moment"—that moment when the student needs help in making a choice or a decision—that is when the reference librarian can play an important role. An undergraduate's request for many interlibrary loans, for example, can provide a perfect teachable moment: explaining to the student at the moment of need which items are appropriate and which are not—and why. Several institutions have automated that process, and others are in the process of doing the same. In this case, such automation precludes the possibility of a potentially valuable educational experience. That is why the move toward "disintermediation"—removing the librarian from a procedure that was once performed by individuals and substituting an automated procedure—should be examined carefully to ensure the gain in efficiency is worth the loss of educational benefits.

There is, then, a good case for a continuing emphasis on bibliographic instruction and, one could say, an even greater need for it in the near future. Others are beginning to see it also. Drucker (1994), in his article in the *Atlantic Monthly,* stresses the importance of continued learning in the new knowledge-based society.[5] And in the latest issue of the *Teaching Professor,* there is an item, "Profile of the Autonomous Learner," that calls for developing "information seeking and retrieval skills," which include the ability to "select what is valuable from the mass of information available".[6]

As the faculty begins to understand how easy it is becoming for their students to drown in the sea of information, that viewpoint will be an increasingly prevalent one. Even students will realize that they will not have any problem finding information, but they will still need help in learning how to sift through, how to evaluate, that information. To be sure, machines will perform better some of our more basic and repetitive tasks. But when it comes to helping a beginning student shape a topic, or interpreting something idiomatically American for a foreign-born student, or recommending something that a foreign student might want to read about an aspect of American history or society—or any other question or request requiring the personal touch—it is hard to imagine reference librarians being replaced. Bibliographic instruction will change, but its thrust will remain very much the same. And so the title, *Plus ça change...*

---

[5] P. Drucker, "The Age of Social Transformation," *Atlantic Monthly*, 274 (November), 53-80.
[6] "Profile of the Autonomous Learner" (1994). *The Teaching Professor,* 8(9), 3.

25

The Academic Library in Transition, But to What?
(1995)

Readers should note the audience for which this piece was prepared: a relatively small group of older adults, mostly members of the Friends of the Library at a small evangelical college in Oregon. Thus the religious allusions.

The existing library was woefully inadequate, and the administration hoped either to build a new one or renovate the present one. I had been there as a building consultant; now my role was to provide the image of what a modern academic library might be like. Even though this was only a little more than a decade ago, my predictions probably sounded far-fetched to that audience; now, however, they look bland. The electronic project I was working on seemed at the time creative and very useful, but even more creative developments in electronic information soon overtook it and it died less than a year later.

I did, though, manage to get in my oft repeated concerns: the library's role in the teaching/learning process; the problems of information overload; the critical place of reference librarians even in tomorrow's library...

— Evan Ira Farber, 2006

A few years ago the editor of the *American Scholar* wrote about the excessive use of the expression — "we're in a transitional phase." That expression, he noted, may well be as old as humankind. Indeed, he went on, its first use may have been by Adam. As they were sent forth from the Garden of Eden, Adam undoubtedly tried to reassure Eve: "Don't worry, my dear, this is just a transitional phase." Well, overused as the expression may be — and as inappropriate as it may be for ascribing it to Adam — there's not much question that it *is* appropriate to apply it to today's libraries and librarians.

Of course libraries have been in transitional periods before: from papyrus to parchment, from parchment to paper, from individually handcrafted, beautifully decorated incunabula to mass produced publications, from handwritten accession lists to card catalogs — and now to computer screens — the history of changes could go on and on. This period of transition, however, is different — it's not taking place over centuries, it's not a gentle transition, not one of just a few degrees. It entails powerful, radical changes — and no one can be certain of when or what the end of the transition will be.

Talk given at "Celebrating 100 Years of Library Service; Friends of the Library Banquet," Edward P. Kellenberger Library, Northwest Christian College, Eugene, Oregon, October 13, 1995.

Transition, radical change, then, is one given we must consider.

Another given is the role of the college library—that is, pretty much as we know it today. In almost every talk I've given to college faculty and administrators, I've started with this admonition: I know you talk about the library being the heart of the college—it's not. This may sound heretical coming from a librarian, but you know as well as I do that what *is* at the heart of the college is the teaching/learning process. It's that process that goes on between teachers and students, where teaching leads to learning. The library's role? It's primarily to *enhance* that teaching/learning process, to make it more effective. That means not only making sure students have materials available to them—books, periodicals, and other sources of information—but also making sure that students know how to use them, how to find information for themselves so that, after they leave their classrooms and their teachers, they can continue to learn on their own—they can use libraries for lifelong learning. Of course the library fulfills many other purposes: to provide recreational reading material; to serve as a place for study or quiet reflection; to collect and preserve archival materials reflecting the institution's mission and heritage; and others…but its primary purpose is to enhance the teaching/learning process. And it's by how well it does that its effectiveness should be evaluated.

That, I insist, is a given when we talk about the role of the undergraduate library.

We have these two givens, then—one, libraries are rapidly changing and, two, the library's role in the educational process. What will their relationship be, say, in ten or fifteen years? Or will there be any relationship? Let me turn to some of the changes.

Just think about what academic libraries were like when most of you were students. If you wanted some information from the library then, you had to go to the building—in the rain, or the snow, perhaps—if the library was open—and then you had to see if the library held the material that contained the information you wanted—and if it did, it may have been checked out, or missing—if the library didn't have it, or you couldn't find the library's copy, you asked for an ILL—filled out a form, had it approved, and then waited probably for weeks before it came. Now, at some colleges, students have computers in their rooms, and can connect with the library, and not only find out what their library has, and whether or not the books they want are checked out or not, but can also see what other libraries have, and if the book they want is at another library but not theirs, they can automatically request it in seconds. If they're looking for periodical articles, they can search electronically from their rooms—and then, at many places, print out the text of those articles. And soon, I'm convinced, they'll be able to print out portions of, or even entire contents of many, books in their rooms. If that prediction seems extravagant, I'm basing it somewhat on experience.

This past year I've been working with a publisher on an electronic project. What it involves is photocopying the indexes from many books, converting the photocopies into electronic form, and then integrating all the entries into one massive, instantly accessible index. A student, then, will be able to look up a name, or a subject—let's say the Oregon Trail—and find out immediately not only what books mention it, but on what pages in those books. Then the student can see if the book is in the library or, if not, order the appropriate pages, and have them delivered. All that part of the project is in place. The next step for the project is to have the books available electronically, so the student won't even have to wait for the pages to be delivered; as soon as the student chooses what pages she wants to look at, they'll appear almost instantly on her terminal screen...

Now this is just one project, by one publisher. There are many others, not just by publishers—there are many other projects, by libraries, by foundations, by the government—let me cite just one, the American Memory Project. This is a project administered by the Library of Congress, but with a number of cooperating organizations; about forty libraries, from school to major university libraries, some corporations, including Apple Computers, IBM, and the Pioneer Electronic Corporation of Japan, plus a couple of major foundations. The ultimate objective is to provide immediate, online access to the collections of the Library of Congress—over 100 million items—books, pamphlets, manuscripts, films, photographs, diaries, etc., etc. It's somewhat breathtaking. Not only will all those materials be accessible, but users will be able to reproduce them, edit them, incorporate them—manipulate them in any number of ways because they have been digitized.

Let's assume that this project, and others like it, will be successful—and they will be. What are the implications for libraries?

Almost any book, any magazine, any newspaper will be accessible to any person with a computer at home. There will be a marvelous benefit to libraries—just one: rare manuscripts, collections of valuable documents, can be looked at without touching the originals. One of my predictions is much more radical: I think that libraries will not have to check out books or other materials; rather, they'll give them away by making instant copies—and that will be more efficient than a circulation system...but that's an aside...

Let me turn to another, closely related development, the Internet—it's a fascinating development; think of the social or political implications of being able to communicate with anyone else, or any group, or any organization in the world.

186

But I'm not here to talk about the social or political aspects of the problems of the Internet...but, rather, what it has to do with libraries. Well, what it's permitted is users of the Internet to have access to libraries and to everything on those libraries' servers. I can, for example, from my office in Indiana, get access to the University of Oregon library network—look at their holdings—and I can read whatever they put on their local network (let's say, the text of the Portland *Oregonian*). Now, that's fine—and it's a marvelous resource for scholars, because there are thousands of resources now, and there are more being added all the time. It may be possible some day to look at all 100 million items in the LC from one's desk. That's part of the future.

But put these developments together. On the one hand we have the ability of individuals to access library networks on their own computers—that is from their offices, from their studies, from their dorm rooms. On the other hand, we have libraries, publishers, foundations, governments, making more and more information available online...not just new information, but transforming what used to be on paper into an electronic format.

There are all kinds of implications here for libraries. But it seems to me that two stand out. The first relates to the amount and kinds of information available; the second, to the fact that users don't even have to go into a library to get that information—all they need is a monitor and a connection to the Internet, or whatever the Internet will become.

First, as to the amount and kinds of information available. Focus on that word "information". Note, I did not use the word "knowledge" and certainly not "wisdom." To be sure, there's a lot of knowledge to be gained from using libraries, and perhaps even wisdom. But neither of those should be confused with information. Information consists of data, facts, statements, opinions—perhaps unproved, even unsupported. Information has no inherent validity or worth—it's *what one does* with information that makes it important, and one very important job of education is to help students learn how to shape information into knowledge and, ultimately, one hopes into wisdom. Does the amount of information available contribute to knowledge? It can, of course. (Whether or not it can contribute to wisdom is something else: we have much more information, but are we much wiser than Aristotle, or Plato, or than Buddhist monks?) The danger that really concerns me is of *too much information*, of information overload—especially for students, who can just be confused by too much and simply give up. When one is faced with too many choices the result is confusion, withdrawal, or pick the easiest option. And then there's the problem of reliability. With printed materials we have filters, that is criteria we can use: the academic credentials of the author; the scholarly reputation of a publisher; book reviews; footnotes and bibliographies. With electronic information, some of those filters remain; but on the Internet, almost all information looks the same—anyone can say anything.

One of the advantages of electronic information is that it is not bound by limits of time and space. "Print media, in contrast," according to an editorial in *Internet World* (4/95), "is finitely determined by the editor and the space afforded within a publication." But there is another way of looking at the difference between the two. And that is, like so many aspects of our existence, placing limits leads to desirable behavior patterns. Ask any parent if he or she believes in placing limits on his or her children. I suppose we can liken the limitless horizons of electronic communication to a completely permissive upbringing of children. The result: lack of self-imposed discipline...

A comment in *The Economist* a few months ago put it this way: "The trouble with the information age is that it seems to place no emphasis on differentiation...In, with the computer, came the raw, untreated flow of data; out, at least by implication, went the ability to discriminate between useful and useless, good and bad, interesting and dull." It seems to me that for students, who don't yet have the ability to discriminate, who lack the filters to separate the informational wheat from the chaff, this is the real danger, especially when combined with too much information.

The second implication of the new technology is that users can bypass the library, can get whatever information they need from their monitors at home. Or, I should say, whatever information they *think* they need. One of the primary responsibilities of librarians has been to help users formulate their questions, to shape their topics. Now, there's no question that computers are getting smarter and smarter and, with the continuing development of expert systems, computers will be able to help users somewhat the way a good reference librarian would. The trouble is, only somewhat—and too often the help that a reference librarian can give is to offer advice—to act, as someone has said, as a forest ranger in the wilderness of information. If users bypass the library, they'll miss this.

These two implications—one relating to the amount of information available and its lack of authenticity, and, two, users having access to all this without the intermediation of librarians—tells me that libraries have got to change a lot. Now, that change, that transition, won't necessarily come tomorrow.

For a while—ten to fifteen years, probably—library users will still mostly depend on traditional materials—books and periodicals. And some materials probably will always be available in paper format—fine printing, poetry perhaps, other works valued for their artistic merit. But as more and more items are put in electronic form, and as users in fifteen years (today's pre-schoolers, let's say) who are even now comfortable with using computers, have computers that are simple to use, users will more and more prefer getting information in electronic form.

My own experience with undergraduates tells me that some of them will always need reference librarians to serve not as "information navigators"—or not *just* as "information navigators"—but as persons who can provide the helpful advice that can only be conveyed by reassuring, understanding, perhaps sympathetic words, an attitude that demands eye contact, personal presence.

So libraries will, in a sense, be living in two worlds. Not only because of the time it would take to digitize all the materials now in libraries, but also because some of that material—perhaps much of it—is better used in traditional paper and print form—that is, in books. As one writer put it [Sven Birkirts in *The Gutenberg Elegies: The Fate of Reading in an Electronic Age* (Boston: Faber and Faber, 1994), p. 196], "using computers, all the tapping of keys and monitoring of monitors cannot slake some irrational deeper wanting...literature remains the unexcelled means of interior exploration and connection-making...." What he's saying, I think, is that there's something almost spiritual in the use of printed matter—at least some printed matter—which is lost even if the same material is used through a computer.

So libraries will have to straddle the centuries. Can they do it without becoming schizoid? I think so...

There's a classic work in anthropology—*Ishi in Two Worlds* [by Theodora Kroeber, University of California Press, 1976]—the story of an American Indian who actually had to live in two cultures. He was a member of the Yahi tribe, a tribe that, in order to survive, had remained concealed from civilization. Ishi was brought from this utterly primitive existence in the California hills to San Francisco, and much of the book is devoted to how he coped. It wasn't easy, but he managed. It wasn't easy especially because the change was so sudden. But he had courage, and character, and a sense of self, a sense of self derived from and based on his traditions. Compared to Ishi, librarians have it easy. Our transition is a relatively gradual one. Sure, there are problems, even unforeseen ones, and they will require new approaches, new ways of thinking. And that's not easy, especially for a profession whose practices are based on precedent and tradition.

As I said, Ishi's ability to cope was based on his sense of self. The librarian's counterpart should be our mission, our sense of service, our role in enhancing the teaching/learning process. Perhaps I should give my talk the title, "Keep your hand upon the throttle and your eye upon the rail," the rail in this case being our educational role, the throttle being our means of fulfilling that role.

189

I could even use Quaker terminology. The silent period that begins most Quaker meetings serves as a time to "center down." What that means is for those in the meeting to erase from their minds the everyday matters, and to focus on what Thomas Kelly termed the divine Center—"a divine Abyss within us all, a holy infinite Center, a Heart, a Life who speaks in us and through us to the world." I don't think I'm being sacrilegious if I make the analogy with what librarians do— because I feel that if it's practiced as it ought to be, it approaches the spiritual. In this context, if we focus on our educational mission as our Center, and keep in mind as we do our work, as we make our policies and decisions, librarians will come through the transition stronger, more secure than ever. And the college library will retain, even enhance its role in the undergraduate educational experience—so that our students can cope in the new electronic environment more comfortably and more effectively.

26

Technological Idolatry and the Reference Librarian
(1998)

Larry Oberg, who was Librarian of Willamette University until his retirement a few years ago, and was a good friend of mine for many years, issued Moveable Type, *a very attractive and readable quarterly combining his library's newsletter with essays relating to the world of print or to developments in information technology. When I told him how much I admired and enjoyed the publication, he asked me to write something for it. The piece below was my response.*

What provoked the piece was the confluence of two annoyances, each of which had bothered me for a long time: the reluctance of many reference librarians (even in my own library) to be proactive in helping students, and the assumption that students, and others, are using the library's automated system effectively simply because they are merrily clicking away at the keyboard.
— Evan Ira Farber, 2006

I don't know if Theodore Roszak originated the term "technological idolatry," that handy label for the tendency to love machines or, rather, to love what machines can do. The term appears in *The Cult of Information*, in which he warns readers about the computer's peculiar power to spellbind its users.[1] Roszak, a distinguished historian, was seeing too many students who not only regarded the computer as the single key for unlocking the universe of information, but who also felt that if it comes from the computer, it's got to be true. Every reference librarian recognizes this attitude and most of us try to counter it.

Roszak's observations are persuasive. Recently, while looking through the book, a question occurred to me: isn't the enthusiastic adoption of technology by academic librarians dangerously close to the troubling manifestation of technological idolatry? Troubling, I say, because that enthusiasm may be causing librarians, quite inadvertently,

---

[1] Theodore Roszak, *The Cult of Information: A Neo-Luddite Treatise on High-Tech, Artificial Intelligence, and the True Art of Thinking* (New York: Pantheon Books, 1986). A slightly revised edition was published by the University of California Press in 1994.

Farber, Evan Ira, "Technological Idolatry and the Reference Librarian," *Moveable Type*, Volume 5, Number 2 (Spring 1998). http://library.willamette.edu/publications/movtyp/spring98/evan.htm

to pay less attention to their primary mission, that of enhancing the education of their students.

A recent article suggests that a reference librarian who roves around the reference area, rather than sitting at the reference desk, increases the number of reference encounters and produces more sophisticated and more thorough reference service.[2] When reference librarians used to see students at the card catalog, flipping through card after card, going from one tray to another, they knew those students needed help. Is using an online catalog that much simpler? Whenever I approached students (or even faculty members) at a catalog terminal, looked over their shoulders and saw that they were going from screen to screen, apparently in no systematic sequence, I asked if they were finding what they needed. Their replies invariably indicated that they weren't taking advantage of the system's versatility or helpfulness.

Why should we assume that simply because users are seated at a terminal, clicking away on keyboards, they're finding what they want or need, or even asking the right questions? Do we assume that the software is so perceptive, so sophisticated, that it can replace even a brief reference interview? If we think along those lines, if we let the machines do what we were trained to do, haven't we also been seduced by technological idolatry?

I see another problem: reference librarians, rather than watching out for students who may need help, spend much of their time focusing on the terminal on their desks. They read e-mail and consult other reference librarians around the country on all sorts of matters. These are often discussions that could improve the library's services. But isn't there a cost? Most students who might ask for assistance are hardly going to interrupt librarians who are focused on the screens in front of them. So we miss opportunities for individual instruction, the most productive kind of education.

What can we do? In the short run, we can be more skeptical of the efficacy of online searching and emphasize the limitations of electronic sources in our instruction. In the long run, as more and more students come to do online searching from outside the library, we can incorporate automated instruction into our technology, thereby helping to ensure that students will search systematically and critically. If we are to confront the mindset of technological idolatry we must, in a sense, fight fire with fire.

But, even if some group develops the ideal automated program for teaching information skills, there's one step I would insist be

---

[2] Eileen H. Kramer, "Why Roving Reference: A Case Study in a Small Academic Library," *Reference Services Review* 24 (Fall, 1996): 67-80.

included: At some point during the search process, the student must talk with a reference librarian. No matter how effective automated instruction becomes, there's no substitute for a reference librarian who can help a student shape a topic, suggest an unusual source and offer an encouraging word. That role is extremely important; let's be sure to keep it in mind.

27

Faculty-Librarian Cooperation: A Personal Retrospective (1999)

The issue of Reference Services Review *in which this piece appeared contained the papers given at the LOEX 25th anniversary conference. This was the second paper I'd given at a LOEX conference, and both focused on working with faculty. The earlier paper was given in 1976 so one could reasonably assume that in the intervening 23 years I learned a lot about BI programs other than our own and, indeed, that our own program changed a lot. Of course I learned a lot, and that learning— from visits, from reading, and from personal contacts—served to modify and to improve many aspects of our instruction program. But there was one constant: whereas years ago I claimed that course-related instruction was the most desirable approach for attaining a successful program—a claim that some librarians disputed—I came to believe that it really was the* only *approach to use, and just about everything else I had to say about BI, then or later, rested on that belief.*

— Evan Ira Farber, 2006

Introduction

Over the last several decades, many librarians who have taken part in course-related bibliographic instruction have written and spoken about a problem that every one of them has encountered—the problem of cooperation with teaching faculty. The large number of articles in periodicals, plus chapters in books, and presentations to conferences that dealt with the problem all attest to the problem's prevalence, persistence and importance. Whatever their format, these statements have almost always been based on first-hand experience, experience gained as the authors or speakers had tried to implement or to improve a program of bibliographic instruction.

History of the problem

Given the fact that for at least a century a number of college librarians had either provided or attempted to provide instruction in use of their libraries, one might have expected that the problem would have been discussed some time ago. But that does not seem to have been the case. For example, Harvie Branscomb and Louis Shores, both of whom

Farber, Evan, "Faculty-Librarian Cooperation: A Personal Retrospective," *Reference Services Review*, Volume 27, Number 3 (1999), pages 229-234.

wrote what are now generally considered classics in the history of bibliographic instruction, did not even consider the problem. Of course, neither had first-hand experience with trying to implement a program and both of them wrote long before the bibliographic instruction movement really got underway. Harvie Branscomb's *Teaching with Books: A Study of College Libraries*, provided a convincing rationale for college librarians who were interested in making their libraries more effective participants in undergraduate education. His premise, based on a survey of some 60 colleges that in particular examined students' use of their libraries, was that the libraries were sadly underused. He suggested a number of ways to correct the situation, most of them involving a more active role for college librarians. He also clearly saw the need for students to become more proficient in using the library, but he felt the teaching faculty was the appropriate vehicle, with the librarians playing a helpful but subordinate role. "The point which should be guarded against is the library taking over all responsibility for library instruction".[1] One can hardly fault Branscomb for that attitude. Although at the time of the survey he was a university library director, he was primarily a scholar and teacher, and immersed in that "faculty culture" that Larry Hardesty so trenchantly described and analyzed in his article, "Faculty Culture and Bibliographic Instruction: An Exploratory Analysis".[2] Because Branscomb's views were, in a sense, restricted by his own academic role and status, he could not foresee the resistance by teaching faculty to innovations such as bibliographic instruction.

Library college movement

If one considers the range of cooperative working relationships between teaching faculty and librarians as a spectrum, surely at one end of that spectrum is Louis Shores' Library College Movement, which envisioned all courses being taught in the library by "library-trained, subject matter experts." Shores' views, published from the 1930s into the 1950s, attracted a number of librarians initially; as a matter of fact, I was one of those idealists intrigued by his views, but along with many others I soon recognized the limitation of that idealism, the practical impossibility of sustaining those views in a real academic setting. It may be an oversimplification of their ideas, but not, I trust, a distortion of them, to say that Branscomb thought of librarians almost as handmaidens of the teaching faculty while Shores saw the two roles melded into one.

---

[1] H. Branscomb, *Teaching with Books: A Study of College Libraries* (Chicago: American Library Association, 1940) 208.
[2] L. Hardesty, "Faculty Culture and Bibliographic Instruction: An Exploratory Analysis," *Library Trends*, Vol. 44 No. 2, pp. 339-67.

There must be—I know there are—many other possible relationships, but it seemed to me many years ago and still seems to me that the most sensible, most practical relationship is a cooperative one, in which teaching faculty work with librarians.

Educating the library user

Less than a decade after the interest in the Library-College Movement had subsided, John Lubans' landmark book, *Educating the Library User*, was published.[3] It was a substantial work, containing 38 contributions by librarians from academic school and public libraries discussing and describing their approaches to and programs of user education. My contribution to that collection was a description and rationale for our program of course-related bibliographic instruction at Earlham. At one point, while discussing the role of librarians as instructors, I offered some of my reasons why our program did not accept the conclusions of either Branscomb or Shores: teaching faculty are discouraged from giving library instruction or even from preparing explanatory materials for assignments that entail bibliographic tools, without consulting with librarians. While the teaching faculty have the central responsibility for the educational enterprise, librarians can help them carry out that responsibility much more effectively and at the same time enhance it. While the two groups—teaching faculty and librarians—can and should work together, neither can do the other's job.[4]

All instruction librarians will recognize that there's a major gap between the "should work together" and the reality of most institutional situations. That gap, of course, is the crux of the problem. Certainly I recognized the problem, but felt this way: one must come to the conclusion (regretfully, perhaps) that only by working through the courses, and that means through individual faculty members, can the objectives of library instruction presently be achieved. Working with faculty, then, becomes a given.[5]

Monteith Library experiment

That was hardly an original position. In 1966 Patricia Knapp's *The Monteith College Library Experiment* was published. It certainly was—and perhaps still is—one of the most important and influential works in the development of library instruction. The book described a

---

[3] J. Lubans, *Educating the Library User* (New York: R.R. Bowker, 1974).
[4] E. I. Farber, "Library Instruction Throughout the Curriculum: Earlham College Program," in Lubans, J. (Ed.), *Educating the Library User* (New York: R.R. Bowker, 1974) 145-62. P. 157.
[5] Ibid, p. 160.

research project that was concerned with "exploring methods of developing a more vital relationship between the library and college teaching".[6] The project, implemented in 1960-1962, was based on the conviction that the key to library instruction was in the structure of the relationship between librarians and faculty. In an earlier article, Knapp had clearly spelled out the importance of involving the teaching faculty: instruction in the use of the library will be really effective only if it is presented by the regular teaching faculty as an integral part of content courses in all subject fields. The cooperative efforts of most of the faculty must be enlisted in working through the processes involved, and the whole faculty must be committed to the fundamental value of the project.[7] And a few pages later she commented that "the librarian must convince the faculty that library instruction is necessary; he must educate the faculty on the potential role of the library and assist it in planning instruction"[8] She then went on to suggest steps that should help implement that effort.

As intelligent and logical as Knapp's approach was, and although she occasionally seemed to recognize that most teaching faculty were fairly traditional and conservative in their teaching, I always wondered why she did not recognize two factors: one, how readily the attitudes behind their practices can translate into resistance, resistance not only to a librarian's overtures but to almost any educational innovation;[9] and two, that such resistance was easily overcome in the Monteith experiment because it was an experiment and had the full support of the college's administration. It is perhaps unfair to fault her because it is only with a good bit of experience and a number of frustrating encounters in that experience that one can see how prevalent that resistance is. But I digress.

Educational worth of course-related instruction
If at one time I advocated course-related instruction "regretfully," as I noted earlier, after several years more experience with

---

[6] P. B. Knapp, *The Monteith College Library Experiment* (New York: Scarecrow Press, 1966) 11.
[7] P. B. Knapp, "A Suggested Program of College Instruction in the Use of the Library," *Library Quarterly*, Vol. 26 No. 3, pp. 224-31. P. 226.
[8] Ibid, pp. 230-231.
[9] C. Kazlow, "Faculty receptivity to Organizational Change: A Test of Two Explanations of Resistance to Innovation in Higher Education," *Journal of Research and Development in Education*, Vol. 10 No. 2, pp. 87-98. See also, R. I. Evans, *Resistance to Innovation in Higher Education: A Social Psychological Exploration Focused on Television and the Establishment* (San Francisco: Jossey-Bass, 1968).

our program, and with many opportunities to hear about and observe other approaches, I realized that even from an educational perspective course-related instruction was the most effective one. And so I became even more convinced that cooperation between librarians and classroom teachers was a necessity. That conviction meant that the other Earlham librarians and I worked continually and energetically with a wide variety of teaching faculty—a wide variety of personalities, of disciplines, of teaching styles.

At the same time we saw that many other academic librarians agreed on the advantages of course-related instruction and, because the cooperative relationship that undergirded that approach worked so well at Earlham, we began offering workshops on our program, initially on our campus, and subsequently around the country. The most effective ingredient of those workshops was the series of presentations by the teaching faculty who described how and why they worked with librarians in particular courses, in many cases in both planning assignments and providing the instruction.[10]

Earlham's impact

My increasing optimism about the possibilities of cooperation with the teaching faculty was due, I am sure, to a number of factors. First was the continuing growth and improvement of our own program where we saw even closer and more creative working relationships develop between instruction librarians and faculty. Second was the increasing interest shown by others in our program in a wide variety of institutions, some of which I had written off long ago as unsuited because of the size or other institutional characteristics, or simply as shortsighted, or even more often, as smug. Third was the striking growth of the bibliographic instruction movement, a growth accompanied by an intellectual ferment and proliferation of activities that had to make anyone who participated in the movement excited about its present and confident about its future.

That optimism was tempered by the realization that, as I wrote in 1985, "if the library is to take an active role in the teaching-learning process faculty cooperation and support are essential. That cooperation and support have not been forthcoming very often."[11] And certainly not as often as I would have liked. One reason was that, in the words of one

---

[10] L. Hardesty, J. Hastreiter, and D. Henderson (Eds), *Bibliographic Instruction in Practice: A Tribute to the Legacy of Evan Ira Farber* (Ann Arbor: Pierian Press, 1993).

[11] E. I. Farber, "The Library in Undergraduate Education," prepared for the Carnegie Foundation for the Advancement of Teaching. P. 66.

college president, "Academic faculty are, for the most part, not predisposed as scholars to recognize and to acknowledge a legitimate educational role for the library and for librarians"[12] On the other hand, my optimism resurfaced in that same paper's last section, "Conclusion: problems and prospects":

> Faculty attitudes are changing and will change even more. Certainly a factor will be the improving quality of librarians. Also, the impetus of the bibliographic instruction movement will make it a part of most college teachers' stock in trade, and they will be working more closely with librarians in constructive ways. The new library technology should change attitudes in several ways. A study of faculty perceptions showed that, for newer faculty, their most negative feelings about the library resulted from "their perception of adequacy of the collection in their areas." When technology permits access to so much material, the cause for that negative attitude should disappear. In addition, faculty will increasingly recognize the importance of instruction by librarians to help them find and evaluate all the material available to them and their students.[13]

Impact of electronic resources

I was rather prescient in that prediction, I think, and ten years later, when the potential of the new information technology had become obvious, I was able to write that:

> In the past, one obstacle bibliographic instruction librarians faced was that so many faculty taught just as they were taught. Now, however, faculty recognize that their teaching toolkit must include the Internet, or Dialog, or whatever electronic resources are appropriate for their courses. Because librarians are the ones to show their students how to gain access to those sources and to demonstrate what they provide,

---

[12] Ibid, pp. 68-69.
[13] Ibid, p. 71.

> faculty members are much more willing to
> accept librarians as teaching colleagues—not
> fully accepted in all cases, but at least as
> colleagues to teach and work with.[14]

No amount of prescience, however, could have anticipated the Internet, and certainly not the amount and variety of data available on it, ranging from absolutely useless, even at times dangerous information, to newsworthy, helpful, and important material. On the one hand the Internet's availability, ease of access, and immediate response make its use very tempting for students, most of whom are primarily interested in convenience and in saving time; on the other hand, its anarchy and absence of structure make its use a problem for even the sophisticated user. Teachers used to have some control over the sources their students used—reading lists, reserves, the library's collection—but the allure of instant information on the Internet has changed all that. The major problem with this changed situation is, of course, that most students are unable to discriminate.

Yet that is nothing new; in the pre-electronic era, students typically thought that if they found any books or articles on their topics in the library, they were worth using. It was difficult enough to teach them that not everything in print was valid, and that there are criteria, intellectual filters one can use to separate the wheat from the chaff, the scholarly from the spurious. With the Internet, however, because it is so volatile in so many dimensions, teaching students how to use it intelligently is a formidable task—and some would say, impossible, just now. But there is no question that in time (and I think in just a few years) it will become less volatile, more structured, and as it does there will be ways of determining criteria for the evaluation of sources. The teaching faculty is increasingly aware of the educational challenge the Internet poses, and also aware that they do not have the time or expertise to keep up with the continual changes and improvements. They know that while they can provide some guidance in helping students find and evaluate information, they'll have to depend on librarians to really do the job. This attitude was nicely expressed by James Wilkinson, director of Harvard's Derek Bok Center for Teaching and Learning:

> [T]he ordering of information on the Internet
> or in keyword search does not allow the user to
> discriminate between what is more or less

---

[14] E. I. Farber, "Plus ça change?," *Library Trends*, Vol. 44 No. 2, pp. 430-38. P. 432.

important. The information superhighway, in other words, provides too much information and too little organization. Who will perform the complex triage that separates what the researcher needs to know from the mass of second- or third order information? Some traffic-watchers on the information superhighway have argued that programmable "agents'" (that is, electronic instructions) can do this work for us. But I think that a far better human agent is at hand—reference librarians.[15]

Ideal cooperative relationship

When that cooperative relationship works well, it can result in assignments that approach, if not reach, what I consider the ideal: where both the teacher's objectives and the librarian's objectives are not only achieved, but are mutually reinforcing—the teacher's objectives being those that help students attain a better understanding of the course's subject matter, and the librarian's objectives being those that enhance the students' ability to find and evaluate information.

Where will instruction librarians find the time? The one-shot, one-class period of library instruction has always been hard enough to get, yet once gotten rarely seemed enough to provide as much instruction as one felt appropriate.

But now, with teaching the variety of databases within the library or available online, added to all the basic instruction, 50 minutes is hardly adequate. The required time, I think, will become available because basic instruction, which now takes up so much of a librarian's time, will be taken care of by expert systems built into many databases. These systems will guide users, help them select the appropriate databases, instruct them in using the database, then help in selecting items from the databases.

A precursor of these systems is Ohio State University's The Gateway to Information.[16] But as effective as it is, it is still relatively primitive, only a beginning to a very sophisticated technological development.

---

[15] J. Wilkinson, "Homesteading On the Electronic Frontier: Technology, Libraries, and Learning," in L. Dowler (Ed.), *Gateways to Knowledge: The Role of Academic Libraries in Teaching, Learning and Research* (Cambridge, MA: MIT Press, 1997) 186-7. Pp. 186-187.

[16] Virginia M. Tiefel, "Library User Education: Examining Its Past, Projecting Its Future", *Library Trends*, Vol. 44 No. 2, pp. 318-337.

The future

That time is some years away. Until then, instruction librarians will continue working with faculty, constantly improving instructional approaches and procedures. Expert systems, after all, are only as good as the expert opinions and practices on which the systems are based. But even when expert systems become a standard, perhaps even a major component of library instruction, there will still be a role for instruction that is tailored to a unique or experimental assignment. As long as the separate course is the keystone of higher education, and as long as students need new information for fulfilling assignments in those separate courses, cooperation between faculty and instruction librarians will still be an important factor.

28

College Libraries and the Teaching/Learning Process:
A 25-Year Reflection
(1999)

This article was first published in the May, 1999 issue of the Journal of
Academic Librarianship. *I don't remember exactly the genesis of the article's
publication, but I think I was asked by members of the Journal's Board to write
something appropriate for its 25th anniversary. Again, I'm not sure how I chose
this particular topic but in retrospect it was an obvious choice perfectly suited to
my special concern—the library's role in the teaching/learning process—and,
indeed, a topic various aspects of which I'd written and spoken about many
times. However, while among those many articles and talks I had touched upon
particular developments in BI, I had not really used as a framework a broad
historical perspective and this seemed to have been a perfect opportunity to do
that. Perhaps just as important, it seems to me now, was the fact that when I
thought about writing this article I'd been retired for four or five years, and it
didn't make sense to me to speak from the same platform as I had as a
practicing librarian, a role I had played for twenty-five or thirty years. The
works of elder statesmen, as I thought of myself, usually took advantage of their
authors' experiences rather than trying to keep up with contemporaneous
developments. Besides, since I really hadn't kept up with those developments,
using an historical approach was safer. In any case, I think the article stands
up well.*

*There is an ironic footnote to all this. In the same issue of the JAL the
editor commented on the recent sale of the journal to a commercial publisher
and regretted the consequent protest and resignation of a number of JAL's
editorial board. Among those who resigned were several librarians I'd known
for a long time, and who may well have been responsible for asking me for the
article. Whether members of the new editorial board, most of whom I did not
know, would have approached me I'll never know, but I suspect not.*

— Evan Ira Farber, 2006

Twenty-five years? For some librarians—this one, for
example—1975 does not seem like such a long time ago, but when
considering the ways libraries operated and the issues librarians were
discussing then, the difference between then and now is striking. For
many librarians in the early 1970s microforms still seemed to be on the
cutting edge of technology. OCLC, or as it was known then, the Ohio

Farber, Evan, "College Libraries and the Teaching/Learning Process: A 25-Year
Reflection," *The Journal of Academic Librarianship*, Volume 25,
Number 3 (May 1999), pages 171-177.

College Library Center, had only recently agreed to extend its services beyond the borders of Ohio; though it was still relatively unfamiliar to many librarians there was a beginning recognition in the profession that OCLC's primary use was not for catalog card production, but for a variety of other library functions. Some librarians even had begun to think that the traditional card catalog might not be with us very much longer. One could go on and on recalling the limited views and practices of the early 1970s, a time just before discussions about the use of computers in libraries began to occupy many conferences and workshops, as well as so much of the content of professional publications. Those discussions soon led to many changes, and the contrast between librarianship 25 years ago and librarianship today is almost inconceivable.

Of course, college libraries were affected by those same changes, but any returning class of 1973 had little trouble in recognizing the library when its members returned for their 25th reunion in 1998. Sure, the card catalog was gone, and there were clusters of terminals and printers in its place and perhaps elsewhere around the building, but there was still the familiar circulation counter, the clearly visible reference librarian's desk, the display of current periodicals and recent book acquisitions, the scattering of study carrels through the stacks, and overall, one hoped, an atmosphere conducive to study and reflection. What had really changed was not visible: the services provided by the library, the resources available through it, and the means by which those services and resources were acquired and distributed. Though invisible to the uninitiated observer, they had made an enormous difference in the ways the library worked and in the services and resources provided to students and faculty. Has there been a comparable change in the educational role of the library over the last quarter-century?

Just about 25 years ago I wrote a couple of essays commenting on the present state of college libraries; in both I lamented the lack of their contributions to their institutions' educational programs. This lack seemed to me especially deplorable since college libraries had such advantages: a manageable size "that should permit a focus on the kind and level of materials they acquire and distribute, and the relative clarity of institutional goals [that] should point out more or less precisely the services they perform..."[1] The college library "has, so to speak, a captive clientele...With that clientele the library can establish as intimate, as helpful, and as educational a relationship as its imagination, energy, and

---

[1] Evan Ira Farber, "College Libraries and the University-Library Syndrome," in *The Academic Library: Essays in Honor of Guy R. Lyle*, edited by Evan Ira Farber and Ruth Walling (Metuchen, NJ: The Scarecrow Press, 1974) 15.

desire allow."[2] And yet, I concluded, "is there any knowledgeable observer who can say that college libraries are really doing the job they should?"[3] It was, of course, a rhetorical question, but why were they not?

They *should* have been more effective. After all, many college librarians had been giving instruction in the use of the library for over a century. In an 1880 government publication, "College Libraries as Aids to Instruction," Justin Winsor, the Harvard Librarian, had written that the college librarian should become "a teacher, not that mock substitute who is recited to; a teacher, not with a text book, but with a world of books,"[4] and that was not a unique position. Indeed, librarians at many institutions offered courses or lectures on the use of libraries—a Bureau of Education survey in 1914 found that about a fifth of the 446 colleges and universities provided instruction in use of the library.[5] But such instruction was, for the most part, very basic and could hardly be regarded as playing a role of any significance in a student's education. The situation did not change much over the next several decades. A survey of the instructional programs of 157 college libraries taken in 1965 indicated that, while most were offering some form of instruction, there was little enthusiasm for any particular approach, that not nearly enough was being done, and that faculty cooperation was minimal.[6] There were probably a number of reasons for this lack of progress, especially the traditional resistance by academicians to change, but certainly another—resulting from the rapid expansion and growing dominance of university librarianship in the profession after 1900 and especially in the 1920s—was the emphasis on activities that supported graduate and faculty research rather than on those relating to undergraduate education. The educational role of the college library, consequently, remained a supportive, mainly passive one, devoted to getting materials quickly, making them accessible with efficiency, and being available to answer reference questions—at least until the 1960s.

The late 1960s and early 1970s was a socially turbulent period, marked by a variety of social and political movements. Most of them

---

[2] Evan Ira Farber, "Limiting College Library Growth: Bane or Boon?" in *Farewell to Alexandria: Solutions to Space, Growth and Performance Problems of Libraries*, edited by Daniel Gore (Westport, CT: Greenwood Press, 1976) 41.
[3] Evan Ira Farber, "College Libraries and...," p. 15.
[4] *Circulars of Information of the Bureau of Education; No. 1-880* (Washington: U.S. Government Printing Office, 1880) 7.
[5] Henry R. Evans, compiler, "Library Instruction in Universities, Colleges, and Normal Schools," *U.S. Bureau of Education Bulletin no. 34* (1914), p. 3a.
[6] Barbara H. Phipps, "Library Instruction for the Undergraduate," *College & Research Libraries* 29 (September, 1968): 411-423.

expressed a disaffection with one or another area or aspect of American society, calling for change, often radical or immediate change, and higher education was hardly exempt from those feelings. In 1970, Algo Henderson, the founder and director of the University of Michigan's Center for the Study of Higher Education and former president of Antioch College, made a typical call for change: "The colleges and universities have tended to be defensive about their programs and policies rather than open to ideas for change. The times require change. The solutions to problems must be found in action, even if it involves departures from tradition."[7] Similar calls for change, but especially the many educational reforms proposed or actually being tried at colleges and universities around the country, led to the creation of the Carnegie Commission on Higher Education, an exceptionally prestigious body. During the six years of its existence, from 1967 to 1973, the Commission made perhaps the most comprehensive study ever of American higher education. The results of its study appeared in 21 volumes published between 1969 and 1973; the Commission also issued another 80 or so reports by experts on a variety of special topics related to higher education. One might have expected some attention to the role of the library (so frequently referred to by college and university officials as "the heart of the institution") in those thousands of pages, but, as far as I could find, it was discussed in only one volume, and then in just one paragraph. That paragraph acknowledged that while college libraries are usually looked upon as rather passive centers on campus, they "can, and in some places do, play a more active role," and ended with the recommendation that *"The library should become a more active participant in the instructional process with an added proportion of funds, perhaps as much as a doubling."*[8]

What led the Commission to make that recommendation can only be speculated upon. It may have observed the stirrings in academic librarianship, or felt there must be some change, or been influenced by the development of the CLR-NEH College Library Program, a program of the Council on Library Resources. In 1969, the Council, with the cooperation of the National Endowment for the Humanities (NEH), gave grants to 36 institutions to "explore innovative ways of enhancing the library's participation in the education process..." An article reporting the results of the program noted that a team of evaluators, at a minimum, had learned "that the joint program focused the attention of the college

---

[7] *The Innovative Spirit: Changes in Higher Education* (San Francisco: Jossey-Bass, 1970) 301.

[8] *Reform on Campus: Changing Students, Changing Academic Programs* (New York: McGraw Hill, 1972) 50. (Emphasis in the original).

and university administration on the importance of the library in the total teaching effort."[9] It may have gotten the attention of some faculty and administrators, but not of most.

In the early 1980s William Moffett, the Oberlin College Librarian, surveyed a large number of academic librarians as to "what they expect of faculty and administrators and vice versa." The results were not encouraging. A typical comment was that "The library's presence is accepted as a given, but it is not seen as a vital resource for the intellectual endeavors of the institution."[10] In a talk to academic librarians, Gresham Riley, President of Colorado College, was not any more encouraging. He commented that "faculty are, for the most part, not predisposed as scholars to recognize and to acknowledge a legitimate educational role for the library and for librarians...[They are] likely to be influenced by the local conditions which prevail at their college or university (in particular, the attitude of key administrators as to the role of the library)."[11]

The literature of higher education of the period reflected that same obliviousness to the library's potential. If one samples the spate of books on the changes and reforms in higher education in the 1960s and 1970s, one looks in vain for any discussion on the educational role of the library. A case in point: in 1981, Arthur W. Chickering and Associates, a group noted for their innovative views of higher education, came out with *The Modern American College: Responding to the New Realities of Diverse Students and a Changing Society*.[12] In over 700 pages the 42 chapters in the book treated just about every aspect of college teaching and learning, yet there is not one mention of the library. For a librarian who was devoted to making the college library an integral component of undergraduate education, the continuing lack of interest in the library's educational role by the higher education establishment was somewhat discouraging. It was very little comfort to remember what C. P. Snow

---

[9] Nancy E. Gwinn, "Academic Libraries and Undergraduate Education: The CLR Experience," *College & Research Libraries* 41 (January, 1980): 11.

[10] Moffett, "What the Academic Librarian Wants from Administrators and Faculty," in *Priorities for Academic Libraries*, edited by Thomas J. Galvin & Beverly Lynch (New Directions for Higher Education, no. 39, September, 1982) 15.

[11] Gresham Riley, "The College Viewpoint," in *Academic Libraries: Myths and Realities: Proceedings of the Third National Conference of the Association of College and Research Libraries, April 4-7, 1984, Seattle, Washington* (Chicago: Association of College and Research Libraries, 1984) 12, 13.

[12] Arthur W. Chickering & Associates, *The Modern American College: Responding to the New Realities of Diverse Students and a Changing Society* (San Francisco: Jossey-Bass, 1981).

was supposed to have said about the British resistance to changes in higher education: "I once thought it was easier to start a revolution than to change the examination system of Oxford or Cambridge. I now think I was too optimistic."

Academic librarians, however, had seen the need for an increased instructional role on campus and during the 1970s the bibliographic instruction movement had made considerable progress. Whatever the reasons—perhaps a new generation of reference librarians and library administrators, or perhaps a by-product of the experimentation and innovation in higher education generally—the movement had taken off. Whereas the annual number of articles on the subject averaged 35 between 1958 and 1971, in 1974 *Library Literature* listed more than 70. A number of organizational developments also reflected the increase in interest and practice: among others, the CLR-NEH programs which started in 1969, the establishment of LOEX in 1972, and, in 1973, the formation of both the Library Instruction Round Table and the Bibliographic Instruction Section of the Association of College and Research Libraries (ACRL).

The June, 1984, issue of the quarterly series, *New Directions for Teaching and Learning* was devoted to "Increasing the Teaching Role of Academic Libraries." That is some indication of the movement's success, because the series has always focused on higher education, and this was the first time the library was featured. In his introduction to the issue, Tom Kirk, then the Librarian of Berea College, noted that the "professional focus of academic librarians has shifted from a passive and, at best, responsive role to an active involvement in the educational program of the institution." He then listed a few of the forces that had led to this shift, especially the tremendous increase in the amount of accessible information, the new technology to help retrieve information, and the changes in educational practices and policies...[13]

About the same time, in the summer of 1984, I had read in *The Chronicle of Higher Education* that the Carnegie Foundation for the Advancement of Teaching was planning a "comprehensive study" of undergraduate education. "There is an urgent need to bring colleges and universities more directly into the debate about the purposes and goals of education, said Ernest I. Boyer, the Foundation's president."[14] The remainder of the article touched on several reasons for the study which was to be published by Harper & Row in 1986, but none of the reasons,

---

[13] Thomas G. Kirk, "Editor's Notes," *Increasing the Teaching Role of Academic Libraries* ("New Directions for Teaching and Learning," Number 18, June, 1984) p. 1.

[14] *The Chronicle of Higher Education* (August 8, 1984), p. 3.

of course, related to the library. Since I knew Ernest Boyer (he had served briefly as a member of the college's Board of Trustees) I wrote him saying that I hoped some attention would be given in the study to the role of the college library. I got a prompt response asking if I would be willing to do a background paper on the subject for the study. Willing? I leapt at the opportunity and the following March sent him an 85-page paper, "The Library in Undergraduate Education."

The Introduction noted that, while I thought I could be objective in writing about the role of the undergraduate library "I know I'm not disinterested...I believe that the extent of that role can make a real difference in the quality of undergraduate education...Moreover, because college libraries will be changing so much in the coming decades, it is especially important to look at what they've been doing and what they should be doing."[15] The paper treated three developments that at the time seemed to me were having a significant effect on the role of the library: the financial retrenchment that so many colleges were facing, the impact of technology, and instruction in use of the library. "Those three developments have come together in the last ten or fifteen years, and the combined impact will be increasingly evident."[16] As one might guess, I gave most attention to the development and importance of bibliographic instruction.

College: The Undergraduate Experience was published two years later.[17] Though the role of the library and librarians only got seven or so pages, some of the comments in those pages that related to that role were notable:

> The college library must be viewed as a vital
> part of the undergraduate experience...The
> library staff should be considered as important to
> teaching as are classroom teachers. Since the
> library expresses the philosophy of education
> and the distinctive characteristics of the college,
> its role should be to "bring students, faculty, and
> books together in ways that would encourage
> learning, intensive scholarship, and casual
> browsing."

---

[15] Evan Ira Farber, "The Library in Undergraduate Education; Prepared for the Carnegie Foundation for the Advancement of Teaching" (unpublished paper, Earlham College, Richmond, Indiana, March, 1985), p. 1.

[16] Ibid., p. 6.

[17] Ernest L. Boyer, *College: The Undergraduate Experience in America* (New York: Harper & Row, 1987).

We further recommend that every
undergraduate student be introduced carefully to
the full range of resources for learning on
campus. Students should be given bibliographic
instruction...

For the library to become a central learning
resource on the campus, we need, above all,
liberally educated librarians, professionals who
understand and are interested in undergraduate
education, who are involved in educational
matters...[18]

Boyer's final chapter, "Epilogue: Guide to a Good College,"
included a number of questions which, "when taken together, provide for
students and their parents a guide to a good college."[19] One of those
questions was "Are those who direct the library also considered
teachers?"[20] Today those comments and that question may seem
obvious, even superfluous, but for an eminent authority on higher
education, a former university administrator, President of the Carnegie
Foundation for the Advancement of Teaching, to say that was
enormously gratifying to anyone promoting the role of librarians in the
teaching/learning process. The book was widely and favorably reviewed
in the popular press; librarians also welcomed it. Outside of the library
press, only one reviewer noted the brief discussion of the role of the
library. Frederick Weaver, a Hampshire College faculty member, called
the book "a comprehensive, knowledgeable and humane survey" and
noted that a "strong part is the report's discussion of the library and the
need to integrate the library into the curriculum through bibliographic
instruction."[21]

While Boyer's recommendations regarding the role of the library
may not have influenced college faculty and administrators as much as
librarians had hoped, other developments did, or at least had a greater
potential for so doing. One of those was the adoption by accreditation
groups of statements relating to the library, statements which may well
have been influenced by Boyer's comments. In the fall of 1989, the
Middle States Commission on Higher Education held a workshop to
discuss the recently adopted standard on bibliographic instruction.[22] As

---

[18] Ibid., pp. 164, 165.

[19] Ibid., p. 287.

[20] Ibid., p. 292.

[21] *College Teaching* 35 (Summer, 1987): 119.

[22] Marilyn Lutzker, "Bibliographic Instruction and Accreditation in Higher
Education," *College & Research Libraries* News 51 (January, 1990): 14-18.

an official step by an organization that had real clout, that standard was most significant. It stated that "the centrality of a library/learning center in the educational mission of an institution deserves more than rhetoric and must be supported by more than lip service. An active and continuous program of bibliographic instruction is essential to realize this goal."[23] To implement the standard the workshop suggested that members of evaluation teams should have "an understanding of the relationship between library use instruction and the wider educational process of the institution." And, because the standard also declared that excellence in the professional staff of the library is "measurable in part by the extent to which they are active participants in the academic enterprise, not merely custodians"[24], evaluation teams should also discuss the extent to which faculty "are committed to library research for undergraduates...as well as the extent to which they view librarians as resource people who can not only offer students instruction in library use, but also help faculty in designing research projects."[25] A few years later, Howard Simmons, then the executive director of the Commission on Higher Education of the Middle States Association of Colleges and Secondary Schools, recalled that workshop and reiterated the important role of the library. "If we are to be serious about improvement in the teaching-learning cycle...the library ought to play a pivotal role...And to make it work, librarians need to be empowered. I decided that the influence of an accrediting agency would help them do so. I saw this also as a way of improving the college curriculum."[26]

The Southern Association of Colleges and Schools' 1992 standards echoed the implementation of instruction in library use and the cooperative working relationship of librarians and teaching faculty:

> Basic library services must include an
> orientation program designed to teach new users
> how to obtain individual assistance, access to
> bibliographical information and access to
> materials...
> The library must provide students with
> opportunities to learn how to access information

Ms. Lutzker, Chief Librarian of the John Jay College of Criminal Justice, also participated in the workshop.

[23] Ibid., p. 14.

[24] Ibid., p. 17.

[25] Ibid., p. 16.

[26] Mignon Adams, "The Role of Academic Libraries in Teaching and Learning: An Interview with Middle States' Howard Simmons," *College & Research Libraries News* 53 (July/August, 1992): 442.

in a variety of formats so they can continue life-long learning.

　　Librarians must work cooperatively with the teaching faculty in assisting students to use resource materials effectively.[27]

　　One hopes that the phrase "a variety of formats" does not allude to microforms and other print-based formats, but rather implies a recognition of the uses of electronic information. In any case, because of the prestige—and clout—of an accrediting association this development was a most significant one; it surely helped focus the eyes of college and university administrators on what their libraries were doing to teach students to make more effective use of library resources. But whether or not it could change the attitudes of most faculty members toward the role of the library was another question. The "faculty culture" and its resistance to bibliographic instruction has been insightfully discussed by Larry Hardesty.[28] Though the resistance has ameliorated over the years, it still seems to be a major obstacle to enhancing the educational role of librarians. However, in the last few years what has helped to blunt that resistance, and at the same time suggested a more prominent role for librarians, has been the impact of electronic information.

　　It was a development that was predictable, certainly to anyone familiar with the social history of major technological developments. There is a maxim in that field of study that goes like this: the first stage of a major technological advance permits us to do what we did before, but better or faster, or both; the second stage permits us to use the advance to do things we had not been able to do before; in the third stage it changes the way we work, or live, or even how we think. One can readily apply these stages to the use of computers in libraries. At first, computers permitted us to do some of our standard operations—for example, keeping records, producing catalog cards, creating bibliographic lists—better or faster, or both. In the second stage we were able to use computers to permit access to databases from long distances, to automate the card catalog and let users create their own subject headings—to do many other things we could not do before but which we now take for granted. We are now in the third stage, and computers are changing just about every aspect of librarianship, with the possible

---

[27] *Manual for the Institutional Self-Study Program of the Commission on Colleges, Southern Association of Colleges and Schools.* (Atlanta: Southern Association of Colleges and Schools, 1992).

[28] Larry Hardesty, "Faculty Culture and Bibliographic Instruction: An Exploratory Analysis," *Library Trends* 44 (Fall, 1995): 339-367.

exception of archival preservation: building design, professional education, financial requirements, administrative concepts, even standard definitions. They are also helping change faculty attitudes toward the role of librarians. Should they also change our approach to library use instruction which, until recently, has been the most important factor in helping librarians play a more significant educational role?

One librarian who thinks that the practice of bibliographic instruction now demands a new model is Verlene Herrington.[29] She feels that the changes computers are making in libraries can be regarded as a paradigmatic shift, a shift so profound that "basic principles must be examined, revised, or even discarded."[30] Her new model would change the role of the instruction librarian: "Instead of focusing on teaching, instructional librarians could collaborate with systems personnel in developing user-friendly interfaces and the content for the online subject guides."[31]

No one believes more than I that there is a crying need for more helpful screens and commands, but it is hardly necessary for the instruction librarians in hundreds of academic libraries to work on that need. The basic beliefs, or "worldview" (to use Ms. Herrington's term) of instruction librarians do not need to change much, a point I made in an article a couple of years ago.[32] What instruction librarians need to do—and what many, maybe most, have been doing—is instruct students and faculty how to make more effective use of electronic information resources. That basic, and what seems to me obvious, purpose is what we did for the world of print. The resources now are different; the methods of instruction are also, but not quite as, different; our clientele, however, is very much the same, and so is the rationale for our purpose.

In my paper for the Carnegie Commission I had written that "Faculty attitudes are changing and will change even more...The new library technology should change attitudes in several ways...faculty will increasingly recognize the importance of instruction by librarians to help find and evaluate all the material available to them and their students."[33] That belief was shared by many librarians and more than a few faculty members. Timothy Heiskel, a Henry Luce Fellow at Harvard, wrote, in 1988, about the impact of electronic information on scholars and teachers

---

[29] Verlene J. Herrington, "Way Beyond BI: A Look to the Future," *Journal of Academic Librarianship* 24 (September 1988): 381-386.

[30] Ibid., p. 381.

[31] Ibid., p. 384.

[32] Evan Ira Farber, "Plus ça Change...," *Library Trends* 44 (Fall, 1995): 430-438.

[33] Evan Ira Farber, "The Library in Undergraduate Education ...," p. 71.

as well as students, all of whom will need to be instructed with reference "to the possibilities and actual techniques of electronic research:"

> [I]t is becoming clear that major new
> commitments to teaching tasks are emerging
> within the university independent of the
> traditional mechanisms of control by the
> faculty…Faculty who wish jealously to guard
> their role as teachers may find they muzzle or
> restrain the teaching role of the professional
> librarian whose expertise in these realms they
> can barely hope to match…Few faculty are even
> aware that there is a problem here; even fewer
> have helpful suggestions. *Librarians may have
> to take the initiative in this realm, as they have
> in so many other domains related to the
> information revolution.*[34]

In the many conversations I have had over the years about developing a working relationship with the teaching faculty, I often commented that it seemed to me the more prestigious the institution, the more resistance there would be to working with librarians. That inverse correlation has not always turned out to be the case, fortunately; finding the occasional exceptions to my too-facile generalization were always — somewhat perversely, perhaps — gratifying. Weiskel's statement just cited may have been one such case; another was the recent book, *Gateways to Knowledge: The Role of Academic Libraries in Teaching, Learning, and Research,*[35] a collection of papers given at a conference hosted by the Harvard College Library. In the book's Preface, Lawrence Dowler, Associate Librarian of Harvard College and editor of the volume, in commenting on the contributions, said "Most surprising is a tendency to define the library's role not as a passive agent within the university but as an active partner contributing to the educational mission of the university."[36] James Wilkinson, Director of Harvard University's Derek Bok Center for Teaching and Learning, focused on that role in his essay:

---

[34] Timothy C. Weiskel, "The Electronic Library: Changing the Character of Research," *Change* 20(6) (November/December, 1988): 43-44.
[35] *Gateways to Knowledge: The Role of Academic Libraries in Teaching, Learning, and Research*, edited by Lawrence Dowler (Cambridge, MA: The MIT Press, 1997).
[36] Lawrence Dowler, "Preface," *Gateways to Knowledge*, p. xvii.

A point of entry for libraries to aid learning through technology lies first in aiding students and faculty to maneuver onto the information superhighway… [Librarians] can offer useful filters to students and faculty in need of them…Clearly, this filtering must be done intelligently…But who better suited to the task than those who understand both the available resources and the needs of the client—the librarians?

And a few pages later:
What are libraries for? To their two traditional roles as custodians of knowledge and hosts for creative research, I would suggest that we add a third role—as locus and advocate for electronic teaching. This role will mean creating new partnerships among librarians, faculty, and students and pursuing an ongoing effort to master technologies subject to constant change.[37]

The "gateway" concept of the library, as seen in this volume of essays, is nothing really new; it serves as the point of access to other research resources, a very traditional role for an academic library. What is new is the emphasis on using electronic technology, and how that changes so much of what the library does and how it does it. And what is especially important is the recognition of the role of the librarians in this new environment.

What has happened, it seems to me, is that the recognition of the educational role of librarians now is a result of the convergence of two developments: one, the widespread success of bibliographic instruction; and two, the impact of electronic sources of information. The first development got librarians recognized by faculty as colleagues who permitted their students to make more effective use of the library, and thus to do better work, more satisfying for the teacher; the second, the new world of electronic information, has made faculty and administrators aware that they, as well as their students, need assistance in sorting through the myriad of available databases so that faculty members can use them in their teaching and research.

---

[37] James Wilkinson, "Homesteading on the Electronic Frontier: Technology, Libraries, and Learning," in *Gateways to Knowledge*…, pp. 191-192, 195.

The first development can be quickly illustrated by the
difference in the language of advertisements for reference librarians
between, say, 1970 and 1990. In the earlier period it was rare to find a
phrase that asked applicants to give instruction. Twenty years later it
was almost as rare to find an ad for a reference librarian that did not
mention user or bibliographic instruction, or some other phrase alluding
to that activity. In the last few years the user instruction responsibility
has been supplemented—not replaced—with technological duties, and a
concomitant role in the educational process. A recent ad for a
Reference/Instruction Librarian is a perfect example of this convergence:

> Library faculty members are active
> participants in the overall instructional mission
> of the college, participating in curriculum
> development, direct instruction, outcomes
> assessment, and other teaching endeavors.

And then, under Required Qualifications:

> Experience in library instruction.
> Experience integrating technology with
> reference and instruction.[38]

Another ad, seeking a Reference Team
Coordinator:

> ...responsibilities include proactive
> reference service in an automated environment,
> innovative library instruction, development of
> active working relationship with faculty...The
> successful candidate will have...creative
> teaching ideas; skill in the use of electronic
> information sources, including web-based and
> other Internet sources...[39]

In an essay "What I Expect from a Librarian," an assistant
professor of French recently wrote that she not only expected the
librarians to talk to her classes, but "I especially need your teaching skills

---

[38] Advertisement by Pierce College in *College & Research Libraries News* 59
(June, 1998): 478.
[39] Advertisement by Muhlenberg College in *College & Research Libraries News*
58 (May, 1997): 369.

where new technologies are concerned...As with all teaching, your excitement over a new resource or an idea for incorporating technology sparks my interest. I also like hearing examples of how other faculty use these technologies, and you are positioned to help us network across departments and disciplines."[40]

That need, the realization of teachers that they need to be more familiar with the new electronic resources, has led the reference staffs and computing centers of a number of colleges and universities to offer workshops and other sessions for faculty. A report from the National Conference of the AAHE, in 1998, noted that "in this era of explosive technological advances, on many campuses librarians have been asked to take on an instructional role to the faculty..."[41]

For some, perhaps many faculty members, then, the active participation by librarians in the teaching/learning process is almost a given, not just for their students, but for themselves. What about administrators? There is not much question that college presidents and deans look upon the role of librarians very differently than they did 25 years ago—even differently than they did 15 years ago. President Gresham Riley, remember, commented that faculty do not "acknowledge a legitimate educational role for the library and for librarians" because they are "likely to be influenced by the local conditions...in particular the attitude of key administrators."[42] That was in 1984. In 1998, meeting in a forum at that AAHE Conference mentioned just above, 20 provosts from all over the country discussed various library-related issues, one of them being "How to increase partnerships between librarians and other faculty." Summarizing the discussion, the report stated provosts have seen librarians come out of the library to support learning in new ways...First, the provosts agreed that librarians are providing a necessary service by instructing all, from students to administration, to critically evaluate and choose sources from the wealth of information available...Another idea that was addressed several times was the importance of librarians serving on instructional teams.[43]

Almost anyone who has administered a college library over several recent decades can confirm the improvement in their provost's view of the librarian's role. The change in the expectations presidents and/or provosts have for their directors is clear, and it can be seen by the

---

[40] Aletha D. Stahl, "What I Want in a Librarian: One New Faculty Member's Perspective," *Reference & User Services Quarterly* 37 (Winter, 1997): 135.

[41] Althea H. Jenkins, Laverne Simoneaux, & William Miller, "Provosts, Libraries, and Electronic Information: Reports from AAHE and CNI," *College & Research Libraries News* 59 (June, 1998): 421-422.

[42] See "The College Viewpoint," p. 5.

[43] Jenkins et al., "Provosts, Libraries, and Electronic Information," p. 421.

wording in many of the ads seeking college library directors. Years ago ads stressed administrative experience and ability; rarely was the educational role of the library mentioned, and there was just a smattering of mentions of coping with "automation." Today's ads, while still, of course, seeking applicants with proven administrative talent, frequently emphasize the needs of the library's educational role, especially in conjunction with technology. A few recent examples from representative institutions:

> * The Director will exercise energetic and creative leadership...to develop a vision for the future of the library, including the integration of new information technologies into library instruction and services to support the university's teaching and learning mission.[44]
> * The Director will articulate a clear vision of the library's vital role in supporting the teaching, learning and research activities of students, faculty, and other constituents...Minimum qualifications include...knowledge of emerging technologies and their impact...[45]
> * Qualifications [include]:...Clear vision of the evolving role of the academic library in digital environment and evolving integration of technology into curriculum and teaching...A commitment to user instruction and the educational mission of the academic library...[46]

Of course, not all ads for directors mention or allude to the library's educational role; even so, there is no question that the convergence of the user instruction movement and the impact of the new technologies has given today's college library a much more significant role in the teaching/learning process.

Almost 40 years ago, my boss and mentor, Guy R. Lyle, wrote in his classic *The Administration of the College Library*, that "by mid-

---

[44] Advertisement by Lawrence University, *College & Research Libraries News* 59 (November, 1998): 814.
[45] Advertisement by Concordia College in *College & Research Libraries News* 59 (November, 1998): 813.
[46] Advertisement by Monmouth University in *College & Research Libraries News* 59 (July/August, 1998): 555.

century the college library was beginning to achieve a position of strength in the educational program and commanded greater respect than ever before from the faculty."[47] His optimism, unfortunately, was premature, as I have tried to show above. Guy, who was a real bookman—as well as a superb administrator—remarked to me once that he was glad he would be retiring before technology took over. I wish that he could have seen the situation today, how technology has supplemented the work of academic librarians, and given the college library the educational role he knew it deserved.

---

[47] Guy R. Lyle, *Administration of the College Library*, 3rd edition (New York: Wilson, 1961), p. 10.

29

Working with Faculty: Some Reflections
(2004)

When Inga Barnello told me she was resigning as editor of College and
Undergraduate Libraries *I offered to write something for her final issue. After
all, I'd been a member of its editorial board since its inception and felt some
obligation though I felt that I probably didn't have anything new to say. So I
dredged up the anecdotal pieces that follow. They are hardly profound, but I
did think they were interesting, even useful. I'd used at least two of the pieces in
talks or articles to make a point, and since they always went over well and were
perhaps still relevant for librarians who worked with faculty, were worth
retelling. The context for each piece is contained within it.*

— Evan Ira Farber, 2006

From the 1960s into the 1990s I helped develop and worked in
the Earlham College bibliographic instruction program. It was an
eminently successful program—and continues to be, as a matter of fact—
but also an important one for a wider constituency: it served not only as a
model for other colleges, but also as an example for librarians in many
other types of institutions. The most important working premise of that
program has always been its use of existing courses as the vehicle for the
program. It always has been, in other words, a course-related and/or
course-integrated program. That basic premise meant, of course, that
librarians worked closely with individual faculty members in the planning and implementation of instruction. Consequently, over the years I
learned a lot about ways of facilitating that working relationship and
along the way I occasionally reflected—sometimes mused—about the
process. Those reflections ranged from the obvious to the insightful and
interesting and though I have on occasion shared those which I thought
most useful, I also thought that perhaps today's instruction librarians
might find them helpful.

But, readers might ask—and with justification—those insights,
observations, or whatever you want to call them, date from decades ago.
Are they still useful? Are they not outdated? My response would be
something like the message I spelled out in a paper published a few years

Farber, Evan I., "Working With Faculty: Some Reflections," *College &
Undergraduate Libraries*, Volume 11, Number 2 (2004), pages 129-
135.

ago, "Plus ça Change…"[1] (Farber 1995). Think of the library instruction process as an equation. The basic factors in that equation are four: students, faculty, the sources of information, and the means of presentation. It is what one does with that equation that determines the success of the program. The sources of information have changed greatly—that is, from printed to electronic formats—and so the ways of presenting those sources have also changed. On the other hand, two of those factors, student attitudes and habits, and faculty attitudes and habits are, if not exactly as they were twenty years ago, very close to it. The attitudes and habits of typical students in their search for information can be summarized rather easily: they want the information quickly and easily, and the quicker and easier the better. That, of course, is somewhat of a caricature but, like any good caricature, resembles its target enough to convey the validity of the caricaturist's viewpoint.

Sharing Classes

This first observation resulted from a visit to a university where I had talked to the library staff about instruction. That evening I went out to dinner with the library's head of instruction. During the dinner, when a faculty member she worked with passed by, she stopped him to introduce him to me. "This is so-and-so in the Drama department. We give instruction to all his courses—he's great to work with." I of course was pleased to meet him, which I said, but also commented "You know, that's interesting. I also really enjoy working with our drama people. Why do you think they're so good to work with?" His response, it seems to me, was a very perceptive one. "I think it may be because drama people are used to working with others—the playwright, the set designer, the actors, the costumer, et cetera. So, having a librarian talk to my classes is no problem."

What that incident meant for me was to reinforce my observation (and the observation of many others) that most faculty members don't feel comfortable sharing their classes with others. They're used to—and enjoy—the control, the independence they have. Gordon Thompson, a faculty colleague of mine and a superb teacher of literature, put it this way in his piece Faculty Recalcitrance about Bibliographic Instruction: "Most college teachers are prima donnas. On most campuses, despite their real sufferings and sacrifices, faculty members enjoy an extraordinarily privileged status…Our recalcitrant teachers do not want the sanctity of their classrooms violated".[2] "Prima donnas" may be an

---

[1] Evan Farber, "Plus ça Change…," *Library Trends* 44 (Fall): 430-38.
[2] Gordon Thompson, "Faculty Recalcitrance About Bibliographic Instruction." In *Bibliographic Instruction in Practice: A Tribute to the Legacy of Evan Ira Farber*. (Ann Arbor: The Pierian Press, 1993) 103-105. P. 103.

exaggeration, but I think it is fair to observe that many faculty members have fairly fragile egos, and because someone wants to work with their students, someone who can point out materials and methods with which they may be unfamiliar, they may feel others think them inadequate. Maryellen Weimer, an administrator at Penn State and editor of that very useful newsletter, *The Teaching Professor,* said, "Teachers occupy positions of power in the classroom. They are supposed to know, to be the learned experts, to manage the classroom…If they do not or have not and find that out, from their positions of power, they have far to fall".[3]

How to overcome that reluctance to share their classrooms? First, gain their respect for what we're supposed to do: be a good reference librarian or administrator. Then, indicate an interest in their courses. Some years ago, a survey of 1,680 faculty from a variety of institutions found that 42 percent of them "said that *never* during their entire career had anyone talked with them in detail about their teaching…To talk openly about teaching…implies one has a problem." Yet most faculty members are eager to talk about their teaching. However, they're reluctant to talk about it with colleagues, with department heads, or certainly with deans. Librarians, however, are not threatening, so make an effort to indicate an interest in their courses— notices of new books, or articles they might not see. (But don't point out an article in a journal the faculty member is likely to see.) In sum, keep in mind that most faculty don't feel appreciated and whenever attention is paid to what they do, they are grateful—though it's not often they'll acknowledge this.

Faculty Teaching In New Areas

This insight—that faculty who teach subject matter outside their specialties are easier to work with than those remaining within their specialties—came to me while composing a talk, "Area Studies and Undergraduates: The Role of Libraries," I was to give at a 1987 conference on Asian and African studies in undergraduate institutions. In it I noted that "faculty who teach non-Western studies come from one of two backgrounds: either they've been trained as non-Western scholars, or, more commonly, especially in smaller schools, they've come from a traditional discipline and with the aid of a fellowship, a sabbatical, or other means, and with the encouragement of their home institutions, have done some retraining." So at Earlham for example, there were a number of professors who spent some time studying in Japan, among whom were a psychologist who began to teach a course in cross-cultural psychology,

---

[3] Maryellen Weimer, *Improving College Teaching* (San Francisco: Jossey-Bass, 1990) 17.

222

a philosopher who began a course in Asian philosophy, a musician and a theater person who together gave a course on Asian arts. On the whole, I'd found these faculty members easier to work with than those in traditional disciplines. Why?

My speculation was this: those who have been trained in non-Western studies recognize the problems inherent in doing research in nontraditional areas, and so are more receptive to innovation (bibliographic instruction, as it was then called, was, after all, an innovation) to suggestions and to librarians' assistance. For the other group, those who started out in traditional disciplines and had to retool, so to speak, I had a more complex speculation. First of all, to have left a discipline one was trained in, and to enter an unfamiliar one, indicates an openness to innovation. Second, because they're relatively unfamiliar with the subject matter of the new field, they recognize their limitations and need for assistance. They can appreciate why students need library instruction because they themselves do. Third (and I think this is an especially interesting speculation) is that studying an unfamiliar area and relating it to a familiar area, requires a change in mind-set, a new *Weltanschauung*. The criteria and standards used to analyze and interpret Western psychology, for example, may not do for non-Western psychology. That need for looking through a new prism, so to speak, may loosen the conventional disciplinary framework, and make the scholar more open to other new approaches—in this case, working with librarians.

Time Constraints

Most of my other comments in this piece concern faculty members who are difficult to work with or even approach. This comment concerns two other groups of faculty members: those who claim to be "too busy" to work with a librarian in planning instruction and those who were cooperative in the past—say, last year—but who didn't get in touch with a librarian this year, even though the instruction went well last year.

At one time all first-year students at Earlham took a Humanities course, each section of which was taught by a different faculty member who determined his or her own topic and syllabus. (There were seventeen such sections.) The only common requirement was a "research paper." I taught one of those sections, my subject for the term being the Literature and Art of the Depression. I also agreed to be responsible for the bibliographic instruction to the other sections and during the term got in touch with each of the other sixteen instructors to set a time for talking to their classes. This I did, and gave the instruction. But a week or two before the end of the term, I realized that although I had been very conscientious about providing instruction for the other sections, I had forgotten about doing that for my own! Well, I scrambled and gave it, but really too late in the term.

After the term I reflected on why I was so remiss. What I deduced was that I was so concerned about my students—preparing my lectures or discussion topics, thinking about next term's syllabus, making up or grading an exam, talking with individual students, all those things that are part of any conscientious instructor's working day—that library instruction was not at the top of my teaching priorities. That realization not only made me more understanding of faculty members overlooking the need for instruction to their classes, but, also the need for librarians to take the initiative. We may think of library instruction as essential for a particular class, but even though the instructor may agree, he or she has many other responsibilities that take priority. There were a number of Earlham faculty members whose classes I spoke to each time they taught those classes. One might have expected them to get in touch with me the next time they offered those courses. A few did, but given the priorities of teaching, I realized with most I would have to take the initiative, and I came to accept that as a given.

Faculty Nuisances

This last comment is not based so much on my reflecting on an experience as it is on an observation of an academic dean. I include it not only because it's too good a story to keep to myself, but also because many librarians can appreciate its message.

I was talking to a group made up of college administrators, heads of computing services, and library directors about the changing role of the library in an electronic environment, and while mentioning acquisition policies for some reason alluded to the 80/20 rule. Some of the faces looked blank, so I spent a few minutes saying that studies have shown that about twenty percent of almost any library's collection accounted for about eighty percent of its circulation. Interestingly enough, I went on, that same ratio holds for many phenomena. In retailing, for example, twenty percent of a store's inventory almost invariably accounts for eighty percent of its sales. In the motion picture industry about twenty percent of the films account for about eighty percent of receipts. "And," I added, "I'll bet that in your institutions twenty percent of the students account for eighty percent of counselors' time." They seemed to agree, so I added "And probably twenty percent of your faculty account for eighty percent of your time." At that, one of the audience—a college provost—raised his hand and said, "No, five percent of the faculty account for ninety-five percent of my time," a comment that elicited much laughter and nods of agreement. When later I related this incident to other provosts or academic deans, their response has been similar: approving nods and laughter.

224

What's the message for librarians? It's simple, but useful, I think—that is, on any campus there are going to be a small number of the faculty who will take up a disproportionate amount of a librarian's time. And, of course, for those of you who are library administrators there may be one or two people on your staff who'll do the same thing. How one handles those professors or staff members will depend on any number of factors, but particularly how important that faculty member or staff member is to the running of the library.

Appendix A

Evan Farber Speaking
(2003)

In the fall of 2003, a group of fifty or so college librarians, known as the Oberlin Group, met at DePauw University in Greencastle, Indiana. Scottie Cochrane, director of the Denison University library, was among them and, at a break in the meeting, she asked Tom Kirk, my successor at Earlham, if I'd be there. When he replied no, she and Louis, her husband, decided to stop off on their way home to see me. We met for lunch in Richmond, Indiana, and, according to Scottie's remembrance in a note to me, it was there we decided to do this project, which initially meant her interviewing me and some of my colleagues about my career. A few months later she and Louis came back to Richmond for the interviews. During those interviews and discussions, the project grew from just a biographical work into the idea for a published volume containing some of my key writings plus the biographical material.

Scottie's secretary transcribed the taped interviews, but then Scottie got a Fulbright Lectureship to Thailand. When David Gansz, an Ohio college librarian, discussed with her [at an OhioLINK Independent College Library Directors' meeting, ed.] her lack of time to continue the project, he got together with me and, finding that we were very compatible, began working as editor. Fortunately, David was able to take over the entire project. I'm grateful to Scottie for getting it started and to David for continuing it; his patience, efficiency and demonstrable editorial skills are most impressive. Despite minor additions and grammatical or factual corrections I think the interview retains the flavor and unlabored style of the original.

— Evan Ira Farber, 2006

Farber: I was born in 1922 in the Bronx, New York…Shortly after my birth we moved to Brooklyn and that's where I have my first memories…Shortly after that we moved, first to Manhattan. And then when I was, I guess, maybe five years old, we moved to the Bronx, 1440 Anderson Avenue. I went to PS (standing for Public School) 73, which was about half a mile away…And the neighborhood was great…My father was quite successful, as owner of a dress business. The name of his company was the Estelle Dress Company, Estelle being my mother's name. It was on 36th or 37th street it New York between Broadway and 7th Avenue…Anyway, in 1931 we took the traditional move into the suburbs, to Great Neck…Later on I went to Sunday school there and was bar mitzvahed there. It was a small town then, with only about fifteen or twenty thousand population. A blacksmith still operated not far from our

---

An interview with Lynn Scott Cochrane, December, 2003.

226

home. It was a marvelous place to grow up in because the schools were very good...It's on the North shore of Long Island just outside the New York City limits, sixteen miles from Manhattan...Anyway, we lived there for about two years when my father's business went broke like so many in the early thirties. And so we had to move to a less expensive house, also in Great Neck. From that house I did most of my grade school and then high school. The Great Neck High School was regarded as one of the best in the state. I enjoyed high school very much...

Cochrane: And what did your mother do? Did she stay at home?

Farber: Initially, yes. But my mother, who was very bright, went the traditional route then. She went to Julia Richman High School in New York and then became a secretary. That was never satisfying to her. She also had a lovely singing voice. When we lived in Brooklyn, as a matter of fact, she used to sing on the radio in a local Brooklyn station. And then even after we moved to the Bronx she stayed on that station. I can remember lying on the floor in the living room listening to her sing songs like *Shine Little Glow Worm, Glimmer*. My father was in World War I, but never went overseas. And then shortly after he was discharged, they got married. My mother was always very interested intellectually and regretted that she had never gone beyond high school. And so she supplemented her basic education with a lot of reading. I remember she had a small book group and one of the things they read—for years I had a copy—was H. G. Wells' *Outline of History*. I can remember her marking it all up. Anyway, in Great Neck, she didn't feel worthwhile just taking care of my sister and me. She put my sister in nursery school and then began teaching in that nursery school, and got very much interested in it. A little later on my father had—not quite an affair—but his eyes wandered and it was a friend of my mother's. He told my mother once that he was in love with this woman. She told me later that because of this she wanted to be independent just in case they got separated. Divorce was unheard of in our family. There was only one in our extended family—cousins, aunts, uncles—only one person had been divorced. So she began her career as a nursery school teacher and began commuting, going to New York University for her degree. At that time she was in her forties. Eventually she got her degree and then got her Master's from New York University...And then she became director of one of the first cooperative nursery schools in New York. This was the Great Neck Cooperative Nursery School, which had a fairly distinguished alumni group because there were so many distinguished people living in Great Neck who wanted a good nursery school.

Cochrane: That's a pretty inspiring story isn't it?

Farber: Yeah. And she had a very definite effect on me because of that.

Cochrane: Do you remember the first time you ever went to a library or a librarian?

Farber: Yes. It was when we lived in the Bronx and a few blocks away was the public library. And I can remember even the street that it was on and getting books out. I have no idea what the books were then. But then in Great Neck there was a wonderful public library. At first I used the children's section and read voraciously. And then as soon as I could, went to the adult part of the library and began reading—not very good stuff. I can remember reading Frank Packard's crime stories. Then some pretty good stuff. I got interested in Steinbeck, Dos Passos, that kind of thing, when I was in high school. A wonderful public library; I had a very good experience with it. And I don't think I'd ever thought about becoming a librarian, even though I had such great feelings and remembrances about the public library. The high school library was an attractive and well stocked library. I can remember one book I read there which I bought later on from a used bookstore, because it made such an impression on me. It was a book by M. Ilin, *New Russia's Primer: The Story of the 5 Year Plan*, and it was a pro-Russian, pro-communist thing. And it was interesting…indicative of the library's openness that a high school library had that book…

Cochrane: So you…started school at Chapel Hill?

Farber: Right…Got a degree in Political Science and *still* didn't know what to do. So I decided to go to graduate school. And then went to graduate school, even though I hadn't done very well generally. But the last year, I guess, in Chapel Hill, I'd done fairly well. Got accepted at Princeton and went there for a couple of years. And that was a good, shaping experience except I didn't do very well there, because I had a good time and didn't *really* take my studies that seriously. I enjoyed being there. But then after two years there, there was a shortage of professors, and I got an offer from Massachusetts State—what's now the University of Massachusetts in Amherst. And I taught Political Science there. Again, I had a very good time. I don't think I did a very good job as a teacher because I *did* have such a good time. But also teaching didn't seem to me to be the thing that I really wanted to do for the rest of my life. And so I came back and at Princeton I didn't pass the general exams. So I decided then, well, I still wanted to get a Ph.D. and go back to Chapel Hill. Which I did—first got a master's there in Political Science and then, while sitting in a class—I was going on for the

228

Ph.D.—but sitting in one of the political science classes—this was a public administration class taught by a professor named Harold Wager—in class, Wager read an announcement one day that the library school was looking for students. At that time I had never thought about librarianship as a career even though I was working in the library—and I enjoyed it, but never thought about it as a career. At that time, I was married and besides working in the library took other types of jobs at Chapel Hill, but primarily working in the library in the documents section under a guy named Bill Pullen, who was a marvelous boss and a great scholar. And so I went over to the library school and talked to them about it and it looked so good, so interesting, and so much promise—at that time there was a real shortage of librarians so there were all kinds of opportunities. So I decided to switch. I gave up on going for the Ph.D. I went to library school, and it was great. That decision or that lack of foresight, lack of knowledge of what I wanted to do, of becoming a librarian, later had a great influence on me. I realized that so *many* people, so many students who come to college, don't think about becoming librarians. I point out lots of times that the percentage of high school graduates, or entering college freshmen wanting to become librarians is *zip*...And so the way that influenced me was to realize that you had to be proactive in getting students to think about library school. And so one of the things I've done and that I feel very good about, is talking to students. Anytime I got a student that I could help in reference who sounded interesting and who I thought had the kind of personality that I'd want to go to library school, I'd ask them if they'd ever thought about it. And, of course, no one ever had. A lot of kids worked in the library behind the desk and so I'd take them aside. And anybody who looked, sounded like a live, live body I would talk to about going to library school.

Cochrane: Was Louis Round Wilson there?

Farber: Yeah, he was. I took one of his last classes, called *Libraries in the Southeast*. That's where I wrote my first paper in librarianship. It was a paper on lack of cooperative library planning in the Southeast. It was a good paper, so good that he suggested I send it off to the *Southeastern Librarian*. Which I did and they first accepted it. I found out later that the editor felt that I had some unfavorable things to say about the lack of planning. And so they never did publish it. Wilson was a great teacher. Wonderful! One thing that he told us that I've *never* forgotten. He said he never went into even the smallest library, that he didn't come out with some idea, he didn't learn something from. That's great advice...But I can think of another thing, which had a *big* influence on my life. Guy Lyle came one summer to teach a course in academic libraries and although I didn't need any more courses, I asked him if I could audit the course. So he said fine. It also happened that he loved to play handball and I was a good handball player. And he also liked to play tennis. And so we got along famously. I took his course and enjoyed it very much. And the way it influenced me was that, at that time, he was head of the Louisiana State University Library. But shortly after that he moved to Emory. And not too long after he got there, he wrote to me and asked me if I'd think about coming to Emory.

Cochrane: But you had first been in Alabama?

Farber: Yeah. Right after I graduated I went to Livingston State College in Alabama. It was interesting for several reasons. One, because it had a marvelous president, a guy named W. W. Hill. A guy who most reminded you of the lead in *The Music Man*. He could have sold anything to anybody. But he was a real fighter. He'd say "Mr. Farber. We've got to go out there and beat the bushes for students!" And he really believed in education. He himself was an Appalachian type, came from a poor family but got his Ed. D., from the University of Alabama. It was an interesting place because there I was a Jewish Yankee coming into this place in a small town of eight or nine hundred in the heart of the Black Belt. There was another Jewish faculty member there and a couple other Yankees there. In fact, a pretty decent faculty.

Cochrane: What was the library like there?

Farber: Library was just two rooms—two big rooms, with a collection of maybe forty thousand volumes altogether. I was the only professional. I had a paraprofessional help me and students to do the secretarial work. But it was good. It was good experience.

...But I was glad when I got this letter from Guy Lyle...

Cochrane: So you welcomed the opportunity to go to Atlanta?

Farber: Yeah. That was great.

Cochrane: What kind of place was Emory University at that time?

Farber: It liked to think of itself as the Harvard of the South. And I suppose that a lot of other places, Vanderbilt I know, thought of the same thing...Emory was a school that was really changing at the time. Its new president had come from the University of Chicago, and the Chancellor also came from the University of Chicago. And then it had some very good faculty. But it was also a very stodgy, traditional place. A good library staff. Guy Lyle was a wonderful person to work for, because he had all sorts of ideas. And tried things. My professional development was great because he had done a couple of editions of *Periodicals for the College Library,* and then he asked me if I'd like to take it over. And I said sure. So I did the next two or three editions And that made my name, in a sense, known in library circles. So I was very grateful to him.

Cochrane: So, how long were you in Atlanta at Emory?

Farber: Seven years.

Cochrane: And tell me a little more about Guy Lyle as a person.

Farber: He was somewhat autocratic, not that he felt that he was always right, but that he expected people to shape up and do really good jobs. He came down hard on anybody who didn't shape up. He had strong ideas about the way the library should be kept, and that's one reason I felt here that there shouldn't be hand-lettered signs around, shouldn't have coffee or food in the library. He felt it created an ambience that was not conducive to people watching the rules or taking care of materials. As soon as you got a little bit sloppy your clientele would also become sloppy. And so at Earlham I prohibited anybody putting up signs except in one spot. He had only two rules for conduct in the library. One was if you wanted to put your feet on a chair, fine, but take off your shoes. Oh, no, he had three rules. And the second one was no food or drink. And the kids were very good about that. And the third rule was, respect the rights of others who want quiet. He was a superb boss. I learned a lot from him. He had a good staff and he was very creative, too. At one time we started a little mimeographed publication. He, Ruth Walling, head reference librarian, Tom Crowder, my assistant, and I, would meet once every two weeks and annotate a group of books—usually about 15—that we felt college librarians might overlook simply because they didn't fit into a particular discipline. Things like biographies or poetry or collections of essays on subjects that most colleges didn't collect. We'd read the reviews and write summaries and say why we felt they were appropriate for college libraries. We had maybe a hundred subscribers, but it was really fun doing. It taught me a lot, I think, about book selection and book reviews, which became very important for me later on.

Cochrane: Well, then, how did you come to Earlham?

Farber: Oh. I had never heard of Earlham. I never even knew a Quaker. One day I got a letter from the Dean at Earlham, Joe Elmore, who asked if I'd be interested in applying for the position of college librarian. I always felt, I think, that I missed something when I went only to a large university—missed the intimacy of a small school...He got my name from a faculty member who knew the executive director of ACRL. So I came up to Earlham and just fell in love with the place—got along beautifully with the dean, and liked most faculty members. And everyone liked me.

...I wrote a piece about the library every month, I guess, and sent it to the faculty. That was something I learned from Guy Lyle. He wrote about, not just new books, but new major works, other library developments.

Cochrane: So you did a newsletter every month?

Farber: Yes. And I attached it to the mimeographed list of acquisitions which most libraries were doing at that time. And, of course, everybody looked at those, or at least looked at their portion of them. So I was able to do new things and change things around. One of the first things I suggested was moving from Dewey to LC. And one of the other things I did was something else I learned from Guy, was putting out on the open shelves only the current issues of periodicals rather than a whole year's worth. And at first some faculty objected to it, but I showed them it was to their advantage, really, to having that done. So I was able to change things around.

Cochrane: And Hope was your secretary when you came here?

Farber: She had just been widowed that February. Her husband, who was a school principal, was killed in an automobile crash. And she had three children...I asked Hope if she'd be my secretary; then we started dating. And three years later got married...Hope had two boys and a girl and I had four girls...Four of the children went to Olney, a Quaker boarding school, in Ohio. And the other three went to Richmond's public schools. Hope's three children went to Olney and one of mine did.

Cochrane: Did you become a Quaker?

Farber: No. I'm called an attender. We would go with Hope to meetings, not every Sunday, but maybe one out of two or three or four

Sundays. I'd just spend my time reading the *New York Times* rather than the *Bible*.

...Well, actually, having Hope as my assistant made it easy because she could do so many things that helped, especially the articles and speeches. A couple of things I did were really significant. The paper I did for Ernie Boyer when he was working on undergraduate education. That came from taking advantage of a situation, the situation being that two or three of his children went to Earlham and I got to know him. One of the sons is actually a librarian now, or has a library degree, but then became a minister. Ernie Boyer, Jr. As soon as I read in *The Chronicle* or somewhere that he was working on this, I wrote to him and said I hoped that he was going to talk about the usefulness of the library in an undergraduate education. He wrote me back and said, would you like to do a paper on it? So I did. Seventy pages or something. There's a copy of that somewhere...As I say, that was very creative on my part. It came from some of these talks that I gave on the library's effect on teaching.

Cochrane: How long was Hope your secretary?

Farber: We both retired at the same time, in 1994.

Cochrane: So all those years you worked together? That's amazing to me. And it went well, because you went home together and you worked together and everything.

Farber: Well, she enjoyed it too, because she was more than just a secretary. She was in charge of checking in periodicals which she enjoyed a lot too. She had students working for her several of whom became librarians.

Cochrane: Good. Well, I think you've been a lucky man all told.

Farber: I have. No question about it...

Cochrane: Well. That brings me to Tom Kirk. I read somewhere about how Tom became a librarian. Can you tell me that story?

Farber: Oh, yes. When I came here, Tom and his wife, Betsy, both worked in the library and Tom was very good, as you would expect. He was a biology major. At that time, the science library was at the top of the science building. It was *very* inadequate. To get up there you had to take an elevator; it was hot with poor lighting and everything else. The science faculty was interested in getting the science librarian to be much more important. The science librarian, who was only part time, was married to a guy who was then reference librarian in *this* library. I wanted to let him go, and fortunately he looked at Ball State and became a reference librarian there. He wasn't the kind of reference librarian I really wanted. Tom began helping out in the science library, and when he was in his senior year I asked him what he was going to do. He said well, he was going to graduate and teach high school biology. So I asked him if he would think about becoming a science librarian. And he said he'd think about it and I said I could hire you, pay you a salary during the regular year and help out with your graduate school. You can go to library school in the summers and get your degree over three summers, (I think that was what it was). And we would help pay for his library school. He agreed to that and I got the administration to agree to it in a kind of sneaky way, because I said look, here we can get a full time librarian, not paying him very much, and he'll go on, he'll move somewhere else. And then we'd repeat the plan with another biology major. I guess I really believed that. Anyway, Tom became a librarian. It was very obvious that it made a difference to the science people. And so when we built a new science building the science departments felt very comfortable about putting a sizeable library in their new facility.

Cochrane: That must've felt very good to you.

Farber: Well, it did. There were very few people that I would've been happy about taking my place. I've had pretty good relationships with all the Earlham presidents. Dick Wood, Earlham's president when I retired, had been a good library supporter all along and he understood why I wanted Tom. Tom was undecided because Betsy, his wife, was very happy in Berea. She was teaching and active in the community. And he liked his position. He liked the Berea faculty. But, of course, there was a pull at Earlham. He's a birthright Quaker and coming back to a Quaker school and to his alma mater was important. And then I had Dick Wood, the president, do whatever he could to urge him to come…

Cochrane: And you seized opportunities when they presented themselves—which is the key…Tell me about a fondest memory you have or the thing you're proudest of.

Farber: Well, BI of course. Getting it started and publicizing it, getting out and pushing it. And the thing, again, I think, is taking advantage of a situation. When I was chair of the College Libraries Section I was responsible for the annual program. The program that year was to present our instructional program, and some junior college was also supposed to present its program. We expected maybe two or three hundred people there but it was something like seven hundred people. And I recognized for the first time that there was a real interest in this topic. And a lot of people were groping at it. So that's when I began doing other kinds of things. Like when I was president of ACRL. I had the option of selecting people, choosing people, oh, like Joe Boissé and other people who were interested in instruction to be in key positions so they could carry on later.

Cochrane: How did the conferences get started? The instruction conferences that you had?

Farber: The first one I still have video tapes of. It was in this building. And in a small room downstairs. It got started because...I don't know. I know I got the idea of starting it from—let's see, the first one was what? '75? I guess—something like that...And then people who came to this asked me could I come to wherever. And then Larry [Hardesty], of course, took that and asked me to come to Florida. And then we did that for six, seven years I guess. And, of course, we didn't have any trouble getting faculty to come with me and do them. They still talk about it.

Cochrane: I was in the first group of the *Mentor Program*. And we had our meeting in New Orleans and we were meeting at, I think at Loyola. And they brought in a faculty member you had never even met before.

Farber: Right. Right.

Cochrane: And then you had a session with the person.

Farber: Right. Now that story is interesting. The first, I guess it was maybe the first or second session, workshop that we did. Of course, I like to tell this story. Kathy Milar, a psychology professor, was one of the three faculty members who came with me. But anyway, we were sitting in Larry's office signing releases or whatever we were signing, when Kathy said to me, I want to talk to you about a course I'm teaching next term on women in psychology. So I said, Kathy, let's don't talk about it now. Why don't we talk about it in front of the audience because one thing they're always asking is how do you get to talk with faculty members. So she said fine and that's exactly what we did. After some conversation, I asked the audience if anybody had a suggestion. And, of course, some of the people talked. It worked out so well I decided to do it regularly as part of the program after that. That's how it got started.

235

Cochrane: Yes. Well it makes sense when you think about it but I think it's librarians asserting themselves a little bit too. Where we have a natural reticence sometimes. But we have to assert ourselves and call the faculty member. And usually they're very receptive.

Farber: Right.

Cochrane: But we have to make the effort. They're not normally going to come to us.

Farber: I think that, as you say, we have to make the effort; again, I believe the word *proactive* is the key to most of what I've done in reference work. You know I keep saying to reference librarians, you can't wait for reference questions. You have to go and seek them out. And the idea came to me, I think, from when I was a kid, what a good salesman does. A good salesman, when someone enters a store, a haberdashery, he doesn't say "can I help you?" He says "what size do you wear?" And so you have to talk to him. And it's the same thing with a reference librarian. You don't say "can I help you?" You say "what are you working on?" And people just love to talk about what they're working on.

Cochrane: Tell me what you did when you were hiring a librarian, Evan...How big was your staff? How many?

Farber: The most we had was six professionals.

Cochrane: And what, in your view were you looking for when you were hiring a librarian?

Farber: ...I didn't care too much about their experience. They could get that on the job here. Mostly I was interested in the personality and if they were interested in what students were doing and could relate to students and students could relate to them. That was the main thing—the kind of personality that they had. I can remember the sister of one of our faculty members who applied for a reference position. But she talked and talked and I could see that once a student asked her a question the student could never get away from her. And so I turned her down. But then I advised her. I said "You know one reason is you're *not* a very good listener."

Cochrane: Well, that was of great benefit to her.

Farber: I hope so.

Cochrane: Usually if you are not offered a job nobody ever tells you why.

Farber: Right.

Cochrane: Well, tell me your philosophy of administration or your approach to administration.

Farber: I don't know if I really have a philosophy of administration. It derives from and is shaped by Earlham College. And let me give you an illustration; although it doesn't help answer your question very much. People sometimes ask me, didn't you ever think about going somewhere else? I say only once. And that was Evergreen College, when it was still being planned.

Cochrane: In Olympia, Washington. Right?

Farber: Yes. And I got a letter from the president who described what they were doing. And it sounded very exciting. And I said I would be interested and he and sent me materials on it. And the material said that it was starting out small but they hoped to get to 12,000 students. And I called him up and said there's no point in wasting your time and money and my time. I said I'm really not interested in a library of that size. And the ironic thing is they never got much beyond 2,000 students.

Cochrane: Why do you prefer the smaller size?

Farber: I like the interpersonal relationships that you can have with faculty *and* students. A guy who was working on his masters at the University of Iowa Library School came to Earlham. His project was this library and after he had finished talking to students and faculty and staff he said to me, "You know, students think of this as *your* library, as Evan's library." I said that's one of the nicest things you could've said about me. And I took advantage of that, too, establishing relationships with students. But I realized that was my real strong point. Interpersonal relationships. And that, I would say to library school classes that I talked to about why be a college librarian, that was the satisfying thing. And you couldn't even imagine *any* student at the University of Michigan knowing who was even head of the library.

Cochrane: No. No, that's true. And the emphasis in the research institutions is not on teaching undergraduates.

Farber: That's right. And that's what I was interested in, too. I was interested in undergraduates and teaching them.

Appendix B

A Day With a College Librarian:
Quaker School Library Takes an Activist Role
(1978)

by Pyke Johnson, Jr.

Five years ago when my sons were preparing to go to college I made a number of the obligatory inspection trips with them, and each time I checked out the college library. At the schools I visited, the Lilly Library at Earlham College seemed far and away the best, and so when one of my sons, for his own reasons, chose Earlham (and was accepted), I enthusiastically ratified his choice. This fall, when I returned to Earlham for Parents Day, I made arrangements to go out early and spend a day with Evan Ira Farber, librarian of the college.

Earlham is a Quaker college, inconveniently located in Richmond, Ind., about 40 miles west of Dayton, Ohio. Founded in 1847, it has about 1100 men and women students and a faculty and staff of 150. About 40% of its students come from the Midwest, but another 40% come from between Boston and Washington. It is primarily an undergraduate school, with its only graduate students in the School of Religion. (Western Quakers, whose activities are centered in Richmond, tend to have ministers; but the Clear Creek Meeting, which is located on campus, is a silent meeting.) Despite the Quaker connection, however, under 20% of the students are Friends. The clearest evidences of the Quaker approach are to be found in the consistently poor record of the athletic teams (not even its Frisbee team goes unbeaten); the custom of addressing everyone on campus by first name—from President Franklin Wallin on down; and the fact that decisions are made by consensus (including students) rather than unilaterally or by voting.

I met Evan Farber in his office, which is only lightly supplied with books, most of them of a professional nature, and, at the time of my

Pyke Johnson, Jr., "A Day with a College Librarian," *Publisher's Weekly* (January 9, 1978), 43-46.
Reprinted in:
The Earlhamite: Magazine of Earlham College Alumni, v. 99, n. 2 (Spring, 1978), pp. 13-17.

At the time, Mr. Johnson (father of Tom Johnson, Earlham class of 1978) was Managing Editor of Doubleday and Co.

visit, had a large "Treasures of Tutankhamun" poster on one wall. Evan, a gnomish pipe-smoker, who had just come from his daily round of tennis, launched immediately into a discussion of one of his favorite topics: the difference between the college library and the university library. Defining his terms, he pointed out that the university library is research-centered, whereas the college library is user-centered and, if it performs its function properly, adapts itself to the nature and needs of the institution it serves.

The college library, he believes, should provide its community (students, faculty, and staff) the same kinds of services and materials that the public library offers its community. The Lilly Library does indeed make its resources available not only to junior and senior high school students (and to local collegians home on vacation) but also to other residents of Richmond. It does not, however, attempt to duplicate the functions of Morrisson-Reeves, the excellent Richmond Public Library, and its operations are directed exclusively to the needs of the college.

But the larger responsibility of the college library is to teach the students how to use it, a responsibility which, if assumed at all in universities, is taken over by faculty members. First-year students entering Earlham are given a test on the use of the library; those who fail it (only about 5 %) receive special instruction. After this, instruction is given in conjunction with courses and related to course assignments. During the past year, library staff members talked with almost 100 classes. Smaller classes are brought into the library; larger ones are visited; but all have bibliographies prepared for them. "Almost no student finishes at Earlham," says Evan with understandable pride, "without truly knowing how to use the library."

The Earlham program is becoming increasingly well-known. This year there was an on-campus workshop on teaching students to use library materials. During my visit a similar foundation-funded workshop was just being concluded in the Wildman Science Library, which is housed in a separate building and whose holdings are centered around a large collection of maps housed in wide metal cabinets. Librarians and faculty members from such institutions as Vanderbilt, Johns Hopkins and Arizona State as well as representatives from many smaller colleges have attended these sessions. In addition, bibliographies prepared by the staff have been purchased by more than 200 libraries.

Apart from the library's role in the teaching process, Evan also believes it should help build an interest in recreational reading. As a result, the library has a good collection of current fiction. It subscribes to the McNaughton Plan, run by Bro-Dart in Williamsport, Pa., which enables libraries to receive current books on loan and is widely used by public libraries. Earlham obtains 10 to 12 new novels a month from McNaughton, and at any given time about half of them are in circulation.

Title selection for the McNaughton books is based almost exclusively on the *PW* Forecasts; other current fiction is selected from reviews in the *New York Times Book Review*, the daily *New York Times* and even Gene Shalit's TV recommendations. For current nonfiction, Evan again depends on *PW* (though more selectively), the *Library Journal* and a wide assortment of weekly and monthly periodicals. One of his complaints is that he reads so many reviews he has little time left for reading books.

Poetry Is a Problem

Like many others associated directly or indirectly with getting books to the public, Evan has an uneasy conscience about poetry. He buys most of the books of the Wesleyan University Press, the Yale Younger Poets and the titles strongly recommended by *PW*. But the fact is, these books, even the best of them, are simply not read. During my visit, he and I discussed the subject with Warren Staebler, a sensitive and intelligent member of the English department and a former worker abroad with the American Friends Service Committee. Staebler feels that since the end of the Second World War, poets have become more private and lost their appeal to a broader audience. To show that this lack of interest is in current poets and not poetry itself, however, he instanced the visit last year of Robert Fitzgerald, who had held a large audience spellbound as he talked of his experiences in translating *The Odyssey* and *The Iliad*.

Children's books, except for the Caldecott and Newbery prize winners, are not bought by the library. For the rest, users are referred to Morrisson-Reeves Library in Richmond, with which the college has reciprocal arrangements.

One of the features of the library that had struck me on my first visit was its unusually large collection of periodicals. ("I want students to know that there are more and different magazines than those found on newsstands," says Evan.) The library subscribes to 1300 magazines and newspapers, which are set out on shelves in the center of the building in such a way that they cannot be ignored. They range alphabetically from the *ACLS Newsletter* to *Zygon*, a journal of religion and science. Among the newspapers are ones from Africa, France, Germany and England and also the Indianapolis diocesan paper.

During my visit I passed the periodical section often. Observation indicated that the *New Yorker* was a popular publication, although the area newspapers (Indianapolis, Dayton and Cincinnati) were frequently being read. At one time, three young women were poring over half a dozen back issues of *Win*, looking for ads for homesteads. Also while I was there, the library dealt with a request from a faculty member that a specific East African journal of philosophy be subscribed

241

to. He couldn't recall the name, and after a search, it was discovered that the library was already taking it.

I was also told of a chemistry student who regularly reads *CoEvolution* for its fiction reviews. Through them he had been introduced to the works of Kurt Vonnegut and Tom Robbins. When he discussed this with Evan, he was immediately shown how to look up reviews of earlier books by these writers. Book reviews are very import to Evan Farber. In a panel discussion at the 1976 meeting of the American Library Association in Chicago, he presented his idea that reviews help students recognize that scholars can disagree intelligently on methods and interpretation. Reading them, he feels, helps a student to develop a critical perspective. In many courses students are assigned titles and asked to seek out and report on reviews.

While catering to the recreational reading interests of the library's users, Evan does not neglect the needs of the faculty. Here he places special reliance on *Choice*. This magazine supplies its reviews on individual cards, and when the shipment comes in, they are sorted out by subject and circulated to the appropriate departments. Any faculty member who finds a title of interest initials the card and the book is ordered.

Books are also occasionally bought from the college bookstore, and students are frequently sent there to buy books. The store's manager, Jaipaul Singh, told me that 75% of his space was devoted to books and that students spend an average of $260 apiece during the school year, a figure he felt compared well with the national average of $135. Considering the college's size, the bookstore has an excellent selection of books (including current best sellers) as well as a rack of serious magazines (one full shelf devoted to *Mother Earth News*). It is also a promotion-minded store in the best National Association of College Stores tradition, and Jaipaul is on the NACS Book Selection Committee.

As well as using *Choice* material, Evan also makes copies of other reviews of contents pages of magazines. These he annotates and either sends to interested faculty members or posts on a central bulletin board across from the circulation desk. While I was there the board was filled almost exclusively with notes from Farber, but there was also a handwritten notice from a first-year woman student urging her classmates to read "The Journals of John Woolman," a Quaker classic.

Our conversation in the librarian's office was occasionally punctuated by excursions out into the building, where I was shown something we had been talking about or was introduced to a staff member who could offer further explanation. One such trip was to the terminal that connects the library to the Ohio College Library Center in Columbus. The terminal has a double function. One of its uses is to order catalogue cards. The library's needs are fed into the computer, and a short time later through the mail come the needed cards, arranged alphabetically, ready for insertion into the card catalogue. Cataloguing in Publication information is seldom used by the library, and then usually with new fiction, since most of the CIP data have already gone into the OCLC computer.

Library Loans Handled

The other function of the terminal is to locate books needed on interlibrary loan. I was shown a request for *Individual in Culture Adaptation* by R. B. Edgerton. Basic information was fed into the terminal, which responded with a list of some 30 libraries that had the book. Happily, one of them was at Miami University, 40 miles south in Oxford, Ohio. A van goes between the two schools twice a week, carrying books back and forth and also giving rides to students who want to use the facilities of the larger Ohio library.

The use of the computer means that cataloguing can be done by non-professional help (OCLC can supply cards for almost 95% of the titles Earlham buys), freeing professionals to spend more time with students. The future, as Evan sees it, holds the prospect of the complete replacement by computers of the existing card catalogues. His present worry is that there have not been any studies on where to place them and how to use them. But change seems inevitable and not too unpleasant if one considers that human beings will then be freer to deal directly with other human beings on their personal problems involving the library.

After my morning's conversation, I spent some time walking around the building, which was opened in 1963. It is clean and bright and light. There are many carrels for study and a number of alcoves with comfortable chairs and sofas. The library closes at 11 p.m. but one large room off the entrance remains open until 3 a.m., affording a quiet place for students whose roommates want either to sleep or to use their stereos. One of the most interesting alcoves is called a *tokonoma*, after the section of Japanese homes where pictures are hung. The area is covered with tatami mats, and students are requested to remove their shoes while using it. I saw a shoeless young woman studying Paul Tillich. The library has a general rule that shoes are to be removed before feet are placed on furniture, a ruling that results in a surprising number of bare feet in the building, even in November.

The Japanese room is a manifestation of Earlham's extensive overseas program that offers students and faculty the opportunity to escape the confines of east-central Indiana through off-campus study. Those who want to improve their foreign languages can go to Japan, Colombia, France, Mexico, Germany or Denmark. Others interested in history or political science can take courses in England, Scotland,

Eastern Europe and Washington, D.C. Art and music majors go to New York and Italy. In addition, there are communal studies in Vermont and urban studies in Philadelphia, among 10 such programs in this country. In each case a class goes with a faculty member, lives in local homes and travels around the area. Many Earlham students make one or more I of these trips, usually lasting a 10-week quarter, during their stay at the college. When they come back they can pursue their studies further through the library's collection.

Of the building's three levels, the lowest is devoted to audiovisual materials. There is a language lab, two projection rooms for films and videotaping, record players and a collection of 20,000 art slides. The library lends art reproductions for student rooms. Each year a prize of $50 is given for the best original artwork done by students, and many of the past winners decorate the buildings.

The top level houses a collection of books and documents, with some pictures and furniture, devoted to the college archives and Quaker history. In recent months this collection has received extra use from Friends seeking out their roots. Also housed on the upper level is an extensive collection of government documents. Evan feels strongly about the value of these materials to students. Many libraries tend to hide them away; at Earlham they are readily accessible, and students use them easily.

The staff is friendly and helpful. It is not unusual for a user to be approached by a staff member with the query, "May I help you?" Someone once remarked, "Evan Farber thinks a librarian should be like a clerk in a high-class department store." Farber took it as a compliment. All staff professionals work with users (Farber himself is at the reference desk one night and every fifth weekend), and their desks are out in the open, not behind closed doors.

We lunched in the campus coffee shop. (Check for a filling and digestible meal: $1.40. No martinis.) We sat in a booth with two members of the psychology department, one of whom was Dale Noyd, who received national attention in the '60s when, as a career officer teaching at the Air Force Academy, he refused to train pilots to serve in Vietnam and received a dishonorable discharge. He was hired by Earlham and has been there ever since. Dale reaffirmed the value of the library to the faculty and stated that he had occasionally dropped projects after advice from Evan and his colleagues. His students also use bibliographies prepared by the library.

On the way back to the library I got Evan to tell me something about himself. He is a graduate of the University North Carolina (M.A. in Political Science and B.S. in Library Science). He has been at Earlham since 1962. This fall he was named vice-president and president-elect of the Association of College and Research Libraries

244

division of the ALA. He does a monthly column for *Choice*, evaluating periodicals for college libraries, and not surprisingly, he writes on books and libraries in each issue of the *Earlhamite*, an alumni magazine. He has written or edited three books in the library field. His wife, Hope, who is also a member of the library staff, writes a page for the weekly campus newsletter, annotating seven or eight "New and Readable" books in the library.

Back in the library I was given a copy of the budget. The library spends about $100,000 a year for materials: two-thirds for books, one-third for periodicals, with an additional $8000 going for binding. About 240,000 volumes are in the collection, and about 2000 of them are withdrawn each year. Evan believes that the college library, not being a research library, should continually weed its collection. There is also the matter of space, which has just about reached its limit. While I was there, discards from the history collection were being sold (and bought) for 10 cents apiece.

The library's full-time staff numbers 11, including Tom Kirk and his aides at the Wildman Science Library. They are supplemented by about 45 part-time student workers.

There is no security system, Evan feeling that this would somehow be inappropriate at a Quaker college. Still, about 700 books a year disappear; although about half of them turn up when school closes in June. Evan reports that there is very little mutilation of books. There is a copying machine near the circulation desk, and Philip Shore, the associate librarian, told me that its primary use is by students duplicating their papers and not for copying materials from books.

As a trade book editor, I was interested in the Earlham emphasis on hardcover books for recreational reading, as well as for study. That the program has an effect came home for me in a conversation with Jon Berry, a senior on the student newspaper, who quizzed me on John Fowles' *Daniel Martin*, spoke knowledgeably of the novels of Margaret Drabble and, in general, showed a wider acquaintance with current fiction than most graduates I have met from more prestigious universities. Another senior, a history major and inveterate library user, explained to me, "The original Renaissance Man knew everything; today's Renaissance Man doesn't know everything, but he does know where to find it."

Saturday night I took a last walk around the campus. It was a particularly warm November evening. The football team had lost to Anderson and the soccer team had beaten Principia, but there were no overt signs of despair or celebration. Parents, and their sons and daughters, were leaving a student production of *Antigone*, and farewells were taking place on the steps of the dormitories, from whose windows came the inevitable sound of rock music. Off in the distance shone the bright lights of the Lilly Library, open and in use. And that seemed to me to sum up what this college, or any college, was all about.

About the Author

Evan Ira Farber (b. 1922), received B.A., B.S.L.S., and M.A. Degrees from the University of North Carolina, Chapel Hill, with additional graduate studies at Princeton University. He is a recipient of the Distinguished Alumni award from the UNC School of Information and Library Science, and holds Honorary Doctorate Degrees from St. Lawrence University, Susquehanna University, and Indiana University.

Mr. Farber was Librarian of Earlham College in Richmond, Indiana, from 1962-1994, and is currently Librarian Emeritus. He served as President of the Association of College and Research Libraries, was named ACRL's Academic/Research Librarian of the Year, and received the Miriam Dudley Instruction Librarian Award from the American Library Association.

He is the Editor of: *The Student Economist's Handbook; Classified List of Periodicals for the College Library; Combined Retrospective Index to Book Reviews in Scholarly Journals, 1886-1974*; *Combined Retrospective Index to Book Reviews in Humanities Journals, 1802-1974*; and *The Academic Library: Essays in Honor of Guy R. Lyle.* A Consulting Editor of *College & Undergraduate Libraries* for many years, he also wrote the monthly column "Periodicals for the College Library" which appeared in *Choice* magazine regularly.

Mr. Farber is the subject of the 1993 publication, *Bibliographic Instruction in Practice: A Tribute to the Legacy of Evan Ira Farber.*